THE PICTURESQUE

PAYNE KNIGHT'S "Contrasts" of a picturesque and "improved" scene
(see Plate facing p.2).

Detail from *The Landscape*, figure No. 1.

THE
PICTURESQUE

Studies in a Point of View

BY

CHRISTOPHER HUSSEY

WITH A NEW PREFACE
BY THE AUTHOR

FRANK CASS & CO. LTD.
1967

Published by
FRANK CASS AND COMPANY LIMITED
67 Great Russell Street, London WC1

First published by G. P. Putnam's Sons in 1927

First edition   1927
New impression   1967

Printed in Great Britain by
Thomas Nelson (Printers) Ltd., London and Edinburgh

TO MY FATHER AND MOTHER

WHO EARLY INSTRUCTED ME IN THE PRINCIPLES OF

THE PICTURESQUE

PREFACE TO THE 1967 REPRINT

I CANNOT say there is nothing in this reprinted edition of *The Picturesque* that I want to alter. Written forty years ago, it was something of a pioneering venture in the field of visual romanticism and I am very conscious of its shortcomings, besides the immaturities that it reveals in the author. Many aspects of the subject have since received fuller and more scholarly study, as indicated briefly below, whilst there have been great developments allied to its practical side in contemporary landscape architecture, town and country planning and rural preservation, which had then scarcely begun.

As concern with environment and its aesthetic implications have grown, I have often considered attempting to bring the text up-to-date. But it became increasingly evident that the revisions required are so far-reaching that the book needed to be given an altogether different form—which hitherto it has been beyond my capacities of time and industry to undertake and might unduly tax those of the general reader to peruse.

In view of the continual demand for the original edition, long out of print, I have therefore agreed to the present publisher's offer to issue a limited reprint, in which the only changes are a different frontispiece, the substitution of two illustrations, and certain small literal corrections. If accepted for what it is, an essay on a way of seeing, I believe the book still provides a useful historical introduction to the con-

ception of landscape, that is the appreciation of visual
values, as reflected at the turn of the 18th–19th
centuries in English literature, architecture, painting
and rural management.

A bibliography of works referred to in the text is
given in the Index under " Books, Essays and
Paintings." To add a supplement listing recent
general works on the ways men have seen and sought
to present and shape their environment might be as
daunting to the general reader as I have explained it
is to myself, but its scope can be indicated. It would
range from such classics as Sir Kenneth Clarke's
Landscape into Art (London, 1946) and Dr. E. H.
Gombrich's *Art and Illusion* (London, 1960) to
essays on the aesthetics of practical planning, among
which G. A. Jellicoe's *Studies in Landscape Design*
(London, 1960 and 1966) are notable in suggesting
the effects of contemporary painting on the landscape
of today and the immediate future. Between these
poles are very numerous studies of individual artists,
for the most part contained in specialist publications.
I would mention in particular Denys Sutton's *Gaspard
Dughet* (Paris, *Gazette des Beaux Arts*, 1962) which
justifies ascribing to this painter a greater influence
on the shaping of English landscape than has been
recognised.

No gleaner in the wide field of the Eighteenth
century's fashionable fancies can now dispense with
B. Sprague Allen's *Tides in English Taste* 1619–1800
(Harvard, 1937) or E. F. Carritt's *A Calendar of British
Taste* 1600–1800 (London, 1949). The discovery of
English scenery has its fullest anthology in R. A.
Aubin's *Topographical Poetry in XVIII Century England*
(New York, 1936).

Studies of the lives and works of individual exponents
of the Picturesque are now available in the following
monographs: *William Kent* by Margaret Jourdain to

which I contributed the Introduction (London, 1948);
William Gilpin by W. D. Templeman (Illinois, 1939),
and by C. P. Barbier (Oxford, 1963); *Capability Brown*
(London, 1950) and *Humphry Repton* (London, 1962)
by Dorothy Stroud; and the aristocratic amateurs in
J. Lees Milne's *Earls of Creation* (London, 1962).
Sir John Summerson's *Architecture in Britain* 1530–
1830 (revised edition London, 1963, Ch.28) sum-
marises " The Picturesque and the Cult of Styles "
in relation to the Neoclassical movement.

The three volumes of M. H. Grant's *Old English
Landscape Painters* (London, 1925), Edward Malins'
English Landscape and Literature (London, 1966)
and the recent re-issue by Frank Cass of Elizabeth
Manwaring's *Italian Landscape in Eighteenth Century
England* (London, 1965) are invaluable for further
pursuit of these aspects of the Picturesque, on which
the most comprehensive work of scholarship is
W. J. Hipple's *The Beautiful, The Sublime, and The
Picturesque in Eighteenth-Century British Aesthetic Theory*
(Carbondale, 1957).

AUGUST, 1966.   CHRISTOPHER HUSSEY

CONTENTS

LIST OF PLATES

See also " Notes on the Illustrations," p. 277.

[xiii]

THE PICTURESQUE

[xiv   ]

LIST OF PLATES

[xv]

CHAPTER I

THE PROSPECT

" He talked of foregrounds, distances and second dis-
tances; side screens and perspectives; lights and shades;
and Catharine was so hopeful a scholar, that when they
gained the top of Beechen Cliff, she voluntarily rejected
the whole city of Bath, as unworthy to make part of a
landscape."—Northanger Abbey.

H ENRY TILNEY'S " Lecture on the Picturesque," of which these were the main heads,
was delivered during that same famous walk
when Mrs. Radcliffe's *Mysteries of Udolpho* were dis-
cussed. Having commented on the numerous scenes
of awful grandeur, beauty, and sublimity that compose
that masterpiece, the Tilneys turned " to viewing the
country with the eyes of persons accustomed to drawing; and decided on its capability of being formed into
pictures." Catharine was quite lost. She knew nothing
of taste. Nothing, that is, of the taste for the picturesque, which, in the years when *Northanger Abbey* was
being written, was the latest *chic*.

If it had been no more than a passing *chic*, the picturesque would not be worth more than a casual foot-
note. But Jane Austen was satirizing no precious coterie,
but recording the conversation of typical young persons
of the year 1798. In that year Uvedale Price had
supplemented his *Essay on the Picturesque*, published in
1794, with three additional essays, one of which, *On
Buildings and Architecture*, had put forward the very
point that Catharine Morland was acute enough to
perceive for herself—that Bath was not picturesque.
By then this habit of viewing and criticizing nature as
if it were an infinite series of more or less well composed
subjects for painting had been gaining in popularity all
through the eighteenth century. Henry Tilney, in

deciding on the scenery's capabilities of being formed into pictures, did not think he was conventionalizing his impressions. On the contrary, he thought he was viewing nature in as abstractly aesthetic a fashion as that in which a contemporary young man thinks he guages the significance of a banana on a chair. The picturesque view of nature was then the new, the only, way of deriving aesthetic satisfaction from landscape. Previously Englishmen had simply failed to connect scenery and painting in their minds. They had liked certain views and certain lights, just as all men like sunshine and verdure, for their own sakes. But landscapes as such gave them no aesthetic satisfaction whatever. It was not until Englishmen became familiar with the landscapes of Claude Lorraine and Salvator Rosa, Ruysdael and Hobbema, that they were able to receive any visual pleasure from their surroundings.

Forthwith the picturesque became the nineteenth century's mode of vision. Picturesque scenes and objects appealed to everybody who aspired to the reputation of being "artistic." So long as the convention was accepted there was no question of its aesthetic origins or values. The recognition of the picturesque had become as instinctive as that of day and night. Only when the eye has learnt to see the qualities stressed by painters with other conventions, whether Giotto or Cézanne, are we jogged out of the picturesque habit and enabled to view it as a phase.

The picturesque was the artistic tradition in which I was brought up, and I remember clearly the shock with which I suddenly became conscious that it was only one of many aspects of reality. It happened in the library of a country house built, in 1837, by my grandfather. Through the windows of that room you see, in a valley below, a castle, partly ruined, on an island in a lake. A balustrade cresting a cliff forms the foreground, a group of Scots firs and limes the side-screens. Beyond,

PAYNE KNIGHT'S "Contrasts" of a picturesque and "improved" scene
(see Frontispiece)

Detail from *The Landscape*, figure No. 2.

Plate I. CLAUDE LORRAINE. Narcissus

a meadow melts in the woods, rising to a high sky-line. The reader will find an illustration of the scene in Plate XXI. I had often agreed that it formed a perfect picture, which has time and again been copied by my family, myself included, in water-colours, some of which are hung, with other examples of the family talent, on the staircase. Our pictures might be described as " school of de Wint." For, although many years must have elapsed since my grandmother was taught by that master, his version of the picturesque was handed down as the most artistic. In its derivative way our family *œuvre* is sometimes good.

On this particular evening I was pondering on the happy chance, as it appeared to me, of my grandfather's desertion of the old castle, his building of the new house on this particular spot, and his digging of the stone for building it between the two—in the quarry that makes such a fine foreground to the prospect. It did not occur to me that he was guided by anything more than chance and natural good taste. At that point, however, my eye, ranging the mellow shelves beside me, fell on the book that Henry Tilney had been reading at Bath, *Sir Uvedale Price on the Picturesque*. What was " the Picturesque "? And what could be found to say on it filling so fat a volume? It awoke surmises such as a grandchild of mine might experience on finding books called *Mr. Roger Fry on the Plastic* or *Bell's Significance*.

Sir Uvedale Price was writing about Claude and Salvator, of *banditti* and ruins, cottages, villages, and sandy lanes, shaggy donkeys, Gainsborough, and landscape gardening. Abstract terms like " roughness," " intricacy," " sudden variation," " abruptness," frequently recurred. And before I had read far I reflected that all those scenes which I instinctively called artistic must be " picturesque," and that I was not being original when I sketched a hovel under a gnarled oak but appallingly traditional—the man wrote in 1794! The

very scene before me, so far from being a happy coincidence, must have been planned on picturesque
principles. My grandfather must have evolved it out
of that very book, from which I in my turn have evolved
this one.

It was humiliating, at the time, to find my aesthetic
impulses no more than the product of heredity and
environment. Yet it was gratifying to know the name
of one's subjectivity. Though the knowledge killed my
direct relish of the picturesque, I soon began to appreciate
it consciously, *en vertuose*, disentangling its derivations,
and marking its effects on the arts of two centuries. It
gradually revealed itself as a long phase in the aesthetic
relation of man to nature. At moments the relation of
all the arts to one another, through the pictorial appreciation of nature, was so close that poetry, painting, gardening, architecture, and the art of travel may be said to
have been fused into the single " art of landscape." The
combination might be called " the Picturesque."

The picturesque phase through which each art
passed, roughly between 1730 and 1830, was in each
case a prelude to romanticism. It occurred at the point
when an art shifted its appeal from the reason to the
imagination. An art that addresses the reason, even
though it does so through the eye, does not stress visual
qualities. The reason wants to *know*, not to experience
sensations. The romantic movement was an awakening
of sensation, and, among the other sensations, that of
sight required exercising. Thus the picturesque
interregnum between classic and romantic art was
necessary in order to enable the imagination to form the
habit of feeling through the eyes. Pictures were in each
case taken as the guide for how to see, because painting
is the art of seeing, and in landscape painting the visual
qualities of nature are accentuated. As soon as the
imagination had absorbed what painting had to teach it,
it could feel for itself, and the intermediate process, of

proving the truth of the visual sensation by a comparison to painting, could be dropped. In the great romantic epoch, which followed upon the picturesque phase of each art, the artist's vision is only one among his other equally intense sensations.

While the picturesque phase lasted, the art it produced consequently accentuated visual qualities at the expense of rational ones on the one hand, and of associated ideas on the other. Thomson's poetry, while it has more glow and freedom and colour than Pope's, pleases the mind less, owing to its comparative lack of intellectual content. And stimulates the imagination less than Gray's or Coleridge's, owing to its weaker associations. Picturesque art is imperfect art, but not necessarily bad art.

One of the most curious characteristics of the picturesque phase is the succession with which it affected the various arts. Poetry had " had the picturesque " and recovered from it, sixty years before architecture caught it. Intermediately gardening, travel, and the novel were in turn infected. So far as there is an explanation, either available or desirable, it lies in the relation of each art to imaginative experience. Poetry is the art to which imaginative experience is most necessary, architecture the most rational and physical of the arts. Romanticism may have helped to produce that precocious phenomenon Vanbrugh, but it could not radically affect this stronghold of reason and symmetry till it was at full strength. Even then it failed to produce a genuinely romantic architecture. Its result was not a " movement " but a pastiche. Still, for what it is worth, the " gothistic " architecture of the late eighteenth century may be compared to Byron and Scott.

An appreciation of scenery is a very late acquisition in the development of the western mind. The reason for the delay can be found in the teaching of Christianity, but more precisely in the material and social conditions that prevailed for a long period in Europe. In China, on the contrary, the feeling for nature has been, since a time long before the Christian era, of a kind unknown in Europe till the close of the eighteenth century. The Chinese did not merely love nature; they were in love with her. So were the European romantics; but whereas their love was a pagan ardour tinged with mysticism and poetry, the Chinese love of nature grew directly out of a ritual worship.[1] The elaborate political organization of China was complete at a period when Europe was still barbaric. Consequently the minds of poets and artists turned for solace from the restrictions and system of cities to the hills and rivers, which were not only the abodes of gods, but also of holy men. At an early period the religious fervour for wild places began to transform itself into romantic aestheticism. A somewhat similar association of gods and landscape prevailed in Greece when the belief in the gods was spontaneous. But the humanistic mentality of the Greeks led them rather to suggest a grove by a statue of the dryad of the place than, as in China, to suggest the idea of divinity by a picture of a grove. This humanistic bias has remained inherent in the western mind, was reiterated in the Christian conception of a personal Deity, and strongly reinforced by the Manhood of Christ and the sanctification of the Virgin and saints. In China, Mr. Waley makes it clear, no conception of a personal Divinity competed with the feeling that the beauty of nature was itself divine.

A further bar to the love of nature in the west was the conversion, by early Christian teachers, of the ancient gods of wood and spring into evil spirits, and of Pan into the Devil. Whereas in China the holy men retired to the mountains to be closer to the divine beauty of nature, in the west hermits who withdrew to " deserts "

[1] *An Introduction to the Stuay of Chinese Painting*, by Arthur Waley, p. 137.

were believed to be peculiarly subject to the forces of evil. Thus the forests and mountains and rivers of Europe were not only considered vaguely sinful, but positively dangerous. Not until the dissociation of nature and sin had been set going, was the existence of beauty in inanimate nature even remotely recognized. An early exception was Bishop Ulrich of Augsburg, elevated to that see in 925. He is the first recorded admirer of the Falls of the Rhine at Schaffhaussen.

In China the comparatively peaceful condition of the empire, and the high organization of communications eliminated the fear of bodily harm from landscape. Similarly in the west the appreciation of natural scenery is closely connected with the progress of political and material civilization. As soon as the western traveller had decent roads, and was relieved from the fear of robbery and murder whenever he passed by a wood, he began to look about him with relish. For obvious reasons this stage was reached at widely separated dates in various countries. In primitive phases of development man saw with pleasure, and therefore wished to be reminded of only what Ruskin called " the available and useful "—fertile meadows, prosperous towns, vineyards, still waterways, young isolated trees. The very sight of mountains and rocks was horrible, recalling arduous journeys and robbers; the forest was similarly connected with wild beasts and outlaws, old trees with goblins, the sea with shipwreck. Landscape in the Homeric epoch and in the Middle Ages is therefore confined to references to " smiling " scenes, gardens, and sheltered nooks.

Next came a phase when man began to interest himself in the history and literature and in the remains of the temples and castles of his predecessors. And lest it should suffer by comparison, he looked for such modern edifices as proved to him the prosperity and greatness of his own age. This phase was reached in Flanders during the fifteenth century by artists of whom Patinir was the most remarkable, and in Italy by the beginning of the sixteenth century. It may be called the period of historic landscape, as selecting principally objects intended to remind observers of a legendary past, such as ruined temples, fantastic hills, groves of trees, and rocks with holes in them. In this kind of landscape little, if any, attempt has been made by the artists to imitate nature. The rocks, trees, and houses are conventional or imaginary shapes. In the case of Patinir and the northern painters the bias is towards the "romance" that lies behind northern civilization, as the classic past lies behind the southern.

In distinction to this purely decorative type of landscape, with historic allusions, I call the next phase, represented principally by Claude, Salvator Rosa, and Gaspar Poussin, Ideal Landscape. By this time the mid seventeenth century, men had begun to love nature and to theorize about her, speculating upon which natural forms were the most pregnant with significance, and why. In the back of their minds they had Aristotle's conception of nature as an immanent force working in the refractory medium of matter, towards a central, generalized form, but invariably deflected from this ideal form by "accident." Accordingly it was the artist's function to do what nature could not do, and to produce such a tree, valley, mountain, leaf, as most perfectly expressed that aspect of nature which he had chosen to portray. A Claude selected and compounded aspects that were calm and idyllic, a Salvator those that accentuated the wildness and fierceness of nature. In neither case was it intended to represent nature as she was, but as she might have been if at liberty to express her moods freely and fully.

With the gradual dwindling of the religious faith that inspired the early and mature periods of Italian art and inhibited the enjoyment of landscape, had grown the divine curiosity of the Renaissance, aided by improved communication, and resulting in the formulation of ideas about the natural kingdom. The acts and beliefs of mankind were viewed in a more rational perspective, and against an ever-increasing background of nature. The Madonna of Leonardo da Vinci, represented against a background of prehistoric rocks and seas, marked a compromise between an early theory of the geological evolution of the earth and the dogma of the eternal existence of Christ. The Madonnas of Raphael were transfigured beings enthroned in the limpid light of heaven against as unearthly a background as possible. The Madonnas of Titian were earthly virgins, warmed by the sun and choosing a leafy shade and flowery bank whereon to repose during the journey to Egypt. The world in which Titian's Madonnas move is as beautiful as the Mother of Christ, and as worthy of being painted. Indeed, it challenged his curiosity still more strongly. He knew why he loved the Virgin, but why did he love the trees and flowers and the blue Alps? Being a painter he left the answer to the philosophers and settled down to paint those aspects of nature that he felt most beautiful—the broad masses of sward and foliage, the light glinting through leaves and catching the tree trunks. He first among Europeans painted nature as he saw it, not as he knew it to be from the testimony of his other senses. He saw mass and did not paint innumerable leaves. He saw mountains and painted them blue, not curious cubes of yellow and brown.

To describe this " painter's view " of nature, the word *pittoresco* was coined, meaning " after the manner of painters." From Titian and Domenichino onwards the fact was accepted that there were " picturesque " aspects of nature, which painters were able to see more easily than ordinary men. Tintoretto and Poussin perfected the technique of rendering picturesque aspects, and Claude took the step of combining the theories of philosophers with the perceptions of a painter. He minutely studied the actual details of natural forms, and from them derived what seemed to him the ideal form to which nature appeared to be tending. He accurately sketched the scenes that he found in the Campagna and among the Alban hills, and applied the same process to them, producing in the finished picture an ideally composed landscape. By a natural extension of the word's meaning, his landscapes were sometimes termed painters' or "picturesque" landscapes, and people began to enjoy actual landscapes that resembled his compositions. These, too, were sometimes termed picturesque, and sometimes beautiful.

Parallel and simultaneous with the development of the "ideal picturesque" in Italy, grew up the naturalistic landscape school of Flanders. Italian classic landscape had owed an impetus to the Flemish fifteenth-century painters. In the seventeenth century the debt was repaid. The wars of independence practically put an end to landscape art in Holland while they lasted, though the tradition persisted in the work of Pieter Breughel where it was mixed up with a feeling for the realities of peasant life. For the time, the course of northern landscape art must be traced in Italy whither, during the last decade of the sixteenth century, Adam Elsheimer of Frankfurt and Paul Bril the Fleming learnt of idealism in landscape from the works of Tintoretto and Domenichino, together with the uses of light and shade in producing a dramatic effect. The landscapes of Bril and Elsheimer have little to tell us of nature, beyond that their painters were fond of trees and were intrigued by curious masses of rock and the splash of cascades. But even that mild interest represented a stride from the village streets of Pieter Breughel and the neat town views of the earlier Flemings. In the daring landscapes of Hercules Seghers the interest has grown into an obsession, particularly with the grandeur of the scenery where the road led through the Alpine passes. " The menace of those solitudes, with the play of stormy light across them, introduced through Seghers a note of serious purpose into Dutch landscape which might otherwise have become too easily optimistic or trivial in its aims." [1] But of incomparably greater and more lasting influence on northern art was the genius of Rubens. He assimilated all the most significant qualities of Italian art of the preceding century, and turned it to expressing his own dynamic and realistic view of matter. His few landscapes have inspired succeeding ages out of all proportion to their numbers and size. They were more realistic than anything hitherto seen in painting by his contemporaries, yet they were bursting with the glow and freshness and drama of Titian's landscape. Above all, the miraculous quality of his paint fascinated later generations. Turner, Constable, and Crome were each decisively affected by *The Château de Stein* in the National Gallery.

Taught by Elsheimer and Bril to look at bosky trees, and by Rubens how to paint broken light and colour, a generation of landscape painters arose in Holland that produced the naturalistic type of picturesque landscape. Within fifty years Ruysdael and Van Goyen, Hobbema and Ostade, Cuyp and Rembrandt had established certain types of landscape and classes of objects as peculiarly suitable for painting. Such were old gnarled trees, sandy banks, water and windmills, rough heaths, rustic bridges, stumps, logs, ruts, hovels, unkempt persons, and shaggy animals. Intermediate between the Italian and Dutch types of landscape were the paintings of Asselyn, Both, Berghem, Pynacker, and their followers, which combined the scenery of Italy as selected by Claude and Salvator Rosa with the Dutch fondness for

[1] Sir Charles Holmes, *The National Gallery—the Netherlands, Germany, and Spain*, p. 172.

minutely observed and rampant foliage, and the effects of light on broken surfaces.

The awakening in England to an appreciation of landscape was a direct result of the Grand Tour fashionable with the aristocracy after the isolation of the country from the rest of Europe during the greater part of the seventeenth century. Not only did the passage of the Alps and the journey through Italy compel some attention being given to scenery, but in Italy the traveller encountered landscape painting. It became fashionable for the aristocracy to pose as connoisseurs, to assemble collections of pictures, and to bring home souvenir pictures of their tour. Simultaneously poets such as Thomson and Dyer devoted their verse to descriptions of scenery, and landowners were busy improving their grounds. Both adopted, as a model of correct composition, the Claudian landscape.

Connoisseurship necessitated some theory of aesthetics. The earlier theories, of Shaftesbury, Hutcheson, and Hogarth dealt predominantly with the grand manner "subject" picture, and architecture. But soon after the turn of the century the massive intellect of Burke established a philosophical theory of a lucidity that those of his predecessors had conspicuously lacked. His *Inquiry into the origin of our ideas of the Sublime and Beautiful* established, for half a century, a wholly objective conception of the effect of visible objects on the passions. The fundamental instincts of man, which gave rise to the passions, were two: self-propagation and self-preservation. Objects were perceived by the senses, and the senses communicated, not with the conscious mind, but with the sub-conscious instincts, begetting passions. Every object perceived must therefore affect one or other of the two fundamental instincts. All those that were in any degree pleasing, attractive, smooth, and gentle affected the instinct of self-propagation and were called Beautiful. All those that aroused passions connected with fear, infinity, difficulty, or pain appealed to the other, and were Sublime. Thought did not enter into the process. It was an instinctive recognition by the sub-consciousness of qualities inherent in the object perceived.

For a time these categories were sufficient to explain all aesthetic pleasure. But in the landscape painting of Gainsborough appeared a great quantity of rough, shaggy, and summarily delineated objects, derived from Dutch landscape, that immediately pleased the connoisseurs but were obviously neither sublime nor beautiful. At the same time a few tourists who practised landscape drawing, of whom the Rev. William Gilpin was the foremost, discovered that many scenes that were beautiful in Burke's sense were unaccountably ill suited to being painted. Gilpin accordingly invented the term Picturesque Beauty to distinguish objects that were actually beautiful and also adapted for use in pictures. Picturesque Sublimity seems never to have been used as a qualifying category, though Gilpin and all other travelling sketchers had to decide repeatedly at what point it ceased to be possible to delineate the sublime.

This was the condition of aesthetic theory in England when, in 1794, Uvedale Price, a Whig squire in Herefordshire, published his *Essays on the Picturesque*, establishing the Picturesque as a third category in addition to the Sublime and Beautiful, which should include the now popular Dutch type of landscape. He was a disciple of Burke's objective theory, but explained—

Even when I first read that original work, I felt that there were numberless objects which gave delight to the eye and yet differed as widely from the beautiful as from the sublime.

The beautiful and sublime, he continued, together formed a category that had always excited admiration, though he would have been nearer the mark if he had said "frequently" instead of "always." The Pictur-

esque, on the contrary, was distinguished by having
been entirely overlooked. Objects had intrinsic qualities
that made them picturesque, as distinct as those that
made other objects sublime or beautiful. Moreover,
the picturesque was equally extended in its appeal to
the senses. There was picturesque music. While a
chorus of Handel was generally acknowledged sublime,
and " Corelli's famous pastorale " beautiful, a " capri-
cious movement of Scarlatti or Haydn " was essentially
picturesque. Thus " picturesque " for Price meant
far more than " suitable for painting "—the definition
that Gilpin had favoured. While the outstanding
qualities of the sublime were vastness and obscurity, and
those of the beautiful smoothness and gentleness, the
characteristics of the picturesque were " roughness and
sudden variation joined to irregularity," of form, colour,
lighting, and even sound. When an uninitiated person
was shown a picture made up of objects in which these
qualities predominated, he would, Price considered, at
first be amazed by their ugliness. But gradually he
might notice that they were selected for some quality
or character; for the variety produced by sudden and
irregular deviation, the strongly marked peculiarity of
their appearance, the manner in which the rugged and
broken parts caught the light, and the contrast that such
lights presented with deep shadows, or for the rich and
mellow tints produced by various stages of decay. Such
objects in real life that the person had previously passed
by without observing, he might now begin to look at
with increasing interest, remembering how Ruysdael or
Teniers, Waterlo or Hobbema, Salvator or even Claude
had treated, or might have treated, such a scene. At
length he would scarcely be able to stir abroad without
recognizing scenes and objects with which pictures had
familiarized him; none of them beautiful or sublime,
but all of them intrinsically and objectively picturesque.
 There the controversy might have rested and, with

many practical men such as painters, did rest, but for the
simultaneous enunciation of the Theory of Association.
This had for the first time been pushed to its full possibilities by Archibald Alison, whose *Essays on the Nature
and Principles of Taste* had immediately preceded Price's
book, having been published in 1790, though by him
ignored. Alison, with a wealth of imagination and
sentiment, denied absolutely the existence of objective
qualities inherent in objects, accounting for all emotions
by the association of ideas aroused in the mind of the
spectator. Anything might be beautiful if it aroused
pleasant and therefore beautiful ideas. Picturesque
objects were simply those that reminded a person of
pictures that he had seen; if he had enjoyed them, the
emotion would be pleasant, and therefore one of beauty.

The truth of Alison's theory cannot be denied. Its
gradual abandonment has been caused, not by any
fallacy, but by its devastating effect on every standard
of beauty. According to it, every man's taste is as good
as another's, and by it are justified the most sentimental
and formless excesses in all the visual arts produced by
the nineteenth century. So long as a picture or building
aroused an agreeable train of thought, it must be
beautiful. The stronger the imagination of the beholder,
the more insignificant might be the objects that roused
him to a fine frenzy. This particular weakness was
admirably dealt with by Ruskin:

Poets and men of strong feeling in general, are apt to be
among the very worst judges of painting. The slightest hint is
enough for them. Tell them that the white stroke means a
ship, and the black stain a thunderstorm, and they will be perfectly satisfied with both, and immediately proceed to remember
all they ever felt about ships and thunderstorms, attributing the
whole current and fullness of their own feelings to the painter's
work.[1]

It was to set in order of moral value the trains of

[1] *Modern Painters*, vol. iii.

thought aroused by pictures and picturesque scenes that the whole panoply of Ruskin's writing was directed.

Price's principal opponent was not, however, Alison, but Richard Payne Knight, a neighbouring squire, residing at Downton Castle, near Ludlow, and one of the group of connoisseurs that frequently appears in Farington's diary. Payne Knight was a disciple of Alison, and supported the theory of association, though with two important exceptions. These were in the case of colour and sound. He maintained that colour as revealed by light did possess objective qualities [1] when perceived abstractly, apart from the object that it denoted. This abstract kind of vision was the painter's, or picturesque, point of view. Nothing was intrinsically picturesque, but many objects, when viewed thus abstractly, had picturesque, or pictorial, beauty. To acquire the painter's capacity for abstract vision, the layman needed to be thoroughly acquainted with pictures. In this way he distinguished between other kinds of beauty, and picturesque beauty. It was he who first traced the origin of the word " picturesque " to the Italian *pittoresco*, " after the manner of painters," and showed that it came into use with reference to the methods of Titian. " This method," he explained, " consisted in a blending and melting of objects together with a playful and airy lightness, and a sort of loose, sketchy indistinctness," in contrast to the minute detail of earlier schools which was rather a literal transcript of " what the mind knew to be, from the concurrent testimony of another sense," than the actual visible appearance, received by the brain through the eye.

Picturesque beauty, according to Knight, was the abstract beauty of colour and pigmentation at which subsequently Impressionism aimed. It was the approach to nature that culminated, in England, in the painting

[1] *Analytical Inquiry into the Principles of Taste*, by Richard Payne Knight (1805).

of Constable and Turner; in France at Barbizon. Another fifty years and Impressionism had broken away from the picturesque scale of colours and class of object in the wholly unassociative colour experiments of Monet and Pissarro. Though modern impressionism developed out of the picturesque, it successfully freed itself from picturesque theory. According to the latter vagueness, irregularity, and an absence of form had become ends in themselves, with a significance corresponding to that which we find in form, decisiveness, and pattern. Picturesque qualities, Knight maintained, were the abstract, emotive qualities that alone had aesthetic value. All other kinds of beauty were associative—with sex, prosperity, wealth, content, and so on—and were non-aesthetic.

The picturesque can thus be seen to provide the first step in the movement towards abstract aesthetic values. But whilst we are able to select, out of the whole range of painting and from a comprehensive view of nature, those qualities that experience leads us to believe to be aesthetic, the early fathers of aestheticism had to discover nature herself. The picturesque provided the earliest means for perceiving visual qualities in nature. It consists in the education of the eye to recognize qualities that painters had previously isolated.

The first part of this book must therefore trace, however summarily, the discovery of visual qualities in nature through the study of pictures. Each art passed through a phase of imitating painting before developing into the romantic phase that came after, when the eye and the imagination had learnt to work for themselves. The period of imitation is the picturesque period.

The art that was earliest affected was that of poetry as being, at the time, the most widely used vehicle of description.

CHAPTER II

IDEAL AND PICTURESQUE LANDSCAPE

Whate'er Lorrain *light-touchd with softening Hue,*
Or savage Rosa *dashed, or learned* Poussin *drew.*
THOMSON, The Castle of Indolence.

§ 1

THOMSON, Dyer, and their immediate followers are usually designated the Landscape Poets. I call them the Picturesque Poets. All poets look at and describe landscape at some time or other, in terms of amenity, classic association, or what not. But these poets look at and describe landscape in terms of pictures. Each scene is correctly composed, and filled in with sufficient vividness to enable the reader to visualize a picture after the manner of Salvator and Claude. Picturesque describes not only their mode of vision, but their method.

Their vision was both realistic and ideal. They saw nature as a composed whole. Yet as a pictorial, not an organic or spiritual, whole. For Thomson the reality of nature was a picture. All through the first half of the eighteenth century, painters and poets considered themselves complementary to each other. The painter must paint as and what the poet sang, and *vice versa*. Du Fresnoy's *De Arte Graphica*,[1] the text-book, for many years, of all artistic perception, fixed for a century this literary view of painting, this pictorial view of poetry.

> Ut pictura poesis erit; simulisque poesi
> Sit pictura; refert par aemula quaeque sororem,
> Alternatque vices et nomina; . . .

---

[1] Published posthumously in 1665. First Englished by Dryden.

Translated by Mason in the middle of the eighteenth century:

> True Poetry the Painter's power displays;
> True Painting emulates the Poet's lays;
> The rival sisters, fond of equal fame,
> Alternate change their office and their name.

But, as regards landscape, the pictorial approach of Thomson and Dyer was something new. Du Fresnoy makes not even a passing reference to landscape painting. Painting for him deals only with " history " and portraiture. Landscape is still the poet's province, as it had been till well after the Renaissance; till, in fact, Claude and the Poussins made their appearance among the poets. Their landscape is poetic landscape: a presentment of what poets had described. Thomson and Dyer enlarged poetic landscape by describing what the painters had borrowed from earlier poets. Finally a Gainsborough or a James Ward completed this house that Jack built, by painting what a Thomson had seen imitated by Claude from Virgil.

The effect on poetry of the picturesque point of view is to be traced in the gradual approximation of described landscape to the landscape painted by Claude and Salvator Rosa.

Mediaeval and Renaissance poetry and painting were free of this trades unionism. Painter and poet put down what to them was the reality of what they felt. No artistic education was needed before his contact with reality could be appreciated. This direct perception need only be indicated to accentuate the obliquity of picture poetry. Here is a troubadour, Guillaume IX of Aquitaine (1071-1127), singing the perennial miracle:

> Ab la dolchor del temps novel
> Foillo li bosc, e li aucel
> Chanton chascus en lor lati
> Segon lo vers del novel chan.

(At the gentleness of spring
The forests shoot, the birdies sing
Each in their peculiar tongue
The verses of a new-made song.)

A simple phenomenon, passionately felt, with no reference to its visual accompaniments. Compare it with Charles d'Orléans, three centuries later:

Les fourriers d'este sont venus
Pour appareillier son logis,
Et ont fait tendre ses tappis
De fleurs et verdure tissus. . . .

Here is a more courtly and allusive view of spring. It is a carpet that is laid. Chaucer, too, saw spring as a garment:

And than bycometh the ground so proude
That it wole have a newé shroude,
And makyth so queynt his robe and faire
That it hath hewés a hundred payre
Of gras and flouris, ynde and pers,
And many hewés full diverse.

There is more than a hint of Van Eyck in Chaucer.

These are detailed, but personal, perceptions. In another two centuries a veil had come between the poet and nature. Shakespeare only once painted a word landscape—the great "impression" in Prospero's invocation to the elves of the hills, brooks, standing lakes, and groves, where all the materials of an ideal landscape are assembled, though not composed. That was the veil—the memory of the classics. Without it Shakespeare was as rich a colourist as Turner, but less precise:

And now they never meet in grove or green
By fountain clear, or spangled starlight sheen. . . .

His impressions glow and sparkle, but have no form.

Plate II. CLAUDE LORRAINE. The Tiber above Rome

V. & A. Museum

Plate III.   LADY DIANA BEAUCLERK.   Group of Gipsies and Female Rustics

But there was another veil over poets; the knowledge that all landscape was also somebody's property. It crops up here and there in Shakespeare:

> . . . your isle, which stands
> As Neptune's park, ribbed and paled in.

And dominates Ben Jonson. The big landscape in *Penshurst*, the most distinctly visualized that had yet been penned, is simply an estate map, with a few dryads and gods illuminated in to fill up blank patches. It is the verbal forerunner of the " prospects of noblemen's seats " painted in the later part of the century by Knyff, Loggan, Badslade. Jonson's, and these painters', approach to landscape was described well by Gilpin, when distinguishing from it the picturesque point of view:[1]

> Where rising from the solid rock, appear
> Those ancient battlements, there liv'd a knight,
> That oft surveying from his castle wall
> The wide expanse before him; distance vast;
> Interminable wilds; savannahs deep;
> Dark woods; and village spires, and glitt'ring streams,
> Just twinkling in the sunbeam, wish'd the view
> Transferr'd to canvas, and for that sage end,
> Led some obedient son of Art to where
> His own unerring taste had previous fix'd
> The point of amplest prospect. "Take thy stand
> Just here," he cry'd, "and paint me *all* thou seest,
> Omit no single object." It was done;
> And soon the live-long landscape cloathes his hall,
> And spreads from base to ceiling. *All* was there;
> As to his guests, while dinner cool'd the knight
> Full oft would prove; and with uplifted cane
> Point to the distant spire, where slept entomb'd
> His ancestry; beyond, where lay the town,
> Skirted with wood, that gave him place and voice

---

[1] *Three Essays . . . to which is added a Poem on Landscape Painting*, by the Rev. W. Gilpin (1792).

> In Britain's senate; nor untrac'd the stream
> That fed the goodly trout they soon should taste;
> Nor ev'ry scattered seat of friend or foe,
> He calls his neighbours. Heedless he, meanwhile,
> That what he deems the triumph of his taste,
> Is but a painted survey, a mere map;
> Which light and shade and perspective misplac'd,
> But serve to spoil.

In *L'Allegro* Milton sketched a completed English landscape, clearly visualized though ideal in the parts:

> Russet Lawns and Fallows gray
> Where the nibbling Flocks do stray,
> Mountains on whose barren Breast,
> The labouring Clouds do often rest:
> Meadows trim with Daisies pied,
> Shallow Brooks and Rivers wide,
> Towers and Battlements it sees
> Bosom'd high in tufted Trees.

With this we have reached observation, if nothing more; the objects are distinctly drawn and coloured, and are relied upon to please the reader. Yet there is no attempt at " composing " the scene; we are told of no misty distance, no cloud shadows or high lights, in spite of the " chiaroscuro " which Burke extolled in *Paradise Lost*—

> From the high mount of God, whence light and shade
> Spring forth.

The most highly approved treatment of scenery during the Renaissance period consisted in personification. Browne, Drayton, and the lesser Elizabethans carried humanism to the pitch of obscurity. Not a natural object could be seen without a goddess or a naiad taking its place in the poet's description. The practice is carried to its extreme in the Court masques for which Inigo Jones designed the costumes and scenery. Among the designs published by the Walpole Society, however,[1] there is one for Davenant's *Luminalia or the Festivale of Light*, performed in 1638, that sets both Davenant and Jones well on the way towards picturesque perception. The former's stage direction refers to the nearer part of the scene being woody " and farther off more open with a calme River, that tooke the Shadowes of the Trees by the light of the Moone." The whole scene " seemed to run farre in from the eye." Here is attention given to visual qualities in reference to their effect on the audience of the masque, and a sketch which sets Inigo Jones beside Claude and Mr. Wilson Steer as a master of " blottesque " impressionism, though it is probable that Inigo drew his inspiration rather from Rubens, with whom he will have been in close contact during his visit to London (June 1629—March 1630).

Ten years later (1640) John Denham published *Cooper's Hill*, of which Dryden wrote, " for the majesty of the style it is, and ever will be, the exact standard of good writing." Its influence undoubtedly was considerable, and out of all proportion to the merits that we should be inclined to allow it. Compared to the descriptive poetry of Thomson and Dyer in the next century, the perception of visual qualities that it evidences is slight. Yet if we compare it to Jonson's *Penshurst*, the advance that it represents is considerable. Denham had learnt to see the Thames Valley and its mild eminences with the magnifying vision that is the surest mark of an acquaintance with Italian landscape art, and he had learnt the pictorial value of contrast. He described how

> the steepe horrid Roughness of the Wood
> Strives with the gentle Calmness of the Flood.

---

[1] Walpole Society. *Designs by Inigo Jones for Masques and Plays. A Descriptive Catalogue of Drawings . . . in the Collection of His Grace the Duke of Devonshire, K.G.*, with Introduction and Notes by Percy Simpson and C. F. Bell (1924).

Such huge Extremes, when Nature doth unite,
Wonder from thence results and thence Delight.

He is familiar with mountains such as never were
seen in England:

But his proud head the ayery Mountain hides
Among the Clouds; his Shoulders, and his Sides
A shady Mantle cloathes . . .
Low at his Feet a spacious Plaine is plac'd
Betweene the Mountain and the Streame embrac't.

Here we find the earliest idealization of vagueness
and distance, such as would follow an acquaintance with
Italian landscape painting. Professor Lascelles Aber-
crombie [1] has traced "the sentiment for views" as it
affected romanticism. The Elizabethan regarded distance as little more than an inhibition to clear seeing.
Looking at a view was waste of time, since you could not
really *see* anything. By the end of the eighteenth
century:

'Tis distance lends enchantment to the view
And robes the mountain in its azure hue.

Vagueness has become the reality, the detailed view of
things irrelevant.

Cooper's Hill, *L'Allegro*, and Inigo Jones's sketch
form a small but unmistakable body of evidence that
the painted landscape of Rubens and Titian and Claude
was beginning to influence the vision of Englishmen.
Envelopement is beginning to take the place of minute
observation. But for the cataclysm of the civil wars
and the Puritan abhorrence of art the picturesque point
of view might have become universal in Charles II's
reign. Actually there are almost as few " landscapes "
in the second half of the century as in the first. Such
as there are, however, give indications of the idealizing

[1] *Romanticism.* Martin Secker (1926).

mental process of which Claude's painting is the fullest expression. The travellers to Italy admire a view because it reminds them of " paradise." Paradise, in fact, becomes synonymous with prospect. Views which do not resemble this ideal conception of what a view should be, are not admired. Thus in Charles Cotton's *The Wonders of the Peak*, published 1681, the view of Chatsworth is not only seen *à l'Italienne*, but ideally:

> The *Groves*, whose curléd *Brows* shade ev'ry *Lake*
> Do everywhere such waving *Landskips* make,
> As *Painters* baffled *Art* is far above,
> Who *Waves* and *Leaves* could never yet make move . . .
> To view from hence the glitt'ring Pile above . . .
> Environ'd round with Nature's Shames and Ills,
> Black Heath, Wild Rock, bleak Crags and naked hills,
> Who is it but must presently conclude
> That this is *Paradise*, which seated stands.
> In midst of Deserts, and of barren *Sands*?

Cotton was a sensitive poet, and a simple man, the angling friend of Izaak Walton. But what a difference between this complicated attempt to portray a whole landscape and the intuitional lines of a Charles d'Orléans or of Cotton himself, when writing of his pastime! The influence that led Cotton to talk of " waving landskips, as Painters baffled Art is far above," may be traced to that remarkable work *Polygraphice* [1] by the quack doctor William Salmon, which, besides giving instruction in all graphic arts, dealt also of " Beautifying and Perfuming, of Alchimy and the Philosopher's Elixir, of Faber's Arcanums, of Chiromantical Signatures," and of several other home sciences. In his chapter *Of Landskip* he thus defines the word:

> I. Landskip is that which appeareth in lines the *perfect* vision of the earth, and all things thereupon, placed

---

[1] *Polygraphice; or, The Arts of Drawing, Engraving, Etching, Limning, Painting, Varnishing, Japanning, Gilding, etc.*, ran through eight editions between 1671 and 1701.

above the Horizon, as Towns, Villages, Castles, Promontories, Mountains, Rocks, Valleys, Ruins, Woods, Forests, Chases, Trees, Houses, and all other Buildings, both beautiful and ruinous.

VII. Make your Landskip to shoot (as it were) away, one part lower than another, that the Landskip may appear to be taken from the top of an hill.

This was the rule for Claudian landscape. In the following sentence we perhaps get the origin of Cotton's remarks about " waving " and movement:

VIII. Let everything have its proper motion, as in *Trees*, when they are shaken by the wind, making the smaller boughs yielding; the stiffer less bending: in *Clouds* that they follow the Winds: in Rivers the general Current.

XII. Lastly, let every site have its proper *parerga*, adjuncts or additional graces, as the Farm-house, Wind-mill, Water-mill, Woods, Flocks of Sheep, Herds of Cattle, Pilgrims, Ruines of Temples, Castles and Monuments; with a thousand such other only proper to particular subjects.

Salmon, or some kindred instructor, had been consulted by Mistress Anne Killigrew, the most celebrated of all the amateur ladies of the time, owing to Dryden's eulogy of her. Others plied the needle, or japanned. As for her:

> Her pencil drew whate'er her soul design'd . . .
> The sylvan scenes of herds and flocks,
> The fruitful plains and barren rocks,
> Of shallow brooks that flowed so clear,
> The bottom did the top appear;
> Of deeper too and ampler floods,
> Which, as in mirrors, showed the woods;
> Of lofty trees, with sacred shades,
> And perspectives of pleasant glades,
> Where nymphs of brightest form appear,
> And shaggy satyrs standing near . . .

> The ruins, too, of some majestic piece
> Boasting the power of ancient Rome and Greece,
> Whose statues, friezes, columns, broken lie,
> And, though defaced, the wonder of the eye.

Mistress Anne obviously had exactly caught the recipe for Ideal Landscape as presented by Claude. Her vision, as Salmon would have said, was " perfect "; her world, in Cotton's phrase, was paradise. The first movement towards appreciation of scenery in England, namely its idealization, can thus be seen to have affected many of the educated class before the close of the seventeenth century. In the love of nature, as in the love of men and women, idealization is the first stage, when eyes are first opened to beauties never before imagined. Analysis of causes, criticism, thought, come after we have found our paradise.

The type-forms of this paradise were to be found on the Grand Tour which, somewhat exceptional in the latter part of the seventeenth century, became the rule after the Peace of Utrecht, 1715. The passage down the Rhone or over the Alps compelled some interest in scenery, whilst the classic scenes of Italy provided visual backgrounds for the familiar Latin poetry. In Italy, too, " Taste " was formed: taste for architecture, pictures, and particularly landscape painting. The collection of pictures became fashionable.

The increase of attention to scenery by travellers will be referred to in a later chapter. Here there is space for only a brief allusion to the development of the collecting habit. It was not a new one. Charles I, the Duke of Buckingham, the Earls of Arundel, Northumberland, and Pembroke formed considerable collections before the Civil Wars. Evelyn further records the collections of Lords Newport, Sunderland, Melford, and Mulgrave. Sir Peter Lely had a famous cabinet, including a Claude; and lesser men, such as William Cartwright, an actor

of repute and a bookseller, amassed as many as 239
pictures, of which about eighty are at present identifiable
in the Dulwich Gallery. He died in 1686.

At the same time engraving disseminated a taste for
landscape. Not only were there the numerous topographical prints of which Pepys was an amateur, but
the Dutch were prolific in the production of more
abstract engravings and etchings. J. Both, Swanevelt,
Berghem, Waterlo engraved and etched as much as they
painted. Rembrandt etched landscapes that were
extraordinarily undervalued, whilst Claude, Salvator,
and Gaspar Poussin employed the medium, the former
for his *Liber Veritatis*. Soon after 1725 an English
school of engravers came into being, of which Arthur
Pond and George Knapton may be considered the
founders, Woollett, Mason, and Vivares the principal
practitioners.

With the dawn of the eighteenth century we find a
new class emerging in society, the Connoisseur, with
Antony Ashley Cooper, third Earl of Shaftesbury, as
the first and one of the greatest. His theory of aesthetics,
contained in the *Characteristics*, provided the rationale of
appreciation during the opening years of the century,
particularly for the group of dilettanti that centred on
Lord Burlington.

Another director of the infant Taste was Jonathan
Richardson, the portrait-painter, who, between 1715 and
1725, published a series of essays on painting and taste
generally. His preliminary task, attempted in his first
publication, *The Theory of Painting* (1715), was to defend
the very position of painting as a liberal art. The course
adopted by Richardson was the usual one at that date—
pointing out the analogy between painting and poetry,
originally made by du Fresnoy. The position faced by
du Fresnoy, in France in the middle of the seventeenth
century, was much the same as that confronting Richardson in England. In each country and epoch an interest

in pictures was beginning to develop. But whilst in each case there existed a considerable body of poets and readers of poetry, neither country at these times possessed an influential native group of painters, working in the country, nor any large body of persons with minds at all sensitive to painting. The task that both du Fresnoy and Richardson felt to be theirs was to create out of an existing respect and feeling for poetry a corresponding respect and feeling for painting.

" The confusion of poetry and painting," says Professor Manwaring,[1] " is important for the better understanding of the popularity of Claude, Salvator, and Poussin, whose landscapes were so easily related to literary conception. This was particularly true of the landscapes of Claude, so naturally reminiscent of Theocritus and Virgil. The likeness between pastoral poets and landscape artists was soon noticed." " The perfection of a Master Painter is, to be able to perform the same Wonders by Colours which the poet commands by Language."[2] All through the century writers and critics exercised their ingenuity in comparing their favourite painters to their favourite writers. Poussin to Theocritus, Raphael to Homer, the Caracci to Virgil, Titian to Ovid, and so on.

The *Observations* of Edward Wright, made between 1720 and 1722, and published in 1730, indicate that Shaftesbury's and Richardson's desire " to persuade our nobility and gentry to become lovers of painting " was in a fair way to success. Wright asserted that Taste was not only fashionable, but " in a way to prevailing," in view of the constant additions being made to the collections of the said nobility and gentry. The year 1730 may, in fact, be taken as the date by which Taste, Connoisseurship, and the connection of landscape with painting was generally recognized. The founding

[1] *Italian Landscape in Eighteenth-century England* (1925).
[2] *The Free Thinker* (1718), No. 63.

of the Dilettante Society in 1734 set a seal on Taste
as a fashionable necessity. Previously the circle of men
of taste had been small. In Queen Anne's reign it was
little larger than that of the Kit Cat Club, with Addison
and Steele, Dodsley and Pope, Vanbrugh and Congreve,
Kneller and a sprinkling of rich men such as the Dukes
of Grafton and Somerset and Lord Carlisle. Perhaps
it was through them that Vanbrugh imbibed, in an
early form, the doctrines of the Picturesque that
strongly animate his architecture.

Pope himself had little appreciation of picturesque
landscape, for all his eminence as a leader of the movement towards " nature." There is no analogy in his
landscapes to those of Claude or Salvator. *Windsor
Forest* contains no trees worthy the name, but saplings
of Raphaelite origin, like those in his grove at Twickenham:

> Here waving Groves a chequered scene display . . .
> There, interspersed in Lawns and opening Glades,
> The Trees arise that show each other's Shades.
> Here, in full light, the russet plains extend,
> There, wrapt in Clouds, the bluish hills ascend.

For the most part his landscapes are crowds of per-
sonifications. Blushing Flora paints th' enamelled
Ground, cheerful Murmurs fluctuate on the Gale,
everywhere are balmy Zephyrs, sylvan Shades, feathered
Quires, vocal Shores, silver Floods, crystal Springs,
Ceres' Gifts, and the Treasures of Pomona (irrespective
of species, let alone of appearance). Pope so far pro-
gressed towards a picturesque attitude to gardening
as to take up the spade against formality and to explain
how gardening was really the same thing as painting.
He might inveigh against terraces " where Grove nods
at Grove," and " half the Platform just reflects the
other." But he only went so far as to prefer a serpentine
to a straight line. His achievement in popularizing

appreciation of landscape goes little further than trans-
mogrifying the nymphs and satyrs of the preceding
generation into " *The Genius* of the *Place* ":

> That tells the Waters or to rise or fall
> Or helps th' ambitious Hill the Heav'ns to scale,
> Or scoops the circling Theatres of the Vale,
> Calls in the Country, catches opening glades,
> Joins willing woods, and varies Shades from Shades.

No visualization here. But once men got into the
habit of pretending that a " genius of the place " was
present in each landscape, it was only a matter of fashion
before they recognized the Divinity of that genius.
Pope's attitude to the picturesque is admirably summed
up in a letter to Richardson (21st November 1739):

> To prefer rocks and dirt to flowery meads and lovely
> Thames, and brimstone and fogs to roses and sunshine. When
> I arrive at these sensations, I may settle at Bath, of which I
> never dreamt, further than to live just out of the sulphurous
> pit and at the edge of the fogs, at Mr. Allen's.

The stage was now set. The caste of connoisseurs
assembled, the painted pictures accessible, and a Taste
for them " in a fair way to prevailing." It remained but
to direct the enthusiasm for art towards the appreciation
of nature. To get men to look at real landscape with a
painter's gusto. That done, and the picturesque point
of view would be delivered into the land. This was the
achievement of James Thomson and John Dyer, the
Picturesque poets. Dyer's *Grongar Hill* was published
in 1726, at the same time as Thomson's *Winter*. The
three following *Seasons* of the latter followed, till the
group was complete in 1730, the date that was suggested
above as marking the first step to Picturesque vision.
The second was 1756, the date of Burke's *Sublime and
Beautiful*. The third is 1794-5, when Uvedale Price
published his *Essays on the Picturesque*, Payne Knight

The Landscape, Humphrey Repton *Sketches and Hints on Landscape Gardening*, and Mrs. Radcliffe *The Mysteries of Udolpho*.

§ 2

The word " picturesque," however, although in use, had not yet become associated with landscape. Steele had used the word in *The Tender Husband* with an eye on the allegorical decorations of a Thornhill:

> NIECE : I would be drawn like the Amazon *Thalestris*, with a Spear in my hand, and an Helmet on a Table before me. . . .
> CLERIMONT : Madam . . . there shall be a Cupid setting away your Helmet, to shew that Love should have a part in all gallant Actions.
> NIECE : That Circumstance may be very Picturesque.[1]

In 1712 Pope had regarded it as a French word, with the meaning graphic or vivid, though the French Academy did not admit *pittoresque* till 1732. It does not begin to be distinguished from " pictorial " until Thomson and Dyer had familiarized the conventions of Italian landscape painting. Gray used the word in its full sense in 1740:

> You cannot pass along a street [in Rome] but you have views of some palace, or church, or square, or fountain, the most picturesque and noble one can imagine.

The achievement of Thomson and Dyer was to bring the body of educated men and women in England up to the stage of appreciation reached by the Italian landscape painters. Where previously laymen had regarded landscape only for its amenity, or historical or economic significance, Thomson and Dyer taught them to look at it as a series of more or less well composed pictures.

---

[1] Act IV Sc. ii. *Dramatick Works* (1723), p. 141.

Perception advanced one stage further on the way towards the understanding of nature. Well into the nineteenth century Thomson was considered " the Claude of Poets," and his pictures of scenery and of rural life the productions of a master. " Who is there," asked Sir Harris Nicolas in his *Memoirs* (1831), "that has reflected on the magnificence of an extended landscape, or viewed the sun as he emerges from the horizon, and does not feel Thomson's descriptions rush upon the mind, and heighten the enjoyment?" Thomson was to Claude what Scott was to Turner. Critics have compared his colouring to that of Rubens, as Ruskin did Sir Walter's to Tintoret's. With the triumph of the a-formal, romantic vision, Thomson gradually ceased to be read, as being too definite and pompous. Ruskin had him in mind when he commented on Scott's

> The blackening wave is edged with white,
> To inch and rock the seamews fly.

" No form in this. Nay, its chief virtue is that it gets rid of form." But to those who remained true to classic traditions, as contrasted with the Gothic revival, to Claude in spite of Turner, Thomson was the poet of nature, and nature was what Thomson showed them.

But to limit Thomson's influence upon his readers to his descriptions of landscape—numerous and ideal though they are—is to ignore the greater part of his work. This, whether it be didactic—" well conned," as Sir Walter Scott called it—or intimate and rustic, is alike distinguished by extreme richness of colouring, *bravura* of technique, and an observation of the surface of objects, even in unimportant details, that is essentially picturesque.

Almost every line presents some turn of phrase or epithet that forces us to visualize the scene, or that fraction of it which is being alluded to. Taking a few

instances more or less at random : of a gleaner addressed
by an amorous Boaz :

> Then throw that shameful pittance from thy hand,
> But ill applied to such a *rugged* task.
> > *Autumn*, 288.

> Here dwells the direful shark. Lured by the scent
> Of *steaming* crowds, of *rank* disease, and death,
> Behold! he, *rushing*, *cuts* the briny flood.
> > *Summer*, 1015.

> > Through all his lusty veins
> The bull, deep scorched, the raging passion feels . . .
> Scarce seen, *he wades among the yellow broom*,
> While o'er his ample sides the rambling sprays
> *Luxuriant shoot.*
> > *Spring*, 792.

These few instances—among hundreds, and taken
from descriptions of minor events—show Thomson's
faculty for what Gilpin called " high colouring " in
connection with his own attempts at picturesque
description :

It is the aim of picturesque description to bring the images
of nature as forcibly and as closely to the eye as it can, by high
colouring. High colouring is not a string of rapturous epithets,
but an attempt to analyse the views of nature : to mark their
tints and varied lights and to express all this detail in terms as
appropriate and vivid as possible.[1]

The use by both Thomson and Dyer of the verb " to
rush " is characteristic of their pregnant eye. The shark
rushes on his prey, the rushing comet to the sun descends.
Scipio restrained the rapid fate of rushing Rome.
Rushing from the woods, the spires seem from hence
ascending fires. To their daily sports, the noble youth
rushed emulous. Columns rush upon the sky. Similar

[1] Gilpin, *Northern Tour* (1786).

lists could be made out for many such words expressing violent and exaggerated movement: shoot, roll, dash, wrap, bend, rear, stretch, nod, rage, gush, sweep, swell, and so on. High colouring and these accompanying *baroque* movements suggest not Claude or Poussin, scarcely even Salvator, but the rush and sweep of Correggio's dome at Parma, of Rubens' apotheoses, of Borromini's and Bernini's plastic tumults.

Whilst Dyer, as an enthusiastic though unsuccessful painter—a pupil of Richardson—continually writes through a picture frame with a brush, and frequently uses the words " picture " and " paint," Thomson very rarely refers, and then indirectly, to painting. " Scenes " occur less frequently with him even than with Pope. On his journey to Italy he was inclined to minimize the good to be gained from " running abroad only to stare " at pictures and statues. " For my part, I, who have no taste for smelling an old musty stone, look upon these countries with an eye to poetry, in regard that the sisters reflect light and images to one another." [1]

Thomson, while undoubtedly sufficient of a *virtuoso* to enjoy, and be enjoyed by, " polished friends," thus gives little evidence of having been consciously influenced by Claude, or Salvator, or by any particular painter. Rather his mind had the mind-form of the epoch. He less had picturesqueness thrust upon him, than he was born picturesque.

The one important exception to his silence regarding painters is, of course, the famous couplet, quoted at the head of this chapter, describing the pictures in *The Castle of Indolence*, and which for the remainder of the century provided the stock epithets for the three painters in question. As Prof. Manwaring puts it, " That stanza . . . was a handy compendium of criticism for the general public."

[1] Letter to Dodington, 28th November 1731,

Grongar Hill—an eminence near Dyer's birthplace, Aberglasney in Carmarthenshire,[1] is in form similar to his "*Country Walk.*" The poet saunters through a summer's day, having summoned the " Silent Nymph with curious Eye " who paints the fair form of things, to aid her sister:

> Grongar Hill invites my song
> Draw the landscape bright and strong.

As he goes, he and the nymphs paint a series of landscapes drawn from the picturesque aspects of Claude's and Salvator's pictures:

> Still the prospect wider spreads,
> Adds a thousand woods and meads . . .
> And, swelling to embrace the light,
> Spreads around beneath the sight.
> Old castles on the cliffs arise
> Proudly towering in the skies!
> Rushing from the woods, the spires
> Seem from hence ascending fires!
> Half his beams Apollo sheds
> On the yellow mountain heads!
> Gilds the fleeces of the flocks
> And glitters on the broken rocks.
>
> Below me trees unnumbered rise
> Beautiful in various dyes
> The gloomy pine, the poplar blue,
> The yellow beech, the sable yew . . .
> And beyond the purple groove . . .
> Lies a long and level lawn
> On which a dark hill, steep and high,
> Holds and charms the wandering eye!
> Deep are his feet in Towy's flood,
> His sides are cloth'd with waving wood,

---

[1] The house remains, but has not been inhabited for some twenty years. Some furniture is still within, many of the windows broken, and there remains a garden with terraces, over-grown. It is reputed to be haunted, by the country people.

Louvre

Plate IV. NICCOLO POUSSIN. Diogenes casting aside his Bowl

Plate V.   SALVATOR ROSA.   Vessels and Ruins

> And ancient towers crown his brow,
> That cast an awful look below;
> Whose ragged walls, the ivy creeps,
> And with her arms from falling keeps . . .
> 'Tis now the raven's bleak abode;
> 'Tis now th'apartment of the toad. . . .
> While ever and anon there falls
> Huge heaps of hoary moulder'd walls.

It is difficult to limit quotation in a passage so correctly " composed " into a " unity." And impossible not to add this delicious and celebrated passage:

> Ever charming, ever new
> When will the landskip tire the view!
> The fountain's fall, the river's flow,
> The woody valleys, warm and low;
> The windy summits rising high,
> Roughly rushing on the sky!
> The pleasant seat, the ruin'd tower,
> The naked rock, the shady bower,
> The town and village, dome and farm,
> Each give each a double charm,
> As pearls upon an Ethiop's arm.

Passages betokening an artist's feeling for plastic form, as seen in the English country-side, uninfluenced by Italian models, are threaded into the more exotic tissue, such as these:

> How close and warm the hedges lie!
> What streaks of meadow cross the eye!

The Country Walk develops this more intimate strain. The fair dawn and the sweet singing of the birds tempt Dyer, like the Troubadours and Chaucer before him, on an adventure.

> Before the yellow barn I see
> A beautiful variety
> Of strutting cocks, advancing stout
> And flirting empty chaff about.

Again his walk takes him in view of an extensive prospect, but to-day he is more intent on the honeysuckle in the hedgerows, the swain asleep by a rivulet, and on himself drowsing upon a couch of moss

> That o'er the root of oak has grown.

On his way home he comes upon that frequent adjunct of the picturesque scene:

> An old man's smoaky nest I see,
> Leaning on an aged tree:
> Whose willow walls, and furzy brow,
> A little garden sway below . . .
> Here he puffs upon his spade
> And digs up cabbage in the shade:
> His gather'd rags are sable brown,
> His beard and hair are hoary grown.

From the top of Grongar Hill the " ever charming landskip " again bursts upon him, and for a moment he loses himself in its familiar profusion:

> Temples! — and Towns! — and Towers! — and Woods !
> And Hills ! — and Vales! — and Fields! — and Floods!

As he drops down to

> The pleasant dome
> The Poet's pride, the Poet's home,

the sleepy sounds of evening, and of toil completed, float up to him and the cottage hearths send up their spirals of smoke.

The *Ruins of Rome*, which Dyer wrote on his return from Italy in 1740, is, as Dr. Johnson considered, disappointing; but only as a Pannini " ruin-piece " is disappointing. The " living interest " of both is confined to a few shepherds and antiquaries, the figures appropriate for such grandeur having long since mouldered into dust—as both painter and poet delight in reminding

us. There is more than a note of Piranesi's later drama
in the passage that most appealed to Dr. Johnson:

> The pilgrim oft,
> At dead of night, 'mid his oraison hears
> Aghast the voice of Time, disparting towers,
> Tumbling all precipitate, down-dash'd,
> Rattling around, loud thundering to the Moon.

Recalling more evidently such pictures as Claude's
Roman Edifices in Ruins are such passages as these:

> the rising sun
> Flames on the ruins in the purer air
> Tow'ring aloft, upon the glittering plain,
> Like broken rocks, a vast circumference,
> Rent palaces, crush'd columns, rifled moles,
> Fanes roll'd on fanes, and tombs on buried tombs.

> Globose and huge
> Grey mould'ring temples swell, and wide o'ercast
> The solitary landskip, hills and woods,
> And boundless wilds.

More Piranesian, again, in anticipation, this picture of
the Temple of Peace, which also contains a definite
instance of Dyer's picturesque mind:

> Three nodding aisles remain; the rest a heap
> Of sand and weeds; her shrines, her radiant roofs,
> And columns proud, that from her spacious floor,
> As from a shining sea, majestic rose
> A hundred foot aloft—like stately beech
> Around the brim of Dion's glassy lake,
> Charming the mimic painter.

An Epistle to a Famous Painter is apparently a posthumous one to Claude:

> Delightful partner of my heart,
> Master of the loveliest art!

[39]

Such an identification is supported by the request that he shall his mysteries impart, by which he shows:

> Seeming Nature's living glow!
> The beauteous shapes of objects near!
> Or distant ones confus'd in air!
> The golden eve, the blushing dawn,
> Smiling on the lovely lawn!
> And pleasing views of chequered glades!
> And rivers winding through the shades!
> And sunny hills!—And pleasant plains!
> And groups of merry nymphs and swains!

The association of ruins with the above—

> Whose columns, friezes, statues lie
> The grief and wonder of the eye![1]

together with cataracts and calm bays strengthens the relation to Claude.

But Dyer, in spite of his obvious delight in the mellow afternoon light of "soft Lorraine," caught that element into his poetry far less than did Thomson. Dyer had little sense of form, or of composition and unity. He groups his mountains and rivers and sunrises in the approved style—was the first Englishman to do so—but the cheerful tinkle of his verse is not full and golden like Thomson's—as though mellowed through and through in a bath of Claudian light.

The first of "*The Seasons*" to be written was *Winter*, published 1726. Prof. Manwaring observes that compared to the other three, this season contains fewer Italian landscapes, as naturally presenting fewer opportunities than the others. She also suggests that the poet, after its publication, found more aristocratic doors open to him, and consequently had better opportunities of

---

[1] A couplet obviously borrowed from Dryden's (see *supra*, p. 27)
Whose statues, friezes, columns, broken lie.
And though defaced, the wonder of the eye.

seeing Italian landscape pictures. But quite picturesque
in the native English, or more accurately Scots, manner,
is this:

> Now, all amid the Rigours of the Year,
> In the wild Depth of Winter, while, without,
> The ceaseless Winds blow Ice, be my Retreat
> Between the groaning Forest and the Shore,
> Beat by the boundless Multitude of Waves,
> A rural, sheltered, solitary Scene.

Summer (1727) is a succession of suggested landscapes, some more elaborate than others. The sunrise
passage is one of the most lovely in eighteenth-century
verse, and is instinct with *il riposo di Claudio :*

> But yonder comes the powerful *King* of Day
> Rejoicing in the East. The lessening Cloud,
> The kindling Azure, and the Mountain's Brim,
> Tipt with aethereal Gold, his near Approach
> Betoken glad : and now apparent all
> Aslant the Dew-bright Earth, and colour'd Air,
> He looks in boundless Majesty abroad.

Colour—golden, ethereal—is Thomson's great contribution to English verse—and landscape. " The
mellowed Treasures of the Sky " shed a diaphanous
haze, whether explicitly or by the music of the sounds,
over all he writes:

> Young *Day* pours in a-pace,
> And opens all the lawny Prospect wide,
> The dripping Rock, the Mountain's misty Top
> Swell on the Eye, and brighten with the Dawn.

Spring (1728) contains the celebrated *Prospect from
Hagley Park*, though this was not written till 1743 in
the August of which year he visited Hagley, and did
not appear till the 1744 edition. In a letter to the
beloved of his youth, for whom his affection never died

though fate prevented their marriage, he describes
Lord Lyttelton's domain:

> The park, where we pass a great part of our time, is thoroughly
> delightful, quite enchanting. It consists of several little hills,
> finely tufted with wood, and rising loftily one above another;
> from which are seen a great variety of at once beautiful and
> grand extensive prospects: but I am most charmed with its
> sweet embowered retirements, and particularly with a winding
> dale that runs through the middle of it. The dale is overhung
> with woods and enlivened by a stream, that, now gushing from
> deep mossy rocks, now falling in cascades, and now spreading
> in a calm length of water, forms the most natural and pleasing
> scene imaginable. At the source of this water, composed of
> some pretty rills, that purl from beneath the roots of oaks, there
> is as fine a retired seat as lover's heart could wish. There I
> often sit, and with a dear exquisite mixture of pleasure and pain
> of all that love can boast of excellent and tender, I think of you.

In such a mood he approached the famous prospect,
though he transferred his amorous sentiments, in the
poem, to the " loved Lucinda " Fortescue, married in
the succeeding year to his host:

> Meantime you gain the Height, from whose fair Brow
> The bursting Prospect spreads immense around;
> And snatch'd o'er Hill and Dale, and Wood and Lawn,
> And verdant Field, and darkening Heath between,
> And Villages embosom'd soft in Trees,
> And spiry Towns by dusky Columns mark'd
> Of rising Smoak, your Eye excursive roams . . .
> To where the broken Landskip by degrees,
> Ascending, roughens into ridgy Hills;
> O'er which the *Cambrian* Mountains, like far Clouds
> That skirt the blue horizon, doubtful, rise.

A century later another Scot, Hugh Miller (*First
Impressions of England*), visited the vantage point after
the principles of the picturesque had been crystallized:

> The entire prospect . . . enabled me to understand what I
> had used to deem a peculiarity—in some measure a defect—in

the landscapes of the poet Thomson. It must have often struck the Scots reader, that, in dealing with very extended prospects, he rather enumerates than describes.

Miller discovered that owing to the clearer atmosphere of England " the picture *must* become a catalogue " and that this view did actually survey about a thousand square miles.

Autumn was considered by Price as peculiarly " the painter's season." He cited the colouring of the Venetian painters, particularly Giorgione and Titian, as being founded principally on autumn tints. The colour schemes of Mola and Domenico Feti were essentially picturesque in their partiality to rich reds and browns. It is significant that Thomson, still in the " ideal " state of landscape perception—though " picturesque " in so far as his vision was analogous to that of the ideal painters—makes no use of autumn tints in his fourth Season (published 1730). The year is " pale descending," the foliage " dusk and dun." The " stooping Forest pours a rustling Shower of yet untimely Leaves." True to his models, who rarely, if ever, portrayed the fall of the leaf; a phenomenon, as Ruskin would have hastened to point out, that was too allusive to death to accord well with their alleged earthly paradise;—Thomson, as yet uninfluenced by the Venetians, did not consider autumnal colouring a circumstance of beauty. It is curious, since the poem contains a refreshing picture of a boisterous August day, with great Poussin white and dark clouds, and bursts of sunlight:

Rent is the fleecy Mantle of the Sky;
The Clouds fly different; and the sudden Sun,
By Fits effulgent, gilds the illumined Field,
And black by Fits the Shadows sweep along,
A gaily chequered, heart-expanding View,
Far as the circling Eye can shoot around,
Unbounded tossing in a Flood of Corn.

Lady Hertford wrote to Lady Luxborough—who had introduced her to Mr. Shenstone—that she had of course read Mr. Thomson's *Castle of Indolence*, published that year, 1748. It had several claims on modish attention, for " it is after the manner of Spenser," and " there are many pretty paintings in it."

The Castle of Indolence, in fact, combined the two tendencies that were influencing English poetry during the middle of the century. On the one hand was the perception of nature through the medium of the ideal landscape painters. On the other the purely literary research into the poetic forms of the past, in which " genuine poetry " was conceived to lie. Milton and Spenser were the particular objects of this retrospective attention. Whilst Burke, the Wartons and Gray, Blair and Young were later to fix their gaze on the mysterious and romantic side of .Milton; Thomson, Shenstone, Akenside, West, and their contemporaries revived the vocabulary and, in less degree, the spring freshness of Spenser's verse. As painters studied the past masters and the antique, so poets looked back to their predecessors as competent to lighten their eyes. Scott and Shelley, Byron and Keats stand on a mountain of enthusiastic and, on the whole, appreciative literary research; on a pyre of ideal and savage landscape canvases. They were only enabled to look so clearly, and so far, over the face of nature by the gradual piecing up of this platform, with pictures, romances, histories, and the labours of scholars.

The achievement of the Spenserians was to " establish communication " between the Claudian mode of vision and the mediaeval-renaissance attitude of Spenser, with Chaucer not far beyond. They enlarged the scope of the beautiful, as the copyists of Milton enriched that of the sublime. If the immediate effect was not to produce any outstandingly fresh point of view, the way was opened that led to Cowper, Coleridge, and Keats.

The Castle of Indolence, though by way of being mediaeval, " wafts " us in a soothed and dreamy condition through the frame and right into the middle distance of some immense and glowing canvas of Claude. We enter the enchanted scene between the familiar *repoussoirs*—

> In lowly dale, fast by a river's side
> With woody hill o'er hill encompassed round.

Once through this guardian valley, the landscape spreads out:

> Was nought around but images of rest:
> Sleep-soothing groves, and quiet lawns between;
> And flowery beds that slumb'rous influence kest,
> From poppies breathed; and beds of pleasant green. . . .

A few distant figures add drowsy animation:

> Joined to the prattle of the purling rills
> Were heard the lowing herds along the Vale,
> And flocks low bleating from the distant hills,
> And vacant shepherds piping in the dale.

Then a great contrasting sweep of shadowed green and a blue distance:

> Full in the passage of the vale, above,
> A sable silent, solemn forest stood;
> Where nought but shadowy forms were seen to move,
> As Idless fancied in her dreaming mood:
> And up the hills, on either side, a wood
> Of blackening pines, ay waving to and fro,
> Sent forth a sleepy horror through the blood;
> And where this valley winded out below.
> The murmuring main was heard, and scarcely heard, to flow.

No wonder that it was a commonplace of criticism to liken Thomson to Claude. Though he was just as frequently compared to Poussin and Salvator, " the savage " appears if frequently, less noticeably in his poetry, however interested his letters show him to have been in the sublime. A single quotation from *The Seasons* will suffice to establish his ability to wield Salvator's dashing brush:

> Now black and deep, the Night begins to fall,
> A Shade immense! Sunk in the quenching Gloom,
> Magnificent and vast, are Heaven and Earth.
> Order confounded lies; all Beauty void . . .
> Drear is the state of the benighted Wretch,
> Who then, bewildered, wanders through the Dark,
> Full of pale Fancies and Chimaeras huge . . .
> Perhaps, impatient as he stumbles on,
> Struck from the Root of slimy Rushes, blue,
> The Wild-fire scutters round. . . he sinks absorbed,
> Rider and Horse, amid the miry Gulf.[1]

In his letters to Mallet, who went to Italy with the Duke of Montrose's sons and, amid much interest from Thomson and Aikman, wrote *The Excursion*, Thomson urges his friend to attempt the Awful:

My idea of your Poem is a description of the grand works of Nature raised and animated by moral and sublime reflections; therefore, before you quit this earth you ought to leave no great scene unvisited. Eruptions, earthquakes, the sea wrought into a horrible tempest, the abyss, amidst whose amazing prospects, how pleasing must that be of a deep valley covered with all the tender profusion of Spring.

On another occasion he quotes some of Mallet's lines in *The Excursion*, with enthusiastic comments:

You paint Ruin with a masterly hand,

> Ghastful he sits, and views with steadfast glare
> The falling Bust, the Column gray with Moss,

That is such an attitude as I can never enough admire, and even be astonished at.

---

[1] *Autumn*, 1138.

> Save what the wind sighs, and the wailing Owl
> Screams solitary—

Charmingly dreary !

> Where the sad spirit walks with shadowy feet
> His wonted round, or lingers o'er his grave.

What dismal simplicity reigns through these two lines ! They are equal to any ever Shakespeare wrote on the subject.

But Mallet's Italian landscapes, though correctly Claudian, lack alike the charming detail of Dyer's or the luminosity of Thomson's. Young—whose *Night Thoughts* and *Meditations among the Tombs* were considered, as Thomson would have put it, " charmingly dreary "—was Miltonic, rather than Ideal. He enumerates certain sublimities, but does not attempt to connect them into a scene:

> Seas, Rivers, Mountains, Forests, Deserts, Rocks,
> The Promontory's Height, the Depth profound,
> Of subterranean, excavated Grotts . . .
> Ev'n *these* an aggrandising Impulse give;
> Of solemn Thought enthusiastic Heights
> Ev'n *these* infuse.

West, Akenside, Blair, and a host of anonymous, or all but anonymous, versifiers followed in the steps of Thomson and Dyer. West copied both their vision and metre. Akenside, as early as 1744, anticipated Burke's categories of the *Sublime and Beautiful*, in *The Pleasures of Imagination*, by enumerating " three sister-graces, whom the painter's hand, the poet's tongue confesses; the *sublime*, the *wonderful*, the *fair*. He unites the two styles of landscape in his description:

> For verdant valleys and surrounding trees
> A solitary prospect, wide and wild,
> Rush'd on my senses, 'twas a horrid pile
> Of hills and many a shaggy forest mix'd,
> With many a sable cliff and glitt'ring stream.
> Aloft recumbent on the dusky ridge
> The brown woods waved.

Blair's *The Minstrel* contained a landscape highly approved by reviewers:

> . . . Rocks on rocks piled, as by a magic spell
> Fenced from the north and east this savage dell . . .
> Southward a mountain rose with easy swell,
> Whose long gay groves eternal murmur made;
> And toward the western sun a streamlet fell,
> Where, through the cliffs, the eye, remote, survey'd
> Blue hills, and glittering waves, and skies in gold array'd.

With the turn of the century poetry was affected by several collateral associations, which, springing originally from " ideal " perception, had taken root and now added their own colour to the view. In the poetry of the Wartons archaeology, Gothic architecture, and landscape gardening appear as subjects equally suitable for verse with cataracts or vales. Dr. John Dalton (born 1709) and Dr. John Brown (1715-1766) were the earliest explorers and celebrators of the Lake District. While the poetry of Gray rose above set pictures and contemporary vogues, his addiction to ruins and romantic country is well known. English poets began to look at English scenery no longer through Italian spectacles. At first they still used a *Claude-glass* bearing the well-known English trademark: *Thomson and Dyer, Opticians.* But soon that too could be thrown away and nature be observed, more clearly than ever, with the naked eye. The poets moved on into a richer, clearer-speaking, informal country, and dismissed, not always very graciously, the guides who had led them among and through

> Delicious Regions, Plains, Woods, Waters, Shades,
> Grottos, Arbours, Flow'rets, Downs, and rural Shades;
> Arcadian Groves, sweet Tempe! Blest Retreats. . . .[1]

The attitude of the finest minds to Italian landscape by the end of the century was that of Cowper in *The Task:*

[1] Henry Brooke, *Universal Beauty* (1735).

> Strange! there should be found . . .
> Who, satisfied with only pencil'd scenes,
> Prefer to the performance of a God
> Th' inferior wonders of an artist's hand!
> Lovely indeed the mimic work of art;
> But Nature's work far lovelier. I admire—
> None more admires—the painter's magic skill,
> Who shows me that which I shall never see,
> Conveys a distant country into mine,
> And throws Italian light on English walls.

Wordsworth confessed that picturesque analysis of scenes " was never much my habit." He exquisitely patronized " th' inferior wonders of an artist's hand," gravely deliberating the spiritual motives that could possess that good friend of his, but essentially picturesque painter, Sir George Beaumont, when he had the impertinence to paint an imaginary castle in one of Wordsworth's favourite scenes. " Upon the sight of a beautiful picture (painted by Sir G. H. Beaumont, Bt.) " ironically sums up the limitations of the picturesque, as exhibited in pictures of which the frontispiece to this book is typical, under the guise of a graceful compliment:

> Praised be the art whose subtle power could stay
> Yon cloud, and fix it in that glorious shape;
> Nor would permit the thin smoke to escape,
> Nor those bright sunbeams to forsake the day;
> Which stopped that band of travellers on their way,
> Ere they were lost within the shady wood;
> And showed the bark upon the glassy flood
> For ever anchored in her sheltering bay.
> Soul-soothing art! which morning, noon-tide, even,
> Do serve with all their changeful pageantry;
> Thou, with ambition modest yet sublime,
> Here, for the sight of mortal man, hast given
> To one brief moment caught from fleeting time,
> The appropriate calm of blest eternity.

> Aerial rock—whose solitary brow

THE PICTURESQUE

From this low threshold daily meets my sight,
When I step forth to hail the morning light;
Or quit the stars with lingering farewell—how
Shall fancy pay to thee a grateful vow?
How, with the Muse's aid, her love attest?
By planting on thy naked head the crest
Of an imperial castle, which the plough
Of ruin shall not touch. Innocent scheme!
That doth presume to more than to supply
A grace the sinuous vale and roaring stream
Want, through neglect of hoar antiquity.
Rise, then, ye votive towers, and catch a gleam
Of golden sunset, ere it fade and die.

CHAPTER III

THE SUBLIME, THE BEAUTIFUL, AND THE PICTURESQUE

§ I

WE have seen how poetry succeeded, during the first half of the eighteenth century, in discovering that visual qualities gave delight apart from the moral or other significance of the objects that they denoted. The discovery stimulated a renewed interest in aesthetics. The need for aesthetics does not arise so long as perception is purely physical, relating to amenity; or purely rational, relating to knowledge. Only recently has the conviction been recovered that art is an intuitional process, and that the painter is to feel intuitively through his eyes, making us to feel through our eyes, and not to think, reason, or know. So late as Ruskin the virtue of our present attitude was denied; the attitude that regards the function of painting as the revelation of those aspects of reality that no other art can express so well. For intuition, the eye must be able to see abstractly, with as few preconceived ideas and as little knowledge as possible. Mediaeval art attained this attitude through the religious conviction that knowledge was vain. We have come to a similar mistrust of knowledge through science. We have found that reality eludes the scientist as successfully as it does the savage. Perhaps more successfully.

The movement away from the conception of art as knowledge began in the eighteenth century with the discovery of visual properties. The Picturesque is a stage in this movement towards abstraction. The progress made by the end of the eighteenth century was largely nullified by the materialism of the nineteenth, when the perfection of scientific methods revived the

[51]

belief that all apprehension was subject to rational explanation.

The extent of the progress towards abstract vision made during the eighteenth century is summarized in two sentences, defining the purpose of painting, from du Fresnoy (1665) and Reynolds (1781). Said du Fresnoy:

The principal part of painting is to *know* what is most beautiful in nature and most proper to that art.

Said Reynolds:

The art of *seeing* Nature is the greatest object of painting, and the point to which all our studies are directed.

It is the difference between reasoning and contemplation, between knowledge and observation.

At the outset we must understand what " Nature " meant to writers and painters during three-quarters of the eighteenth century. The conception first found its way into England from Italy and the classic writers, through Bellori, as translated by Dryden (1695) in *A Parallel of Poetry and Painting*, prefixed to his translation of du Fresnoy. As Reynolds himself most likely drew his main ideas from these translated passages, one or two extracts may be quoted.

Nature had two meanings. In the ordinary sense it meant the sum of visible phenomena not made by artifice. But in relation to art it frequently signified the Ideal Form of any species or, in a sense given it by Aristotle, an immanent force working in the refractory medium of matter towards the highest perfection of form.[1] Bellori, writing in the latter part of the seventeenth century, used " Nature " in both these senses:

Nature always intends a consummate beauty in her productions, yet through the inequality of the matter, the forms are altered;

---

[1] See *The Discourses of Sir Joshua Reynolds*, ed. Roger Fry. Introduction to Third Discourse.

Plate VI.   JAMES WARD.   St. Donats Castle, Bulls Fighting

V. & A. Museum

Plate VII. CLAUDE LORRAINE. The Ford

and in particular, human beauty suffers alteration for the worse, as we see to our mortification, in the deformities and disproportions which are in us. For which reason the artful painter and the sculptor, imitating the Divine Maker, form to themselves, as well as they are able, a model of the superior beauties; and reflecting on them, endeavour to correct and amend the common nature, and to represent it as it was at first created, without fault, either in colour or in lineament.

This, Bellori admitted, was an intellectual conception, and thus the merit of any painter could be gauged by the intellect. He did not maintain that there was a single, invariable Ideal Form, but that it must vary according to the idea proposed by the painter, as one of strength or delicacy, magnanimity or cheerfulness. But in all cases the method must be the same:

Painters and sculptors, choosing the most elegant natural beauties, perfectionate the idea, and advance their art even above nature itself in her individual productions; which is the utmost mastery of human performance.

John Dennis [1] repeated this, the classic, view of the purpose of art:

The great Design of Arts is to restore the Decays that happened to human Nature by the Fall, by restoring Order. The Design of Logick is to bring back Order to our Conceptions . . . of Moral Philosophy to cure the Disorder in our Passions. . . . Those Arts that make the Senses instrumental to the Pleasure of the Mind, as Painting and Musick, do it by a great deal of Rule and Order.

Shaftesbury, in the *Characteristics* and *Plastics*, which began to be published in 1711, identified beauty with reason and virtue, each of which were perceived by the intellect, through contemplation:

What is beautiful is harmonious, and proportionable; what

---

[1] John Dennis, *Essay on the Operas after the Italian Manner* (1706). Included in *Select Works* (1718).

is harmonious and proportionable is true; and what is at once both beautiful and true is of consequence agreeable and good.[1]

Anything that produced an instantaneous, sensuous relish was prejudicial to the moral significance of a picture. Thus colour was to be excluded from " heroic " painting as pleasing the senses instantaneously instead of by contemplation pleasing the mind. This mistrust of visual qualities is the fundamental difference between the poetry of Thomson and Pope. Thomson raised " a separate and flattering pleasure to the senses," Pope appealed solely to the intellect.

The object of the contemplation that Shaftesbury identified with aesthetic appreciation was to be "Nature's genuine Order "; the ideal form and harmony of things existing " before the Fall." These were to be found, for example, in landscape as revealed by Claude and Salvator. In *The Moralists, a Rhapsody* he puts the moral that he draws from scenery:

I shall no longer resist the Passion growing in me for Things of a *natural* kind; where neither *Art*, nor the *Conceit* or *Caprice* of Man has spoil'd the *genuine Order*, by breaking in upon that *primitive State*. Even the rude *Rocks*, the mossy *Caverns*, the irregular unwrought *Grotto's* and the broken *Falls* of Waters, with all the horrid Graces of the *Wilderness* itself, as representing Nature more, will be the more engaging and appear with a Magnificence beyond the Mockery of princely Gardens.[2]

Francis Hutcheson, in his *Inquiry into the Original of our Ideas of Beauty and Order*, carried this intellectual conception further, but at the same time opened a postern in the Castle of Reason. He managed to separate the Sense of Beauty from the Moral Sense, and maintained that the apprehension of beauty was instantaneous, free both of intellect and will. Yet beauty still appealed to the mind. Beauty itself he conceived to consist in

[1] *Characteristics*, vol. iii, p. 182.
[2] *Ibid.*, vol. ii, p. 393.

Order amid Nature's infinite Variety, and Variety amid mankind's Order. The conception is that underlying the earliest efforts of the landscape gardener, with his rectangular lakes fringed by groves, and vistas centering in cascades and obelisks.

The Analysis of Beauty, published by William Hogarth in 1753, marks a big step away from rational beauty, by setting up "the sensibilities" as means to the perception of beauty. Sentiment and grace make their first appearance in the theory of art. In his "line of beauty," derived from the baroque forms of late Italian art, we get the origin of Burke's definition of the quality, and in his denial of beauty to symmetry, simplicity, and distinctness, he foreshadows the coming revolt from classicism. His inclusion of Size as a quality of beauty, however, strained the confines of that category. It becomes clear that not only has beauty grown to be a very different conception to Shaftesbury's Truth and Virtue, but that its attributes have got unwieldy. The word "beauty" was insufficient to describe all that the men of mid-century felt to be significant.

The new word, the new category, was provided by Burke's *Inquiry into the Origin of our Ideas of the Sublime and Beautiful*, published 1756, revised 1765. Vastness became one of the sublime qualities. He was not the first to regard sublimity as aesthetic, but the first to recognize it as a category co-ordinate with the Beautiful, thereby beginning, as the late Bernard Bosanquet recognized, "a great enlargement of aesthetic appreciation." The Sublime had been noted by Shaftesbury as the highest order of scenery. In *The Moralists* he described a tremendous Alpine scene, with precipices, cataracts, and storms:

Here thoughtless Men, seized with the Newness of such Objects, become thoughtful, and willingly contemplate the incessant Changes of their Earth's Surface. They see, as in one instant, the Revolutions of past Ages, the fleeting forms of

Things, and the Decay even of their own *Globe*. . . . The wasted Mountains shew them the World itself only as a noble Ruin, and make them think of its approaching Period.

Shaftesbury makes sublimity, as here described, solely the " moral emblem " of ruin and decay, a *memento mori* on a gigantic scale. It is interesting to find him remarking that it is the " newness " of such scenes that seizes " thoughtless men." When the newness had worn off, the wayfarer, more disinterested, would be struck by the " forces of nature " and the eminently picturesque character of the scenery.

That is what has happened to Burke's Sublimity. He himself saw in Astonishment the most lofty state of the soul, and the most overwhelming emotional product of the Sublime, when " all motions were suspended, with some degree of horror," the mind being so filled with the object that it could entertain no other. Sublimity only remained a defensible category so long as the philosopher was young and naïve.

Burke, and the eighteenth century generally, had all the zest and enthusiasm of children, newly discovering a park full of terrible woods, precipitous hills, and bottomless lakes. Painting and poetry had suddenly enabled them to notice these features, and they attributed the emotions experienced in face of them to qualities in the objects themselves. Thus the " newness " that Shaftesbury was acute enough to see was the emotive quality in sublime prospects, is what is really responsible for an objective view of emotion. To Burke sublimity, as an aesthetic category, still had " newness "; such novelty, in fact, that he erected a complete objective system upon it. We may indeed take it for an axiom that, when any fresh source of emotion is discovered, the tendency is at first to endow that source with " natural properties " causative of that particular emotion. Of late years, for example, certain primitive patterns and forms of sculpture have been considered by many people to have an objective significance for them. When such patterns have become more familiar, the same people recognize that their original emotion was produced by a subconscious association of ideas, of which the pattern acted as a symbol.

Burke opened the way to romanticism. His epigrams, "a clear idea is another name for a little idea" and "no work of art can be great but as it deceives," contain the germs of romanticism in a nutshell. In relating Terror, Obscurity, and the Infinite to aesthetic emotion he provided a basis for the art of the coming hundred years. Indeed, the very existence of aesthetic emotion was first acknowledged by him. To Shaftesbury beauty was ultimately a thought. On Hutcheson it produced an instantaneous sensation which, however, he was unable to explain owing to the intellectual nature of his system. Hogarth got so far as acknowledging the existence of "sensibilities." But it was Burke who sponsored passion and emotion as the products of aesthetic perception. It was this substitution of emotion for reason, and of passion for decorum that made possible the great poetry and the vile architecture of the nineteenth century. He loosed emotion from the corsets of the intellect.

He made all emotion instinctive, eliminating mental processes altogether. Emotive qualities were confined to objects. These, perceived by one or other of the five senses, instantaneously affected one of the two passions, through the imagination.

These passions (or, as we should say, instincts) were those of self-preservation and self-propagation. Objects that affected the former gave rise to fear, and were sublime. Those affecting the latter awakened sensations of sex, tenderness, or pleasure, and were beautiful.

Emotion was only experienced, however, if the immediate physical impulses that the objects aroused were resisted. Flight or indulgence precluded emotion. The physical sensation corresponding to emotion was thus felt only as a result of self-control.

These physical bases of emotion—which Burke took pains to describe—are of great importance for the understanding of eighteenth-century art. He thus defined the sensation of sublimity:

Whatever leads to raise in man his own opinion, produces a sort of swelling and triumph, that is extremely grateful to the human mind. And this swelling is never more perceived, nor operates with more force, than when without danger we are conversant with terrible objects,—the mind always claiming to itself some of the dignity and importance of the things which it contemplates.

His description of the sensation aroused by beauty explains clearly the physical basis for the " waving " and " serpentine " forms predominant in the art of the mid-century, in the lines of Chippendale's furniture, " Capability " Brown's serpentine paths and lakes, and Hogarth's " line of beauty ":

Most people must have observed the sort of sense they have had of being swiftly drawn in an easy coach on a smooth turf, with gradual ascents and declivities. This will give a better idea of the Beautiful than almost anything else.

It was this objective view of emotion, and the establishment of the categories " Sublime " and " Beautiful," each with their attributes, that led to the formation of the third, " the Picturesque," to contain the large number of objects and to account for the pleasure with which they were beheld, that Burke's categories omitted.

The attributes of the Sublime were:

1. *Obscurity*. It induced Terror to a considerable degree, and its judicious use in poetry and painting contributed to this effect. He quoted Milton's gloomy pomp and dusky descriptions where " all

is dark, uncertain, confused, terrible, and sublime to the last degree." In applied art he instanced Historical Painting, in which gay or gaudy drapery could never have a happy effect.

2. *Power.*

3. *Privations* were sublime because terrible. Such were Vacuity, Darkness, Solitude, Silence.

4. *Vastness*, a greatness of dimension. Height he considered the most moving kind of vastness, though possibly it was more so when regarded as depth.

5. *Infinity* had a tendency " to fill the mind with that sort of delightful Horror " which was the most genuine effect and truest test of the Sublime. Such emotion could be induced by the two artificial forms of infinity—*Succession* and *Uniformity*.

6. *Succession* impressed the imagination with an idea of progress beyond actual limits, and thence of the Infinite.

7. *Uniformity* produced the illusion of Infinity because, if the figures of the parts should be changed, the imagination at every change found a check. Hence a *Rotund* form, in presenting no checks to the eye, simulated Infinity. Whether in a building or in a plantation of trees (Capability Brown's " clump ") the *Rotund* had a noble effect. Obviously Burke had here in mind the Pantheon, as he went on to indicate how a cruciform church was less Sublime than a heathen temple, because all of the former could not be seen from any one point. " Nothing is so prejudicial to the grandeur of a building than to abound in angles." Such a misfortune arose from an inordinate thirst for Variety—which was bound to leave very little true taste in him who experienced it.

If the Sublime depended for its effect on surprise, Beauty, he maintained, was equally instantaneous in its

effect, relaxing the nerves and fibres, and thus inducing a
degree of bodily languor. It was Jeffrey who fastened
on this fallacy, pointing out that, if it were true, the most
beautiful of experiences was a hot bath. Burke's Beauty
was wholly sensuous. He disallowed any kind of contemplation or intellectual examination. Accordingly he
ruled out the beauty of proportion, as requiring reference to the understanding. Hutcheson had come up
against the same difficulty in respect of symmetry. He,
however, modified his theory in order to include it.
Burke preserved his theory at the cost of the quality.

The attributes of Beauty were Smallness, Smoothness, Gradual Variation, and Delicacy of form and
colour.

Thus had Burke broken away from a moral conception of beauty, but got only as far as sensuous concepts.
Moreover, his theory did not touch objects that had
neither the smoothness of the beautiful nor the over-
whelmingness of the sublime. These were to be recognized later as forming the third category, the Picturesque.

This extension was to some extent brought about by
the *Discourses* of Sir Joshua Reynolds, delivered between
1769 and 1790. They approach perception from a
different point, since Reynolds was concerned less with
a theory of aesthetics than with the painting of nature.
Whereas earlier investigators had asked themselves
" What is beautiful? " Reynolds inquired " What is
nature?" In the mutation of his answers to this question
lies his importance in the emergence of the picturesque
point of view.

For the *Discourses* show a progressive trend away from
the Grand Style of vision towards the looser emotional-
ism that animated the Picturesque point of view, and
flooded art and criticism as the Theory of Association.
Reynolds uses the word Nature in three distinct senses.
(1) There is the unspecialized sense, of nature as the
sum of visible phenomena not made by artifice: " There

are excellences in painting beyond what is commonly called the imitation of Nature." (2) In the earlier Discourses, in which the Grand Style is his subject, nature is used in the Aristotelian sense, of an immanent force working in the refractory medium of matter towards the highest perfection of form: " The terms beauty, or nature, which are general ideas, are but different modes of expressing the same thing." But Aristotle considered τὸ βέλτιον, which the artist discovers, as an ideal form more perfect and more harmonious than any that nature produces—the form which she is always striving to produce but is always deflected by "accident" from achieving. Reynolds on the other hand conceived the ideal, " natural " form to be the " common form," the average, which might almost be arrived at by taking a compound photograph of all the individuals of a species. This was accepted as beautiful simply by custom, because we were more used to the prevailing type than to the less common divergences, the more extreme of which were deformities. (3) Reynolds's last meaning of " Nature " epitomizes his progress from the categories and generalization of the grand style:— Nature is not only what nature actually produces, or what nature strives to produce, but whatever is agreeable to the affections and predispositions of the mind: " In short, whatever pleases has in it what is analogous to the mind, and is, therefore, in the highest and best sense of the word, nature."[1]

So far as the Picturesque is concerned, this definition sanctioned the literal representation of all natural forms that gave pleasure to the imagination. Painters gradually ceased to speculate on what the ideal form of any class of objects might be, and began to substitute such forms as by usage were established as " artistic," that is to say, picturesque. He made, however, the im-

[1] For an admirable exposition of Reynolds's views of nature, see Fry, *op. cit.*

portant reservation that only the cultivated mind could be relied upon to appreciate artistic truth.

The habit of contemplating and brooding over the ideas of great genius, till you find yourself warmed by the contact, is the only method of forming an artist-like mind. It is impossible, in their presence, to think or invent in a mean manner.[1]

Elsewhere he impressed that the reading of poetry was the best possible way of adapting a mind to paint in the Grand Manner, since for Heroic work he still maintained that a painter must see with the eyes of a poet. But in the case of landscape, when the " artist-like " eye, trained in " the habit of contemplating and brooding upon the ideas of great genius," looked upon the actual face of nature, a " picturesque " attitude was the result. The Picturesque Eye was a form of, if not identical with, the artist-like eye. So, too, the picturesque point of view was contemplative. " Brooding " took the place of reasoning, and a conception of beauty derived from pictures that of a mental concept derived from morality.

The movement of Reynolds's mind from the grand humanistic vision of Burke, towards the picturesque attitude, though it is somewhat obscured by his presidential caution of speech, culminates in the admirable fourteenth Discourse, the last that he made before his eyesight failed, whereupon, with fortitude and dignity, he withdrew from public life. The discourse chiefly deals with the art and personality of Gainsborough, who had recently died, and must be recognized with his friends Uvedale Price and Gilpin, as the part founder of the Picturesque. Early in the Discourse Reynolds suggested the advantage to painters of being able to look at nature through the eyes of acknowledged masters. Most of his teaching had emphasized the necessity for studying their methods, brooding upon their ideas, but

[1] Twelfth Discourse.

he had been reluctant to admit that any save the masters of the Grand Style should be examined with a view to emulation. Hitherto he had conscientiously suppressed his own preferences, in many cases for what he considered inferior excellences. Yet the *Journal* of his tour to Flanders shows him preferring Breughel to Rubens in certain cases, admiring the Van Eycks and, on his visit to Italy, feeling intenser interest in the Primitives than in many more correct but less spiritually true exponents of generalized nature. His own technique and style of painting is a standing testimony to his affection for the Venetians. But, although he knew himself incapable of producing what he conceived to be the highest art, and accordingly contented himself with a style that he preferred and could manage, yet he held it to be his duty to induce others to concentrate on the grand style. This course, though it had deplorable effects on English art, and moved Barry to frenzy against Reynolds who could live on the fat of the land by practising what he refused to preach, was undoubtedly taken with only the humblest and most conscientious intentions.

In this discourse Reynolds was largely occupied in doing justice to one whom, though he had all his life known him as his rival, Mr. Gainsborough, he now did not hesitate to call simply and sonorously, " Gainsborough." In the restrained enthusiasm of the occasion he throws his didactic preferences to the winds, and eats his own words. Whereas he had so diligently repeated " keep your eyes fixed on the higher excellences. Even if you are imperfect, you are imperfect artists of the highest order," now he proclaims, for the first time without qualifications: " We have the sanction of all mankind in preferring genius in lower ranks to feebleness and insipidity in the higher," and confesses his own preference:

I take more interest in, and am more captivated with, the powerful impression of nature which Gainsborough exhibited in his portraits and landscapes, and in the interesting simplicity and elegance of his ordinary little beggar children, than with any works of the Roman School of painting since Sacchi and Maratti—the *Ultimi Romanorum.*

He then recalled some of the habits of Gainsborough, which confirm his position as the father of the picturesque method of seeing. Reynolds himself recognized his essentially picturesque mind:

He had a habit of continually remarking to those who happened to be about him whatever peculiarity of countenance, whatever accidental combination of figure, or happy effects of light and shadow, occurred in prospects, in the sky, in walking the streets or in company.

And from the fields he brought into his painting room stumps of trees, weeds, and animals of various kinds; and designed them, not from memory, but immediately from the objects. He even framed a kind of model of landscapes on his table; composed of broken stones, dried herbs, and pieces of looking glass, which he magnified and improved into rocks, trees, and water.

As to how far the latter practice was valuable in giving hints, Reynolds suggested that the professor of Landscape Painting would inform them. He himself doubted it—though admitted that everything depended on the mentality of the user.[1] Reynolds then made the distinction which separates the picturesque from the ideal in Landscape, Gainsborough from Claude:

If Gainsborough did not look at Nature with the poet's eyes, it must be acknowledged that he saw her with the eye of a painter.

The capacity for seeing nature with a painter's eye was picturesque vision.

---

[1] Constable used to bring home from his walks stones, leaves, and mosses that had caught his eye (C. R. Leslie, *Life of Constable*). Gainsborough may have adopted this practice after seeing de Loutherbourg's *Eidophusikon.* See p. 239 *infra.*

§ 2

The scene now shifts from the studio and the study to the borderland of Wales. In place of the celebrated figures of Burke and Reynolds we find two squires, Uvedale Price[1] of Foxley, Herefordshire (1747-1829), and Richard Payne Knight of Downton, Salop (1750-1824), continuing the analysis of appreciation begun by Shaftesbury. They were not alone. The *Observations on Picturesque Beauty* made by the Rev. William Gilpin of Boldre, Hants, were beginning to be published, while in 1790 the Rev. Archibald Alison published the *Essays on the Principles of Taste* that embodied his theory of the Association of Ideas. The two squires, no less than the two parsons, were characteristic types, not only of the country gentleman of a century ago, but of the " artist-like " mind on the sanctions of which Reynolds depended for his last interpretation of nature. Price was a friend of Reynolds and Gainsborough, Knight one of the principal dilettanti of the day, figuring frequently in the Farington Diary. Both had been brought up amid exceptionally picturesque scenery, had travelled, and were, above all things, interested in the landscape gardening of their seats. Each, moreover, proved to be a writer of considerable ability: Price in a genial and humorous vein, Knight with more incisive brilliance. In their hands the Picturesque ceases to be a mere concept and becomes a set of working principles for gardeners, architects, and travellers. Finding that Burke's *Sublime and Beautiful* failed to account for his pleasure in the lanes and woods and views of Foxley, Price set himself to work out

A mode of study which will best enable a man of a liberal and intelligent mind to judge of the forms, colours, effects, and

---

[1] Price received a baronetcy for parliamentary services in 1828.

combinations of visible objects either in single compositions or else as parts of scenery.

Accepting Burke's objective method and Reynolds's admonition to brood on the works of great masters, Price began not only to look at nature as though it were a series of pictures, but to look at pictures "as a set of experiments of different ways in which trees, buildings, and water may be disposed." His *Essays on the Picturesque* (1794) were, in fact, addressed to his own landed class, and were written under the conviction that

> The study of pictures can only produce any real advantage if we use it as a school in which we may learn to enlarge, correct and refine our view of Nature and by that route become good judges of scenery.

The Picturesque was to be a practical aesthetic for gardeners, tourists, and sketchers.

The attributes that formed his new category of the Picturesque he summarized as the opposites to those of Beauty: namely roughness, sudden variation, and irregularity.

Turning to the works of the great masters, he found that a large number were neither beautiful nor sublime, though they completely confirmed the principles of picturesqueness. For instance:

> Salvator Rosa is one of the most remarkable among painters for his picturesque effects; in no other masters are seen such abrupt and rugged forms—such sudden deviations both in his figures and landscapes; and the roughness and broken touches of his pencilling admirably accord with the objects they characterize.

Guido Reni, on the other hand, was as eminent for the beauty of his celestial countenances, where lines melted and flowed into each other. There is nothing in his pictures " that can disturb that pleasing languor, which the union of all that is beautiful impresses on the soul." Again, " Of all the painters who have left behind them a high reputation, none perhaps was more uniformly smooth than Albano, or less deviated into abruptness of any kind." On the other hand Mola, the scholar of Albano,[1] was as remarkable for his affinity to Salvator:

There is hardly any painter, whose pictures more immediately catch the eye of a connoisseur than those of Mola, or less attract the notice of a person unused to painting. Salvator has a savage grandeur, often in the highest degree sublime; and sublimity in any shape will command attention; but Mola's scenes and figures are, for the most part, neither sublime nor beautiful; they are the most perfect examples of the higher style of the picturesque.

Claude, again, epitomized all that was beautiful. Assuming that Burke was right in predicating that a soft and pleasing repose was the effect and characteristic of the beautiful, could anything be more beautiful than *il riposo di Claudio*? Rubens, on the other hand, was strongly given to a picturesque disposition of his figures —often so as to sacrifice every other consideration to intricacy, contrast, and striking variation. In point of brilliancy, and extreme splendour of light, no other pictures could stand in competition. Price particularly admired the dazzle and " flicker " of his effects.

At this point he felt justified in deducing the physical means by which variety and intricacy stimulated the eye. It was, he conceived, by *irritation*, by the quick succession of light to shade, and colour to colour. Rembrandt, he considered, even better than Rubens, achieved this effect in his " rough manner of pencilling," producing what most nearly approached to the glitter and irritation caused by real light.

Yet he did not envisage any development of painting such as pointilism, however he would have approved of

---

[1] P. F. Mola, 1609-1666.

Constable's impressionism. " Breadth," he maintained, of composition and colouring, were as essential to picturesque landscapes as to pictures. Thus twilight was the ideal hour for the painter; and the improver of grounds should attempt to produce the same largeness of masses as twilight showed. Price selected Teniers, Jan Steen, Ostade, and particularly Gerard Dou as examples of how detail could be united with breadth. Similarly autumn, rather than spring, was the painter's season, the latter producing a glaring and spotty effect with its light and brilliant tints.

Thus, however Price and Knight might theorize about light as the cause of picturesque emotion, light effects did not become picturesque till the impressionists had familiarized the world with their renderings of them. Sir George Beaumont, who used to paint from nature, included a fiddle in his sketching apparatus, since " a good picture, like a good fiddle, should be brown," and maintained that there ought to be one brown tree in every landscape. Sir George Beaumont's brown tree has, in fact, survived to our own day, and may be taken as the hall-mark of the picturesque mentality.

Richard Payne Knight inherited Downton when he was fourteen years old, in 1764. By a curious coincidence Price had also come into Foxley at the same early age. The next thirty years were spent by both the friends severally in travel to Italy, in fulfilling the duties of Whig members of Parliament, and in remodelling their houses and grounds. Knight, in addition, made several excursions into scholastic literature, but in 1794, the same year as Price published the *Essays*, turned his talents to the picturesque in *The Landscape. A didactic poem*, which he dedicated to Price:

> How best to bid the verdant Landscape rise
> To please the fancy and delight the eyes; . . .
> T' adorn, arrange, to separate and select

[68]

Plate VIII.   SIR THOMAS LAWRENCE.   Homer reciting the Iliad

Plate IX. SIR THOMAS LAWRENCE.

Portrait of Richard Payne Knight

With secret skill and *counterfeit neglect*
I sing—Do thou, O Price, the song attend.

The poem, of its kind, is far from bad. It was a bitter
attack on Capability Brown and Repton, and Knight
had some of Pope's acid in his pen, charged with
which the rhyming couplet is the most deadly literary
weapon.

Up to this time Price and Knight seem to have been
on terms of intimacy, their widely different tempera-
ments finding common ground in their enthusiasm for
the picturesque and their objection to the Brown-Repton
school of landscape gardeners. But in a note to the
second edition of *The Landscape*, Knight criticized
Price's distinction between the Beautiful and the
Picturesque, and, in reply, Price in 1801 published
*A Dialogue on the Distinct Characters of the Picturesque and
Beautiful*, where Knight's contentions were apparently
discredited.

Knight's contention was that the picturesque consisted only in a manner of viewing things—with an eye
and mind educated in the principles of painting; and
that picturesque beauty was simply the beauty of visible
objects; called so because painting, by imitating the
visible qualities only, isolated beauty from whatever
irrelevant qualities or circumstances might tend to
conceal it.

The *Dialogue* provides an entertaining approach to
picturesque doctrine. Three gentlemen meet at an inn
door, Mr. Howard (who sustains Knight's part), Mr.
Hamilton (Price), just returned from a tour together
through the north of England, and Mr. Seymour, an
intelligent but inexpert party, eager to learn the mysteries of the picturesque. The friends accordingly set
out for " a seat in the neighbourhood where there was
a very numerous and well chosen collection of pictures,"
comprising examples of most of the Dutch and Italian

painters popular at the time. On the way they passed several picturesque scenes, debating as they went.

The first " scene " in their walk " might have been painted by Morland or Teniers." It was a hovel beneath a gnarled oak, with an aged gipsy, a rusty donkey, mellow tints, and dark shadows. Mr. Hamilton discovered in this singular scene " The two qualities of roughness and sudden variation, joined to that of irregularity," which he considered were " the most efficient causes of the picturesque." Mr. Seymour protested that it was merely ugly, while Mr. Howard pointed out that the scene had a beauty belonging exclusively to the sense of vision, made up of light variously gradated, and quite independent of the persons and things that composed it. It was that abstract beauty that the painter perceived and was able to transmit in a picture. It might, therefore, be termed Picturesque Beauty. A layman could not perceive this beauty until it was separated in the artist's imagination, unless he was himself possessed " of a painter's eye trained by the love and study of pictures." Rembrandt, Ostade, Teniers, and other Dutch painters had produced the most *beautiful* pictures by the most exact imitation of the most ugly and disgusting objects in nature. In the originals of these, animal disgust and the nauseating repugnance of appetite, overwhelmed every milder pleasure of vision, which a blended variety of mellow and harmonious tints must *necessarily* produce on the eye, in nature as well as in art, if viewed in both with the same degree of abstracted and impartial attention. Mr. Seymour could not bring himself to view the scene thus abstractedly, withholding the operation of his mind. Whilst Howard might see in it only light and colour, he himself was painfully conscious of its squalor and poverty. " I can imagine," he admitted, " a man of the future, who may be born without the sense of feeling, being able to see nothing but light variously modified, and that such a way of considering nature would be just. For then the eye would see nothing but what in point of harmony was beautiful. But that pure abstract enjoyment of vision, our inveterate habits will not let us partake of." And even if the colours in the scene *did* match harmoniously, and " the wild and singular appearance of the blasted oak, its bark full of knobs, spots, and stains, please the painter more than a tree in full vigour," he could not bring himself to call the whole or any part of the scene *beautiful*. Could not some term be invented to describe this class of objects which, obviously not beautiful, was yet stimulating to eyes accustomed to painting?

" The term you require," said Mr. Hamilton, " has already been invented, for, according to my ideas the word Picturesque has exactly the meaning you have just described. The set of objects we have been looking at struck you with their singularity; but instead of thinking them beautiful, you were disposed to call them ugly. Now, I should neither call them beautiful nor ugly, but picturesque; for they have qualities highly suited to the painter and his art, but which are, in general, less attractive to the bulk of mankind."

Having crossed a wild common, the party began to enter a hollow lane. " The banks were high and steep; and the soil, being sand mixed with stone, had crumbled away in many places from among the junipers, heath and furze, which, with some thorns, and a few knotty old pollard oaks, and yews, clothed the sides.

" A little way further, but in sight from the entrance, stood a cottage, which was placed in a dip of the bank near the top. Some rude steps led from it to the lane, and a few paces from the bottom of these steps, the rill which ran on the same side of the lane, had washed away the soil and formed a small pool under the hollow of the bank. At the edge of the water, some large flat stones had been placed, on which a woman and some girls were beating clothes; and a little boy stood looking on; some other children sat upon the steps, and an old woman was leaning over the wicket of the cottage porch, while her dog and cat lay basking in the sun before it.

" ' I wonder,' said Mr. Seymour, ' why they do not clear the sides of this lane a little, and let in the sun and air; the soil, indeed, is naturally dry, but there are ruts and rough places, over which I have already stumbled two or three times; it is really impossible to walk three together.'

" The two others were so occupied by the scene, that they hardly heard what he had said, or missed him as he passed on before them. And the whole way up the lane, they met with so many interesting objects, that they were a long while getting to the top of the ascent; where they discovered their companion seated under a spreading tree, and gazing with delight on what they began to look at with no less rapture ":—an extensive view over a rich, green country, in which a river wound by the village, church, and mansion, whither they were bound, the horizon being bounded by hills " of the most graceful form." At their feet the lane widened out, forming a frame with its shaggy banks, while clumps of fern enriched the turf of the foreground.

Having wondered what had detained his friends for so long in the lane, where he had noticed no gipsies, asses, or hovels, Mr. Seymour demanded whether this fine prospect was beautiful or picturesque. Mr. Howard replied it was indifferently either. Mr. Hamilton called it beautiful, since it must inevitably appeal to all mankind, in distinction to the lane that they had just passed through, which was picturesque; " and that it does not suit the general taste, you yourself have given a strong proof, who seem by no means insensible to another kind of scenery. Nothing detained you there, everything detained us."

They soon dropped down to the village, by which

stood the object of their walk. *En route* their eyes were caught by the parsonage house, " which exhibited a singular mixture of neatness and irregularity. Something seemed to have been added by each incumbent, just as a room, a staircase or a passage was wanting; there were all kinds of projections—of differently shaped windows and chimneys—of rooms in odd corners —of roofs crossing each other in different directions. This curious old fabric was kept in the highest order,— part of it was rough cast, part only white-washed, but the whole of a pleasing quiet colour; vines, roses, jasmines and honey suckles flourished against the walls, and hung over the old-fashioned porch, and a luxuriant Virginia creeper grew quite to the top of a mossy stone chimney." Mr. Seymour was charmed with the neatness and cheerfulness of the whole, but, in view of its extreme irregularity, could not venture to call it anything but odd. Mr. Hamilton pointed out that its irregularity alone rendered the building picturesque, though its clean colour and bright flowers prevented it from being, like the mouldy gipsy's hovel, *merely* picturesque. Age and decay might reduce it to utter picturesqueness. For the present it partook of the beautiful as well.

The incumbent then appeared, together with his daughter.

SEYMOUR (*as they were walking on*): "I think that there is a sort of resemblance between the good old parson's daughter and his house. She is upright indeed, and so are the walls, but her features have a little of the same irregularity, and her eyes are somewhat inclined to look across each other like the roofs of the old parsonage. Yet a clear white skin, clean white teeth, though not very even, and a look of neatness and cheerfulness, in spite of these irregularities, made me look at her with pleasure; and I really think, if I were of the cloth, I should like very well to take the living, the house and its inhabitant. You, Hamilton, I suppose, were thinking how age and neglect would operate upon her as upon the house, and how simply picturesque she would become, when her cheeks were a little furrowed and weather-stained, and her teeth had got a slight incrustation."

HAMILTON: " No, indeed. I thought of her much as you did; for I was reflecting how great a conformity there is between our tastes for the sex, and for other objects, though Howard, I know, holds a very different opinion. Here is a house and a woman without any pretensions to beauty; and yet many might prefer them both, to such as had infinitely more of what they and the world would acknowledge to be regularly beautiful. [But then, again, deprive the woman, or the house, of those qualities that belong to beauty, though they will not alone confer that distinction, and you will hardly find any man fond enough of the picturesque, to make that sort of proposition.] "

The last sentence, enclosed by brackets, was added in the later edition in consequence of Knight's ridicule of the passage in his attack on the picturesque as a category, in his subsequent work *On Taste :*

My friend Mr. Price indeed admits squinting among the irregular and picturesque charms of the parson's daughter, whom, (to illustrate the picturesque in opposition to the beautiful) he wishes to make appear lovely and attractive, though without symmetry or beauty. He has not, however, extended the details of this want of symmetry and regularity further than to the features of the face; though to make the figure consistent, the same happy mixture of the irregular and picturesque must have prevailed throughout her limbs; and consequently she must have hobbled as well as squinted; and had hips and shoulders as irregular as her teeth, cheeks, and eyebrows. All my friend's parental fondness for his system is certainly necessary to make him think such an assemblance of picturesque circumstances either lovely or attractive; or induce him to imagine that he should be content with such a creature, as a companion for life;

and I heartily congratulate him that his fondness did not arise at an earlier period, to obstruct him in a very different choice.[1]

The discussion of the category to which the parson's daughter properly belonged brought the three friends to the picture gallery. Mr. Seymour, feeling that he had already " had a very good lecture from real objects," was partially converted to Price's view of picturesqueness as an objective category comprising all rough and abrupt objects. Knight, in the person of Mr. Howard, was, however, given a good run for his contention that picturesque beauty was the abstract beauty of coloured light, so called because pictures separated it from other irrelevant qualities.

The technical brilliance of a Rubens was admired, and Mr. Seymour noticed the resemblance of a Claude to the view by which he had recently been captivated on their walk. " What a picture," he exclaimed, " to have in one's sitting-room! a scene where one imagines that every other sense must be charmed besides that of seeing! " He believed that even people without a painter's eye must be charmed by such a picture. This was true. The immense popularity of Claude and his imitators was owing as much to the ideal nature of his scenery as to his colouring, which a few critics appreciated, and his mastery of design, which was largely ignored. Ideal landscape had, by 1800, been accepted as the type of beauty both for painters and poets. Howard next gained a point over Hamilton by getting Seymour to agree to the beauty of colouring in a Teniers depicting a woman washing " tripes, guts, and garbage." To which Hamilton countered with a Magdalen by Guido, Seymour confessing that it was still more beautiful. A Caravaggio, in contrast, was found to be excessively powerful with its polarized light and black shadows, though Seymour disliked the characters represented in

[1] Price married Lady Caroline Carpenter in 1787.

comparison with the Magdalen of Guido. A Salvator canvas, of a landscape with banditti, carried Seymour off his feet:

> There is a sublimity in this scene of rocks and mountains, savage and desolate as they are, that is very striking; the whole, as you say, is a perfect contrast to the Claude; and it is really curious to look from one to the other. In that, everything seems formed to delight the eye and the mind of man—in this, to alarm and terrify the imagination; in the Claude, the inhabitants inspire us with ideas of peace, security, and happiness—in this of Salvator, (for I now recollect and feel the full force of those lines I only admired before)—
>
>> Appears in burnish'd arms some savage band;
>> Each figure boldly pressing into life,
>> And breathing blood, calamity and strife." [1]

" Why, Seymour," said Mr. Howard, " you talk with more enthusiasm than either Hamilton or myself." "Where," replied Mr. Seymour, " there is so much poetry in pictures it is unnecessary to have a painter's eye to enjoy them, although a knowledge of the art would greatly enhance the pleasure." This is our old friend *ut pictura poesis*, but by this time come to be a commonplace such as only a Seymour would remark. The " poetry of painting " led Hamilton to point out a Bacchanalian scene of Nicolas Poussin in which Seymour approved the glow and riot of the colouring. He still more admired a *Deluge* by the same painter, for its leaden colour and monumentally simple design, thereby earning Howard's approval. " You have," he said, " perhaps unknowingly, been paying yourself a compliment in showing so much admiration of Poussin; for he has been called *le peintre des gens d'esprit.*" With a Rembrandt of a butcher's shop Howard again stressed the abstract nature of picturesque beauty. In going through the village they had passed a real butcher's shop

[1] From Knight's own poem *The Landscape.*

with averted gaze, but in the picture Seymour was delighted with "the blended variety of mellow tints" in the carcass of the ox.

So they continued, first one then the other connoisseur gaining possession of Mr. Seymour's ear, but neither entirely convincing him, till at length Mr. Howard got tired and allowed Mr. Hamilton and his disciple to enter the Saloon alone in order to see a pair of Panninis of St. Peter's. Mr. Seymour was ravished by the opulence and majesty of the pile which, owing to the war, he had been unable to visit. The occupation of Rome by the French even caused him to fear that the basilica might come to some hurt. Hamilton seized the opportunity. " I wish your fears may not be too well founded," he said, " and I own I feel just as you do. Now, if Howard were here, he would comfort you, though I cannot. For, according to his system, it will become still more beautiful, when it is in the state you have just been describing with so much horror. He must acknowledge, (for nothing is more generally acknowledged) that a ruined building is more picturesque than it was in its entire state; therefore, according to him, it must be more beautiful, for he says that the picturesque is merely that kind of beauty which belongs exclusively to the sense of vision; in other words, that it is the beautiful in visible objects."

This was final. Mr. Seymour owned that he had often heard it observed that ruins were more picturesque than entire buildings, and now, looking at the picture, there did seem something very contradictory in the idea of its becoming more *beautiful* by destruction.

Thus, as soon as Price got away from pictures to buildings, he was able to make his case—to his own and to the not very subtle Mr. Seymour's satisfaction. If every object must be labelled " sublime," " beautiful," or " picturesque," as by his notion it must be, a ruin, a hovel, a sandy lane, and a rambling vicarage clearly were picturesque. It was a piece of sophistry, as objectivism must always be. But the description has stuck, and such objects are loosely termed picturesque to this day.

Four years later Knight returned to the charge [1] with his more defensible argument for the subjectivity of beauty, sublimity, and picturesqueness. He based his aesthetic on Alison's theory of association, but made one important exception. Colour, alone among visible phenomena, made a direct physical impression on the eye, producing " a varied irritation of the organic nerves." Thus colour could objectively produce a physical sensation quite distinct from the mental sensations produced by associated ideas. Abstract perception, from which he realized art alone could proceed, was the power of discriminating between visual and associated impressions. He quoted the observation of the Scots philosopher, Thomas Reid, that the visible appearance of objects of sight is scarcely ever regarded by us, or made a subject of reflection, but serves only as a sign to introduce to the mind something which may be as distinctly conceived by those who never saw.

An apt criticism of the majority of pictures.

But he failed to carry the process one step further— that one step which would have set up " the visible appearance " of things as the primary concern of painting. In fact, he denied the truth of such a conception. While children were delighted with every gay assemblage of colours, the habit which they acquired as they grew up, of spontaneously mixing intellectual and imaginative association with organic perception, resulted in men rejecting all works of art in which some intellectual or imaginative association was not predominant. As a humanist, as an associative thinker, and as a colour impressionist, he was not prepared to throw association overboard, though he maintained that ultimately, if all

[1] *Analytical Inquiry into the Principles of Taste* (1805).

association was wiped out, as in the case of a man born blind recovering his sight, beauty would depend exclusively on colour—a theory that Turner carried into practice in his last phase.

With his strong attachment to associated ideas Knight was unable to overlook the " subject " of a picture. It is clear that his personal predilection was for sentiment—" those tender feelings which we call pathetic "—in the choice of subjects. He noted three " of the most interesting and affecting pictures that the art has ever produced," one of which was in his possession, and in all of which he much admired the " pathos ": " Mr. West's *General Wolfe*, Mr. Westall's *Storm in Harvest* [Plate XII], and Mr. Wright's *Soldier's Tent*." A choice that, to-day, would scarcely be made in order to bolster up the cause of " subject " in painting.

More significant is the complete blindness of all these writers to *form*.

Had Knight included form as well as colour among the legitimate objects of abstract vision, he could have anticipated Cézanne and Mr. Clive Bell. But form, he was careful to prove, had no direct significance to the eye, its appreciation being in his view an operation of the understanding.

The Picturesque, then, according to Knight, was a mode of vision. The objects described as " picturesque " clearly had no special properties—apart from their colour—since they had no significance for people unacquainted with painting. Yet the very relation to painting, expressed by the word Picturesque, implied an association of ideas on the part of all subsequent observers. For nobody could see picturesquely who had no recollections of pictures, besides the power of abstract vision, to associate with objects perceived. Apart from such colouring and lighting as gave abstract pleasure, the enjoyment derived from, for instance, ruins, lanes, hovels, and gipsies consisted entirely in their association with pictures in the memory of the observer. Classical scenes appealed to the learned, wild mountain scenes to the romantic. There were pastoral scenes and prosperous scenes and so on, without end.

All these extra pleasures are from the minds of the spectators; whose pre-existing trains of ideas are revived, refreshed, and re-associated by new, but correspondent, impressions on the organs of sense, *and the great and fundamental error, which prevails throughout the otherwise able and elegant " Essays on the Picturesque " is seeking for distinctions in external objects, which only exist in the modes and habits of viewing and considering them.*

Price, Knight considered, " had viewed nature and examined art with the eye of a painter, the feelings of a poet, and the discernment of a critic; but not having been accustomed to investigate and discriminate the operations of the mind, he unfortunately suffered himself to be misled by the brilliant, but absurd and superficial, theories of the *Inquiry into the Sublime and Beautiful.*" Knight continued that he had long been puzzled by Price's philosophy " in spite of many discussions which we have had to explain it." At length, however, in *The Dialogue*, he found a sentence that gave him a complete key to it:

"All these ideas," says the interlocutor, who sustains his own part in his dialogue, "are originally acquired by the touch; but from use they are become as much objects of sight as colours." When there is so little discrimination between the operations of mind, and the objects of sense, that ideas become objects of sight, the rest follows of course.

This sums up the weakness of Price's theory of the Picturesque. He mistook subjective associations for objective qualities, as Burke had done before him.

Knight, it will be seen, denied the real existence of all categories, the Sublime and Beautiful no less than the Picturesque. He dismissed Burke with ridicule, quoting how, having asserted that sublimity proceeded

" from whatever is fitted in any sort to excite ideas of pain or danger," he immediately qualified the statement by adding

When danger or pain press too nearly, they are incapable of giving any delight, and are simply terrible; but at certain distances, and with certain modifications, they may be, and they are, delightful, as we every day experience.[1]

" It were to be wished," remarked Knight, " that the author had informed us, what the particular delights were, which pain and danger every day afford us; and at what specific distances, and under what particular modifications, they do afford them." As for astonishment being a primary cause of sublime emotion, he thought its fallacy could not be better shown than by applying the theory to Burke's character:

He was certainly a very *respectable* man; and *reverenced* by all, who knew him intimately. At one period of his life, too, when he became the disinterested patron of remote and injured nations, who had none to help them, his character was truly sublime; but unless upon those whom he so ably and eloquently arraigned, I do not believe that it impressed any *awe*.

If during this period he had walked up St. James's Street without his breeches, it would have occasioned great and universal *astonishment*; and if he had, at the same time, carried a loaded blunderbuss in his hands, the astonishment would have been mixed with no small portion of terror; but I do not believe that the united effects of these two powerful passions would have produced any sensation approaching to sublime, even in the breast of those who had the strongest sense of self preservation.[2]

Knight's conception was reflected in the painting of the period. No longer was the sublime attempted in the grand manner, or the beautiful in scenes of smooth and undulating classicism. Instead, painters selected scenes of sentiment: cottage doors, maidens, pleasant country-

[1] *Sublime and Beautiful*, pt. i, section vii.
[2] Knight, *op. cit.*, p. 374.

[81]

sides; or painted, with superb vigour, scenes adapted to brilliant impasto. There was in the one camp a Westall, a Stothard, an Ibbetson. In the other a Morland, de Loutherbourg, a Rowlandson or Thomas Barker. These may be called picturesque painters, with their sentiment and sensuous feeling for texture. The most prominent among them will be found grouped in the appendix attached to chapter vii.

The artists who were to demonstrate the truth that Knight had shied at, and were to evolve impressionism, were as yet industriously picturesque. Through that vision Crome, Constable, and Turner were to reach a true art.

Chapter IV

PICTURESQUE TRAVEL

The first source of amusement to the picturesque traveller is the pursuit of his object and searching after effects. This is the general intention of picturesque travel.—Rev. William Gilpin, *Three Essays* (1792).

THE impulse of the traveller for pleasure, apart from gain, is, in every variety of degree, to satisfy his craving for the ideal, or to drug his craving by the belief that it is being satisfied. The picturesque traveller is the traveller who has a conception of an ideal form of nature, derived from landscape painting, and whose purpose it is to discover ideal scenes in existence. Not that he often succeeds, for obviously the fact that the object of his search is ideal makes it unlikely that it is also actual. But, as Gilpin puts it, it " amuses " him to pursue. It is the *expectation* of new scenes, perhaps the ideal scene, opening to his view, that sets him off and keeps him going. It is the Pleasure of Hope, *per se*. So Campbell introduced his poem of that name (1799) with its famous line:

Why to yon mountain turns the musing eye,
Whose sunbright summit mingles with the sky?
Why do those cliffs of shadowy tint appear
More sweet than all the landscape smiling near?—
'Tis *distance* lends enchantment to the view,
And robes the mountain in its azure hue.

But that is where the picturesque traveller parts company with the purely romantic. Campbell enjoyed a prospect, even if the one he describes is correctly Claudian in composition, for its very unattainability, mystery, possibilities. The romantic mind, stirred by a view, begins to examine *itself*, and to analyse the effects

[83]

of the scenery upon its emotions. The picturesque eye, on the contrary, turns to the scene:

When the mind has a little recovered its tone, from the *general* impression of such a scene, it feels a new pleasure in examining more minutely the several picturesque ingredients which produced it,—the stillness and purity of the air—the strong lights and shades—the tints upon the mountains—the polish of the lake.[1]

Here, in a region perhaps that the world had hitherto considered without an ameliorating feature, the picturesque traveller might exclaim:

Here is beauty indeed—Beauty lying in the lap of Horrour![2]

In the accounts of grand tours made between 1640 and 1730 a pictorial view of landscape is exceptional. In each case it can be traced fairly exactly to the actual sojourn in Rome, where the works of Claude and Salvator were to be seen. The notes upon scenery thence onward tend to become more frequent and picturesque. The supreme experience of the tour was the crossing of the Alps. In each case the comments made upon this adventure may be taken as a test of how far the relish of grand landscape had overcome the natural distaste of danger and discomfort.

John Evelyn's record of his travels (1644-1648) through France, Italy, Switzerland, and Savoy, makes delightful reading and gives evidence of a precocious interest in what Shaftesbury was afterwards to call the "virtuoso sciences." The scenery that most appealed to him was the rectangular and fruitful. This he habitually compared to "paradise," in the manner of

---

[1] Gilpin, *Northern Tour to the Lakes, etc. Made in* 1772. Published 1786, vol. i, p. 22.

[2] *Ibid.*, p. 125. The remark is attributed by Gilpin to a certain Mr. Avison, organist of St. Nicholas, Newcastle-on-Tyne. He published a work on music in collaboration with J. Brown of the *Estimate*.

Plate X.   THOMAS GIRTIN.   The Sandy Lane

Louvre

Plate XI. NICCOLO POUSSIN. Winter (The Deluge)

Cotton. The phrase accentuates the beginning of the
" ideal " phase of perception. Another kind of landscape that he could appreciate even before reaching
Rome—though he refers to it more frequently afterwards—is the amphitheatral type, evidencing some
familiarity with ideal landscape which usually adopts
this form of composition:

A most goodly prospect towards the sea and city [Naples],
the one full of galleys and ships, the other of stately palaces,
churches, monasteries, gardens, castles, delicious fields and
meadows, Mount Vesuvius smoking, the Promontory of Minerva
and Misenum Capreae, Prochyta, Ischia, Pausilipum, Puteoli,
and the rest, doubtless one of the most divertissant and considerable vistas in the world.

The Bay of Naples might be dubbed the parent of all
Ideal Landscape. The amphitheatral form is there seen
at its most obviously impressive, in that the view
immediately proclaims itself a unity, perfectly composed
and balanced. A Claude had only to adopt this principle
of composition and to include similar cities, sweet
meadows, and distant sea to interest at once anybody
who had seen the prototype.

Evelyn had gone to Italy by sea from Marseilles.
He returned, however, over the Alps. At first he did
his best to admire the distant view of the mountains,
on the advice of the aged Earl of Arundel, with whom
he had become friendly at Venice, and who seems to
have attained to a picturesque point of view. But as he
drew nearer, the knowledge that he would have to climb
up those tremendous rocks was sapping his power of
pictorial appreciation. When he landed at the far end
of Lake Maggiore " and at the very foot of the Alps
which now rise as it were suddenly after some hundreds
of miles of the most even country in the world, where
there is hardly a stone to be found," he viewed them
with still less favour. It was " as if Nature had here
swept up the rubbish of the earth in the Alps, to form

and clear the plains of Lombardy." After passing up a narrow valley, he was fairly in the mountains, had to take to an ass instead of a horse, and lost all vestige of pleasure in what he saw.

The next morning we mounted through strange, horrid and fearful crags and tracts, abounding in pine trees, and only inhabited by bears, wolves, and wild goats: nor could we see anywhere above a pistol shot before us, the horizon being terminated with rocks and mountains. . . . Some of these 'vast mountains were but one entire stone, betwixt whose clefts now and then precipitated great cataracts which made a terrible roaring echoing from the rocks and cavities. . . . The narrow bridges, in some places made only by felling huge fir trees, and laying them athwart from mountain to mountain, over cataracts of stupendous depth, are very dangerous. In some places we pass between mountains that have been broken and fallen on to one another, which is very terrible.

The people have monstrous goitres, the lodgings are cold and horrible. Next day the party is involved in an affray with a community of *crétins*, and is detained in a foul lock-up. Soon after they are released the sumpter horse slips down a frightful precipice and glissades two miles down a slope of snow. When at length Evelyn got down to Geneva, no wonder he looked back at the road he had travelled as " melancholy and troublesome." But as soon as he was a respectable distance away from the " horrid mountains " and seated comfortably in a boat on the lake, he could appreciate " one of the most delightful prospects in the world, the Alps covered with snow, though at a great distance."

The general view prevailing during the latter half of the seventeenth century was that the Alps were a necessary evil. " High objects," said Dryden, " it is true, attract the sight; but it looks up with pain on craggy rocks and barren mountains, and continues not long on any object, which is wanting in shades of green."[1]

1 Dedication to *The Indian Emperor* (1667).

The craggy rocks had to be negotiated as best as might be, for the sake of what lay beyond. In the same way we subject ourselves to the Channel crossing, during which, however enthusiastic we may be for seascapes and pictures of tempests, we do not feel called upon to admire the magnificent force of the waves. It was Italy that made the Alps endurable.

John Dennis, the critic and playwright, was perhaps the first Englishman who recorded an appreciative opinion of the Alps. His letter describing his journey in 1688 must have been considered merely perverse by its recipient:

I am delighted, 'tis true, at the prospect of Hills and Valleys, of flowery Meads and murmuring Streams, yet 'tis a delight that is consistent with Reason. . . . But transporting Pleasure followed the sight of the Alps. . . . Ruins upon Ruins, in monstrous Heaps, and Heaven and Earth confounded. The uncouth Rocks that were above us, Rocks that were void of all form, but what they had received from Ruine : the frightful View of the Precipices, and the foaming Waters that threw themselves headlong down them, made all such a Consort [concert] to the eye, as that sort of Music does for the Ear, in which Horrour can be joyn'd with Harmony.

Elsewhere he exclaims that these scenes of " dreadful depth," precipices and torrents, " gave us such a view as was altogether new and amazing "; the sense of all this produced in him different emotions, viz., a delightful Horrour, a terrible Joy, and at the same time that he was infinitely pleased, he trembled. This was the stuff that the Sublime was made of, and a man who could feel thus crossing the Alps was ready to enjoy Salvator Rosa, even more than Claude, when he reached Rome.[1]

The less romantic Addison is usually taken as an example of the type of man who was disgusted with mountains, on the strength of his relief at " the sight of a plain " after crossing the Alps in about 1700. He

[1] Manwaring, *op. cit.*, p. 6.

was not much interested in pictures—referring only to
" gay, gilded scenes and shining prospects " in connection with painting when he wrote to Lord Halifax.
But after he had " done " Rome and its galleries, and
assimilated unconsciously the point of view of Claude
and Salvator, a fresh attitude is traceable in his observations. The gilt and shine has come off his prospects.
We are told appreciatively of " broken and interrupted
scenes," " infinite variety of Inequalities and Shadow-
ings " and, in a prospect near Tivoli, that " the *Roman
Painters* often work upon this Landskip." At Albano
he paints a Claudian, amphitheatral scene, and on the
journey home he sees the Alps with a reformed eye.
About Geneva they " make a Horizon that has something
in it very singular and agreeable." He appreciates the
contrast of hills covered by vineyards and pasture, with
" huge Precipices of naked Rocks . . . cleft in some
places so as to discover high mountains of snow." His
horror is agreeable. As yet, however, there is no verbal
connection of romantic scenery with the artists who
popularized it.

On the contrary, the association called up in the
minds of most men was with Poetry. As yet the Englishman regarded verse as the descriptive art *par
excellence*. The impressions of Italy in 1714, recorded
in the letters of Bishop Berkeley, are those of a man who
still sees with a poet's and not with a painter's eye. As
he crossed the Alps in January and thought himself
lucky to get over with only four falls, and the loss of
sundry possessions, he might be excused any preoccupation with sublimity. Nevertheless, writing to
Pope afterwards, he thought it would

be worth a poet's while to travel, in order to store his mind
with strong images of nature. Green fields and groves, flowery
meadows and purling streams, are nowhere in such perfection
as in England. But if you would know lightsome Days, warm
suns, and blue skies, you must come to Italy ; and to enable a

man to describe rocks and precipices, it is absolutely necessary that he pass the Alps.

Or alternatively brood upon pictures that isolated the visual qualities of such scenes.

This was actually how the picturesque point of view came into being in England. Few of those who popular- ized it had been out of the country. Gilpin, who had not crossed the Channel, did not hesitate to affirm that " England exceeds most countries in the *variety* of its picturesque beauty, and surpasses most." His reasons were the prevalence of hedgerows, enriching the land- scape, the predominance of oak over other kinds of trees, the frequency of parks, the vaporous atmosphere, and the large number of Gothic ruins. Had Gilpin only been familiar with Claude and Salvator, he could scarcely have justified his assertion on such grounds. But, by 1780, an English school of landscape painters [1] had joined the poets in illustrating English scenery. Gainsborough, while he observed the rules of the pictur- esque as deducible from Italian and Dutch masters, yet selected typically English scenes, saw them from an English point of view, and thus gave his pictures a native stamp. As the English landscape could now be compared to English painting, it naturally resembled painted landscape more closely, appealed more fully to English minds, and was therefore more picturesque than before Gainsborough's revelation of it.

Ruins, mentioned by Gilpin among the picturesque ingredients of English scenery, had appealed to a few travellers even before the civil wars, who felt the same kind of curiosity in them as in " natural wonders "— caves, stallactites, and lakes reputed bottomless. The entertaining journal[2] kept by a lieutenant of the Norwich

[1] See Appendix.
[2] *A Relation of a Short Survey of 26 Counties* . . . by a Captain, a Lieutenant and an Ancient, all three of the Military Company in Norwich. Edited by L. G. Wickham Legg (1904).

Military Company of a tour made in 1624 shows three men diligently inspecting churches, castles, and ruins with curiosity if not with pictorial appreciation. At Warwick they found it difficult to decide whether they were most impressed by "the sumptuousness of the Building, or the strength of the brave, ancient, high towers." They are relics of a mysterious, glamorous past that the lieutenant somehow regrets. But his romanticism did not enable him to appreciate the Lake district—"nothing but hideous hanging hills and great Pooles, that in what respect of the murmuring noyse of those great waters, and those high mountainous, tumbling rocky Hills, a man would think he were in another world." Wokey Hole, near Wells (Plate XIII), was more in his line. "Some of the caverns were like churches, some like butteries and kitchens. Some Roomes were very strong and like wee know not what, and with the continual dropping and distilling of the waters, such strange Shapes and several Formes were congealed, as there did palpably appeare to our fancies, men and women and other Creatures in that glitt'ring Diamond sparkling hollowness, as made us gaze and wonder." He felt the lack of a pictorial standard of comparison.

In 1700 the Rev. James Brome [1] explored the same caverns—"the most admirable piece of Nature's workmanship." As he got deeper into the "Sibylline Grotto," "dreadful apprehensions" began to seize him; the utter darkness, accentuated by the candles that his guides held, begot "both horrour and astonishment." Brome felt the emotions that Burke subsequently identified as Sublime. Neither Snowdon, nor any of the Welsh mountains, caused him any excitement whatever, though the passage of Penmaenmawr startled him: "on the one side huge Stones over our Heads,

---

[1] *Travels over England, Scotland and Wales*, by James Brome, M.A., Rector of Cheriton in Kent, and Chaplain to the Rt. Hon. the Earl of Romney (1700).

as if ready to fall upon us, and on the other side the raging Ocean, lying for a wonderful depth underneath it."

Celia Fiennes' journeys, made a few years earlier, were begun, she says, to regain her health by variety and exercise.[1] She had wide powers of observation, an active mind, and a downright personality which never suffers a certain " Freedom and Easyness " of syntax to obscure her meaning. She was most precise in describing the houses she visited, the gardens, and particularly the ornamental devices for sousing incautious visitors. What later became romantic or picturesque scenery left her cold, or rather hot, for she was principally concerned in such spots with the exertion of going up and down hill.

On the whole she enjoyed the Lake District: the surprise of finding lakes, of rowing over to islands that one found to be much larger than they seemed from the shore, the potted char, the oatcakes. But when she describes her journeys from one to another, the breathlessness of her transit communicates itself more than usually to her style.

I rode almost all the waye in sight of the great Water [Windermere], so I gained by degrees from Lower to higher hills wch I allways went up and down before I came to another hill. At last I attained to one of these hills or ffells of Rocks wch I passed on the side much about the Middle, for Looking down to the bottom it was at Least a Mile all full of those Lesser hills and jnclosures, so Looking upward I was as farre from the top which was all Rocks, and something more barren tho' there was some trees and woods growing in ye Rocks and hanging over all down ye Brow of some of the hills. From these great ffells there are several springs out of ye Rocks in the way, when something obstructs their passage and so they Come with more violence, that gives a pleaseing sound and murmuring noise.

---

[1] *Through England on a Side Saddle*, with an Introduction by the Hon. Mrs. Griffiths.

The circumlocution describing a cascade in the last sentence shows how completely unromantic was Mistress Fiennes. She had not even a vocabulary, still less a gusto. Young or Gilpin like as not would have described the trickle as a fearful cascade dashing itself athwart, etc., with a sound like the sublimest tempest, etc. For this lady who, on a surface that is not horizontal, feels like a fish out of water, a stream that falls vertically instead of flowing flatly is an oddity that none the less makes a curiously pleasing, murmuring sound. No associations, no horror, no pictures.

Defoe's *Tour through the Whole Island of Great Britain*, taken between 1724 and 1727, contains criticisms of "improvements" and occasional, but not picturesque, descriptions of the varieties of art and nature. The second Earl of Oxford, part collector of the Harleian Manuscripts, and the friend of Swift, Prior, and Pope, kept diaries of his tours about the year 1723, which show him a fairly intelligent observer of Gothic architecture, and occasionally struck with scenery of a smiling character. Of Durham he found "the whole situation somewhat romantic, but to me not unpleasant . . . but others of better judgement condemn this site, to whose opinion I always submit my own, to my great advantage and instruction." This is an early and significant instance of romantic scenery being "not unpleasant." But, as the context shows, the Earl's advisers were less susceptible to that magnificent scene where the cathedral towers above the wooded Wear. Perhaps as a result of their disapproval he was more orthodox in his comments for the future. The only sight that pleased him in Scotland was that of the plantations at Kinnoul: "This is the finest sight I have yet seen, or expect to see, in the whole of the kingdom of Scotland, and is a great example and encouragement for setting about the improvement of the country. Indeed the spirit of planting seems of late years to have stirred a little among

the nobility and gentry." Scotland might be barren
and mountainous, but by planting it could be brought
to resemble more nearly the ideal landscape of the
painters.

That phrase, " the spirit of planting," is perhaps a
symptom of the stirrings of romanticism. It seems to
indicate something less rational than " the habit " or
" the practice " would imply, something less trivial than
" the fashion." Sir John Vanbrugh uses it in 1721 in a
similar context:

> There are several gentlemen in this part of the world [York-
> shire] that are possessed of the Spirit of Building.[1]

Planting and architecture, we are to understand, however playfully the word was used, were the result of
some afflatus, similar to that which the German romantics of a century later conceived to be the nature of
genius. Vanbrugh's romantic and picturesque tendencies, which will be considered in the chapter on Picturesque Architecture, are further suggested in the same
letter by his appreciative reference to the scenery of
Northumberland:

> If I had had good weather on this expedition, I should have
> been well enough diverted in it, there being more valuable and
> agreeable things and places to be seen than in the tame South
> of England.

This is the exact reverse of the opinion of such tourists as have hitherto been quoted. Though they show
an increasing awareness of the ideal element in " tame "
scenery, they indicate only a rare susceptibility to the
sublimity of " wild " country. As yet, moreover, not
one of the travellers quoted has mentioned the word
picturesque nor given evidence of a mind in any way
affected by picturesque theory. The years 1738-39
mark clearly the beginning of the cult that was to

[1] British Museum Add. MSS. 33064, ff. 213.

become so fashionable and to have such an important effect on English painting and English life. Professor Manwaring [1] finds the first instance of true picturesque vision in the impressions of a Welsh valley given by Dr. Thomas Herring, subsequently Archbishop of Canterbury. In 1738 the Doctor was so much impressed by " the magnificence of nature " that he feared the sight of the landscape garden at Stowe afterwards would make him smile, and that he would behold " with contempt an artificial ruin " after having been " agreeably terrified with something like the rubbish of creation." He recalled picturesquely a valley with rocky walls, woods, a foaming stream with a rude bridge, a cataract down the mountains which shut in the valley, flocks, and herds, and peasants coming home at evening with full pails. " All these images together put me in mind of Poussin's drawings, and made me fancy myself in Savoy, at least, if not nearer Rome." [2]

In 1739, too, young Horace Walpole and Thomas Gray took their tour through France and Italy, on the way visiting the Grande Chartreuse. Both wrote home ecstatically describing its sublimities, but with a subtle difference. Walpole describes the scenery as vividly as Gray. It is in the conclusions that they differ, as the Romantic from the Picturesque. Gray summed it all up psychologically:

I do not remember to have gone ten paces without an exclamation that there was no restraining: not a precipice, not a torrent, not a cliff, but is pregnant with religion and poetry. There are certain scenes that would awe an atheist into belief. . . . One need not have a fantastic imagination to see spirits here at noonday.

Walpole, while he broke into suggestive exclamations,

[1] *Op. cit.*, p. 170.
[2] *Letters from the late reverend Dr. Thomas Herring* (1777), pp. 39-42.

did not feel with any depth. "Precipices, mountains, torrents, wolves, rumblings, Salvator Rosa!..."

A series of tours over England and Wales was made between 1725 and 1748 by S. and N. Buck in connection with their *Antiquities*. They were topographers like Loggan and Kyp, but artists of a very different order. Where their predecessors had done bird's-eye " scapes " of vast formal lay-outs or colleges, the Bucks went for ruins, castles, and abbeys, which they portrayed with considerable picturesque effect. Their wanderings must have taken them over very difficult country at times, for example, to ruinous castles in Cumberland which, even to-day, are ill served by roads. Their plates show considerable observation of Gothic principles, picturesque composition, a feeling for texture, and a bold use of masses of light and shade.

The blue-stocking ladies, for the next twenty or thirty years, vie with one another in picturesque enthusiasm. Lady Hertford, Mrs. Montagu, Mrs. Delany, Mrs. Carter, Mrs. Vesey, the Duchess of Portland, Mrs. Chapone, and the ladies of the Lyttelton circle show how completely the attitude to nature had been revolutionized since Celia Fiennes had made her tours half a century earlier. Mrs. Delany was a skilful landscape painter, as her sketches now in the possession of Lord Treowen testify, and her letters abound in verbal pictures: " Could I have attended to the beauties *en passant* between dear, sweet Ilam and Sudbury, I should present my dearest Mary with such a mixture of pastoral delights as would have served a Claude or a Shenstone for their whole lives." She introduced landscape gardening into Ireland, though necessarily on a scale even smaller than that employed by Shenstone at the Leasowes, helping Dr. Delany to lay out the little park at Delville. She sometimes describes expeditions to romantic spots, which whenever possible she sketched.

Mrs. Elizabeth Montagu, daughter of an accomplished

amateur landscape painter, had an active eye for the picturesque. In 1754 she went on a "picturesque picnic" with William Pitt and the Wests to Tunbridge:

> We drank tea yesterday in the most beautiful rural scene that can be imagined, which Mr. Pitt had discovered in his morning's ride. . . . He ordered a tent to be pitched, tea to be prepared, and his French horn to breathe music like the unseen genius of the wood. The company dined with us; and we set out, number eight. After tea we rambled about for an hour, seeing several views, some wild as Salvator Rosa, others placid, and with the setting sun, worthy of Claude Lorrain.[1]

These ladies, though their ecstasies sometimes evidence minds schooled in the precepts of Burke, were probably more familiar with the poetry than with the philosophy of the time. Thomson and Shenstone rose in their thoughts at appropriate moments, and their letters do but echo the verses of contemporary poets. Thomson, Dyer, and their followers have been grouped together as the "Landscape Poets";[2] indeed, the unity of attitude, in all arts, towards nature is so marked during the seventy-five years after the publication of Thomson's *Winter* (1726) that it can almost be designated the Age of Landscape. Poetry, Gardening, Architecture, and Painting, and even Archaeology, whenever they have anything to do with the countryside, lose their isolation, as separate arts, and are combined by this picturesque point of view into the single Art of Landscape. The gardener sings in poetry (of a kind) his efforts to copy painters; the architect designs buildings that a painter might have delineated in expressing a poetical conception. The painter illustrates episodes from the poets, in landscapes that a gardener would own to gladly. And so the ring tightens as the dance proceeds. It is this fusion of arts in the warmth

---

[1] *Letters* (1809), vol. iii, pp. 315-316.
[2] H. A. Beers, *History of English Romanticism*, ch. iv.

of enthusiasm for nature, as revealed by painters, that was the biggest achievement of the Picturesque. To this day many persons view life as a succession of "Landscapes with Figures."

The allusions of several travellers to the Lake District have already been quoted. Their, and their successors', reactions to it can conveniently be taken as a gauge of picturesque feeling in England, as the Alps can abroad. Hitherto travellers have got into the Lake District by mistake. Now comes the time of its discovery as a country particularly to be visited. The event is intimately connected not only with "curing the evil itch of over-valuing fforeign parts" as Miss Fiennes put it, but with the development of the picturesque attitude and, through it, of romanticism.

If a few enlightened spirits saw a certain attractiveness in the Lakes and Fells before the middle of the eighteenth century, they were exceptions.[1] It is not until 1758 that we have documentary evidence of anything like a picturesque view being taken of the scenery.

In that year Dr. Dalton, of Queen's College, Oxford, one of Lady Hertford's circle of picture- and naturefanciers, wrote *A Descriptive Poem addressed to two Ladies at their Return from viewing the Mines near Whitehaven*. Almost in the same year Dr. John Brown,[2] of St. John's College, Cambridge, one of the Lyttelton-Gray-Walpole group, and at that time vicar of Morland, near Penrith, wrote a letter to Lord Lyttelton about Keswick, which apparently everyone read. Though it

[1] Sir Daniel Fleming of Rydal had pictures painted of the views from his house in 1652. See W. G. Collingwood, *Lake District History* (1925).

[2] Brown acquired a wide reputation as author of *An Estimate of the Manners and Principles of the Times* (1757), and largely on the strength of it was appointed by the Empress Catharine to reform education in Russia. This was too much for a mind never well balanced, and he cut his throat in a fit of depression.

was not printed till 1767 (at Newcastle), and did not acquire renown till printed in London as a note to Dalton's poem in 1768, it cannot have been written later than 1760, when Brown and Lyttelton quarrelled, and probably before 1756, in which year Brown transferred to a living in Essex.

Dalton, in the iambic measure of Dyer, shows a considerable eye for colour and romance in his descriptions of the scenery to which his poem welcomes the ladies back from infernal regions.

> There the brown fells ascend the sky,
> Below, the green enclosures lye;
> Along their sloping sides supine
> The peaceful villages recline:
> On azure roofs bright sunbeams play
> And make the meanest dwellings gay.

The appreciation of the blue glitter of the slate roofs of Westmorland is unusual and denotes a lively sense of colour. After a description of the course of the river Lowther as compared with Lodore, he breaks off into what amounts to a gloss on the then quite new doctrine of sublimity.

> Horrors like these at first alarm
> But soon with savage grandeur charm,
> And raise to noblest thoughts the mind:
> Thus by thy fall, Lodore, reclined,
> The craggy cliffs, impending wood
> Whose shadows mix o'er half the flood . . .
> I view with wonder and delight,
> A pleasing though an awful sight:
> For seen with them, the verdant isles
> Soften with more delicious smiles . . .
> And last, to fix our wand'ring eyes,
> Thy roofs, O Keswick, brightly rise,
> The lake and lofty hills between
> Where giant Skiddaw shuts the scene.

Of the mighty Skiddaw, " his imperial brow . . . from foul usurping vapours free," he actually cries:

> 'Twere glorious now his side to climb,
> Boldly to scale his top sublime.

It is to Dalton's reference to Keswick:

> nature's pride
> Sweet Keswick's vale . . .

that is appended, in Pearch's continuation of Dodsley's *Miscellany*,[1] the celebrated letter of Dr. Brown, which there is no reason to doubt sent both Arthur Young and Gray to the Lakes in 1768 and 1769 respectively. Young, in fact, almost avows the fact by saying how Keswick had long been a desire with him, and by the closeness with which his account of Derwentwater follows Brown's. The importance of Brown's *Letter* resides in its being the earliest critical and comparative examination of romantic scenery. His *apparatus criticus* is formed as usual on Thomson, painting and horror; his ideal landscape on the amphitheatral form. But he is not *boulversé* by the first hill he meets. Dovedale disappointed him and the "romantic scenes" round Buxton still more so. "They are all but poor miniatures of Keswick."

Instead of the narrow strip of a valley which is seen at Dovedale, you have at Keswick a vast amphitheatre, in circumference about twenty miles. Instead of a meagre rivulet, a noble living lake adorned with every variety of wooded islands. . . . On the opposite shore, you will find rocks and cliffs of stupendous height, hanging over the lake in horrible grandeur, the woods climbing up their steep and shaggy sides, where mortal foot never yet approached; on those dreadful heights the eagles build their nests; a variety of waterfalls are seen pouring from their summits, and tumbling in vast sheets from rock

---

[1] *A Collection of Poems by Several Hands.* 2 vols. Printed by G. Pearch (1768-1770). Vol. i, p. 36.

to rock in rude and terrible magnificence: while on all sides of this immense amphitheatre the lofty mountains rise round, piercing the clouds in shapes as spiry and fantastic as the very rocks of Dovedale. To this I must add the frequent and bold projections of the cliffs into the lake, forming noble bays and promontories. . . .

Were I to analyse the two places into their constituent principles, I should tell you that the full perfection of Keswick consists of three circumstances, beauty, horror, and immensity united; the second of which is alone found at Dovedale. . . . To give you a complete idea of these three perfections, as they are joined at Keswick would require the united powers of Claude, Salvator and Poussin. The first should throw his delicate sunshine over the cultivated vales, the scattered cots, the groves, the lake and wooded islands. The second should dash out the horror of the rugged cliffs, the steeps, the hanging woods and foaming waterfalls; while the grand pencil of Poussin should crown the whole, with the majesty of impending mountains.

He also suggested a pilgrimage to the top of a cliff looking over successive ranges of mountains that " form an immense and awful picture, which can only be expressed by the image of a tempestuous sea of mountains." And he would have the visitor " Walk by still moonlight among these enchanting dales." The letter may be too highly spiced and coloured to be good prose, but it glows and scintillates like a Titian or Rubens canvas. No wonder that the letter was in everybody's hands and that travellers and artists began to brave the " horrors " of the Lakes.

The publication of Dalton's poem and Brown's *Letter* in 1768 had the immediate effect of sending Arthur Young and Gray to the Lakes. The year is thus something of a landmark in the history of the picturesque. But another cause for the sudden " discovery " of the district, and for the more gradual popular appreciation of it, was the improvement of the roads in Westmorland and Cumberland at this date. All over England the appreciation of scenery, the experiencing of romantic

Downton Castle

Plate XII. RICHARD WESTALL. Storm in Harvest

V. & A. Museum

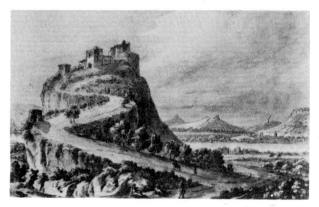

Fig. 1. ROBERT ADAM. Ideal Landscape with Castle

V. & A. Museum

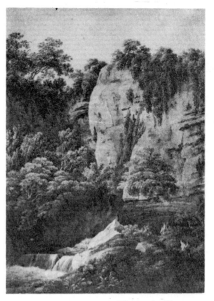

Fig. 2.

MICHAEL "ANGELO" ROOKER

Wokey Hole

Plate XIII

emotions, and the perception of the sublime in nature increased in direct ratio to the number of turnpike acts. Where roads were evil or non-existent, either travellers went not, or were too engrossed in their discomforts to give more than a disparaging glance at the prospect. Whatever the shortcomings of the turnpike system it did at least revolutionize poetry.

We can determine exactly the state of the roads at the time of Gray's and Young's travels, since the latter included a detailed report of those encountered in his *Northern Tour*.[1] The Great North Road by then was fairly good, and turnpike sections, though not continuous, occurred all along its course. But whilst even the North Road turnpikes are accorded restrained praise by Young,[2] once he gets over the Pennines, by a " very rough and broken " road at Greta Bridge, and a " very bad " one by High Force, he finds an immense improvement. The turnpike to Brough, he says, " runs across Stainmore, and is a most excellent one, dry, level, and free from loose stones." The turnpike over Shap is " very good " and to Kendal, though exceedingly hilly, excellent in itself. Evidently Westmorland had been waking up—a surmise that is substantiated by Young's note on the Kendal-Windermere road:

Turnpike. Now making. What is finished is as good, firm, level a road as any in the world. I nowhere remember a better.

The enterprise of the Trustees may have been directly responsible for the visit of the timid Gray, and in any case it was speedily and richly rewarded.

Arthur Young brought a zeal to the cause of agricultural reform to which it is not easy to find a parallel.

[1] Vol. iv, pp. 573 *et seq.*
[2] To Newark. Turnpike good.
  To Bawtry. Very sandy over Shirewood Forest.
  To Doncaster. Part sandy but tolerable.
  To Wakefield. Hilly but indifferent.

Having failed as a practical farmer, between 1768 and
1771 he published his three Tours of England, the
Southern in 1768, the *Northern* in 1770, and the *Eastern*
in 1771, in which he reviewed the progress or lack of it,
that had been made in farming all over the country.
The great improvement in agriculture that took place
during the latter years of the century are directly owing
to his efforts. His *Tours* are to be found in almost
every country house library of the period. But it is
always difficult to make a success of a purely agricultural
book. None realized this better than Young, and the
popularizing of his serious doctrines on enclosure,
fertilizing, and breeding was enormously assisted by his
no less enthusiastic description of landscape, grounds,
and country house picture galleries. Many readers,
particularly abroad, bought his books for them alone.
In the true eighteenth-century manner, both he and his
readers included agriculture in the art of landscape
along with gardening, painting, architecture, and poetry.
Though he usually keeps his artistic and agricultural
comments distinct, sometimes they get mixed up.
Thus of

> The landscape from Mr. Tucker's cabbage field (near Rother-
> ham), situated on the top of a hill; I would at any time, with
> utmost pleasure, ride 40 miles to view such another.[1]

Young was nothing if not picturesque in his view of
nature. Not only did he every now and then make a
drawing himself of some particularly striking scene,
but he constantly passed from galleries with their
pictures of temples, groves, and deserts, " trees finely
done," " the rocks wild and grand," with their Claudes
that he rarely failed to note as " fine," or " very fine,"
on to terraces whence he inspected actual landscapes,
shaped into so many exactly analogous pictures, with
the same sentiments.

[1] *Northern Tour*, vol. i, p. 130.

In moments of emotion he compared real landscape directly to the painted: in the grounds at Hackfall " the outline of the picture is noble—but the filling up of the canvas adds a colouring more than equal to the pencil of a *Claud*." Many of his verbal landscapes describe parks, though a line of demarcation between " made " grounds and " natural " scenery was studiously avoided by improvers of grounds, and consequently Young often includes the view of a country in a garden. At Duncombe Park, among many imposing landscapes, he sketched

a scene more exquisite than any of the preceding. You look through a waving break in the shrubby wood, which grows upon the edge of a precipice, down immediately upon a large ruin'd abbey [Rievaulx], in the midst, to appearance, of a small but beautiful valley, scattered trees appearing elegantly among the ruins, too elegantly picturesque to admit of description. It is a bird's eye landscape; a casual glance at a little paradise, which seems as it were in another region.

Here is, at last, the " paradise " of the mediaeval and sixteenth-century scenic descriptions, viewed distinctly as an ideal, arcadian, landscape, through the imaginary frame of a picture.

Young's relish for wild and moorland scenery was tempered by his conviction that it could be reclaimed and cultivated. He was inclined therefore to prefer the Claudian type of landscape. As he passes into the North Riding we get an example of this preference:

After traversing a vast range of dreary waste, and shut up in a rocky hollow between two wild hills, you break at once upon a view which cannot fail to be astonishing: You look between the two hills on an immense plain, comprehending almost the whole of Cleveland, finely cultivated, the verdure beautiful; and the innumerable enclosures adding prodigiously to the view. In front appears a most picturesque hill, intersected with green hedges,—one of the most truly pleasing objects in the world.

But the Lake District was the objective of his tour, so far as scenery was concerned. There was nothing slipshod about these early picturesque travellers; the approach to a spot was as important as its exploration and analysis. Any advice was welcomed upon the best manner of pursuing the required effects. Young, following Brown, thought the best way of viewing Derwent Water was to row round, landing now and then " for catching the varieties of the prospect." Beginning tranquilly, first his eyes and then his soul were drawn upwards, and his emotions were a crescendo from the detailed beautiful to the obscure sublime. Passing by Wallow Crag and Barrow Crag, he next anchored

in a bay, the environs of which are dreadful; you are under a monstrous craggy rock [Throng Crag], almost perpendicular. Moving the eye from this formidable object, you find the end of the lake surrounded with a chain of them, in the boldest and abruptest style imaginable. The opposite shore of mountains is very great, and the noise of distant waterfalls is heard most gloriously. . . .

From hence you coast a dreadful shore of fragments, which time has broken from the towering rocks, many of them of terrible size, through a path of desolation, sweeping rocks, trees, hillocks, everything, to the water; the very idèa of a small shiver against the boat strikes with horror. . . .

So far, Young had felt emotionally, romantically, rather than seen picturesquely. When the first novelty of mountain country, terrifying to one accustomed to flat country, had worn off, he could view scenes more dispassionately, and criticize their picturesque aptitudes. Thus on " Hullswater " he censured, quite in the manner of Gilpin, the planting of two strips of Scotch Fir across a wooded hillside, " which varies the colour of the verdure and consequently breaks the unity of the view." The approach to Hawswater presented " a sweet landscape which brings to the imagination the idea of an arcadian paradise." There is " a most elegantly picturesque view of a variegated tract of waving enclosures, spreading over hills and hanging in the eye in the most picturesque manner. Three hills are in particular overlooked, cut into enclosures in a charming style, of themselves forming a most elegant landscape, worthy the imitation of those who would give the embellishments of art to the simplicity of nature." Young's approval of enclosures has already been commented on, and Gilpin, we have seen, considered English hedgerows among the picturesque assets of our landscape. But here Young rouses a suspicion that the kind of picture which he would most appreciate would be a picture of an enclosed landscape with well-bred cattle and up-to-date plant. The landscape gardeners, Brown and Repton, were far from considering enclosure a picturesque virtue in a landscape.

Gray, though Arthur Young preceded him in the Lakes, is the greatest pioneer of the picturesque after Thomson, although with him the picturesque was but a means to a fuller emotional appreciation of nature as a whole. The impulse that his writings, and still more his conversation in his circle of friends, gave to the picturesque point of view was largely incidental. He gave as great an impetus to the Gothic revival. With him the picturesque, the mediaeval, the rural were so many doors into the inner chamber of nature's storehouse. As Mr. H. A. Beers remarks, there is, in his Journal of a visit to the Lakes (1769), a certain intimacy of comprehension, a depth of tone which makes his descriptions seem like nineteenth-century work.[1] Mr. John Beresford, too, has recently pointed out [2] how Gray noticed everything, a trait that Johnson, who did not like Gray, freely admitted. While Horace Walpole was not interested in simple ordinary things, Gray " saw with the eye almost as much of a painter as a poet, and

[1] *Op. cit.*, ch. v.
[2] The Author of the "Elegy." *Edinburgh Review*, July 1926.

found always the appropriate image and just epithet."
But by 1769 landscape was to Gray not less but more
than a picture. It had sentiment, character, meaning,
almost personality. As early as 1739, as we have seen,
he wrote to West from the Grande Chartreuse that " not
a precipice, not a torrent, not a cliff, but is pregnant with
religion and poetry." Walpole's more limited mind
took, at the same moment and place, the more detailed
picturesque view. Not that Gray was unmoved by
pictures. On the contrary, when he was with Walpole
in Italy he used his time to far greater purpose than his
dilettante companion, and " studied with much attention the different manners of the old masters."[1] He made
out a list of the principal painters extending as far back
as Cimabue, and another, printed by Mason, " of
subjects proper for painting which he has never seen
executed, and affixed the names of different masters to
each piece, to show which of their pencils he thought
would be most proper to treat it." Salvator Rosa, for
instance, he considered might well have done " Hannibal
passing the Alps; the mountaineers rolling down rocks
upon his army; elephants tumbling down the precipices." Such an exercise was nothing if not picturesque,
though John Evelyn might have said, " Go thou and
do likewise."

Of his journey in the Scottish Highlands in 1765 he
wrote:

The mountains are ecstatic, and ought to be visited in pilgrimage once a year. None but those monstrous creatures of
God know how to join so much beauty with so much horror.
A fig for your poets, painters, gardners and clergymen that have
not been among them ; their imaginations can be made up of
nothing but bowling-greens, flowering shrubs, horse-ponds, Fleet
ditches, shell grottoes and Chinese rails. . . . What a pity it is
that I cannot draw, nor describe.[2]

[1] Note by Mason to first edition of Letters. Quoted by Duncan
C. Tovey, *The Letters of Thomas Gray* (1912), vol. iii, p. 64.
[2] To Mason. Tovey, *op. cit.*, vol. iii, p. 95.

This extract poses nicely the spirit in which the eighteenth century travelled at its best. The arts were united in one great scenic art. While the mountains exalted and terrified the soul, still the eyes wished to note the visual impression in a few lines.

To remedy to some extent his inability to sketch Gray carried with him, and was one of the first travellers to do so, a " Claude Glass," a plano-convex mirror of about four inches in diameter on a black foil and bound up like a pocket-book, which is, as Mason remarked, " perhaps the best and most convenient substitute for a Camera Obscura." The device was, and to some extent still is, employed by landscape painters in assisting them to determine the tonal values of planes. The slight convexity of the glass, moreover, gathers every scene reflected in it into a tiny picture, and, by reducing the colours into a lower ratio, accentuates the tonal values.

> Much will the Mirrour teach, or evening gray,
> When o'er some ample space her twilight ray
> Obscurely gleams; hence Art shall best perceive
> On distant parts what fainter lines to give.[1]

Gray's itinerary was similar to that of Young. According to our ideas he saw very little. He only went from Penrith to the foot of Ullswater, and then to Keswick, where he spent a few days in excursions, but never got up Borrowdale farther than Grange. Then he went by Grasmere to Ambleside and Kendal. Mr. W. G. Collingwood[2] reminds us that later travellers " derided him while they stole his purple streaks to eke out their

---

[1] W. Mason, *The English Garden*, IV, i, 529. Later in the century Thomas West (*A Guide to the Lakes*) recommended the use of *two* glasses, one on dark foil for sunny days and one on silver for dull days. It will be remembered that Charles Gough, who lost his life in the descent of Helvellyn with his faithful dog, and formed the subject of poems by Wordsworth and Scott, was found to have " Claude Lorrain glasses " in his pocket.

[2] *Op. cit.*, p. 158.

patchwork productions," one of them openly asserting
that the poet was so frightened by the " horrors " that
he pulled his post-chaise blinds down and shut his eyes
to the more striking parts of the route. The only
evidence that he was ever turned back by " horrors "
comes in his confession of why he did not see Windermere:

On looking into the best bed chamber (at Ambleside) dark
and damp as a cellar, grew delicate, gave up Wynandermere in
despair and went on to Keswick.[1]

He sees the mountains in the conventional way—
" they rise very rude and awful with their broken tops
on either hand "—but he brings something more to
their appreciation: " . . . Saddleback, whose furrowed
sides were gilt by the noonday sun, while its brow
appeared a sad purple from the shadow of the clouds as
they sailed slowly by it."

. . . To the left the jaws of *Borrodale*, with that turbulent
Chaos of mountain behind mountain roll'd in Confusion;
beneath you . . . the shining purity of the lake, just ruffled by
the breeze enough to show it is alive, reflecting rocks, wood,
fields and the inverted tops of mountains. O doctor! I never
wished more for you; and pray think how the glass played its
part in such a spot.[2]

Gray, like Young, made a point of going to the tops
of hills to see the view. The latter had laid great stress
on the " amazing and most superlative prospect " of
Windermere from the east, and had noted " you look
down . . . (a circumstance of great beauty and which

[1] *Journal*, 8th October.
[2] Oct. 3rd. The Doctor, of course, is Thomas Warton, " who had
intended to accompany Gray to Keswick but was seized at Brough
with a violent fit of his asthma, which obliged him to return home.
This was the reason that Mr. Gray undertook to write the journal "
(Mason).

painting cannot imitate)." Gray, like Gilpin after him, agreed that " birds' eyes " were not picturesque. In one place he approved the choice by George Smith of Chichester [1] of a low view-point, and in another decided that " all points that are much elevated make the parts look poor and diminutive." To which Mason added in a note: " The *Picturesque* point is always thus low in all prospects, a truth which though the landscape painter know, he cannot always observe, since the patron who employs him to take a view of the place usually carries him up to some elevation for that purpose "; a proceeding described by Gilpin in the lines quoted in chapter ii.

At Gordale Scar is a true Salvatorial, romantic picture:

On the cliffs above hung a few goats, one of them danced and scratched an ear with its hind foot in a place where I would not have stood still for all beneath the moon.

There is a gorge and waterfall—

but these are not the things: it is the rock to the right under which you stand to see the fall, that forms the principal horror of the place. From its very base it begins to slope forwards over you in one black and solid mass without any crevice in its surface; and overshadows half the area below with its dreadful canopy. When I stood at (I believe) full 4 yards' distance from its foot, the drops which perpetually distill from its brow fell on my head, and on one part of the top more exposed to the weather there are loose stones that hang in air, and threaten visibly some idle spectator with instant destruction. . . . The gloomy uncomfortable day well suited the savage aspect of the place, and made it more formidable. I stay'd there (not without shuddering) a quarter of an hour, and thought my trouble richly paid, for the impression will last for Life.[2]

---

[1] " The English Claude." Died in this year at Doncaster.

[2] *Journal*, 13th Oct. James Ward's great picture of Gordale Scar, in the Tate Gallery, is unfortunately in too poor a state of preservation to warrant its reproduction.

In the inn where he stayed that night in Malham, three artists had recently preceded him, Vivares (the engraver), Thomas Smith of Derby, and Bellers. It was with such scenes as Gordale Scar in mind that Gray wrote, the following August, to Beattie, of his *Minstrel*:

Your ideas are new, and borrowed from a mountainous country—the only one that can furnish truly picturesque scenery.

Of the tour of the western marches that Gray took in 1770 we have no journal, for unfortunately no Dr. Warton had a bout of asthma. All we have from Gray is a few lines:

the very light and principal feature of my journey was the river Wye which I descended in a boat from Ross to Chepstow. Its banks are a succession of nameless wonders . . . the vale of Abergavenny, Ragland and Chepstow Castle, Tintern, Ludlow, Malvern Hills, Hampton Court near Lemster, the Leasowes, Hagley, and the three cities, lastly Oxford,—no bad harvest to my thinking.

Before another year had elapsed the gentle harvester was himself gathered. But not before he had glanced through the MS. account of an identical tour, taken within a few weeks of his own, by a diffident Hampshire clergyman, William Gilpin, parson of Boldre.

Had he lived [wrote Gilpin] it is possible he might have been induced to have assisted me with a few of his own remarks on scenes, which he had so accurately examined. The slightest touches of a master would have had their effect. No man was a greater admirer of nature than Mr. Gray; nor admired it with better taste.

Which from Gilpin, even for Gray, was praise.

Gray and Young, Price and Knight, are solid bodies with an existence apart from the picturesque. But the Rector of Boldre is a " shy ghost," as misty as his landscapes. His personality is inseparable from our ideas of the picturesque, which his eight books on the subject have to a large extent formed. But apart from it he was a quiet country rector with the ambition of remedying the conditions of ignorance and squalor which he found among his parishioners by establishing a school. As the high priest of the picturesque, he is the original of William Combe's immortal Doctor Syntax, who first sprang into life *In Search of the Picturesque*. And in Peacock's parsons, the Rev. Doctor Folliott and the Rev. Doctor Opimian, we seem to detect not a little of his character. " A humane, tolerant, ingenious, benevolent man " his friend Samuel Pratt tells us. Yet Gilpin cannot have been by any means a nonentity apart from his writing. He was an intimate of the great connoisseur William Locke of Norbury, who assembled about him the finest artists of the day. The Duchess of Portland, Horace Walpole, and William Mason were some of his sponsors to fame, during the ten years that his works circulated in manuscript, and it was Mrs. Delany who sent them to the Queen. At length, in 1782, he took the risk of publishing. For the next seventeen years a succession of *Observations* were printed and eagerly bought. Scarcely any well equipped private library is without at least one of his volumes.[1]

[1] Gilpin's picturesque works in order of publication are: *Observations on the River Wye and several Parts of South Wales, etc., relative chiefly to Picturesque Beauty* (1782); *Observations on . . . the Mountains and Lakes of Cumberland and Westmorland* (1786); *Observations on Several Parts of Great Britain, particularly the Highlands of Scotland . . .* (1789); *Observations on Forest Scenery . . . illustrated by Scenes of the New Forest* (1791); *Three Essays: On Picturesque Beauty; On Picturesque Travel; and On Sketching Landscape. To which is added a Poem on Landscape Painting* (1792); *Observations on the Western Parts of England . . . Remarks on the Isle of Wight . . .* (1798); *Observations on the Coasts of Hampshire, Sussex, and Kent . . .* (1804); *Observations on . . . the Counties of Cambridge, Norfolk, Suffolk, and Essex . . . Also on several parts of North Wales* (1809). The two latter works were published after Gilpin's death in 1804.

The full title of each of his books begins " Observations, chiefly relative to picturesque beauty. . . ." He intended this simply to mean " that kind of beauty which *would look well in a picture*." But as the double term implies, he never distinguished clearly, as did subsequently Price and Knight, between beauty and picturesqueness. A scene was picturesque if it composed well and was harmoniously coloured. He also particularized as especially picturesque, rough and broken objects such as rocks, ruins, and shaggy cattle.

In the Scottish Tour he revealed himself as the romantic that he was at heart. In Scotland he found the limitless, a land in the state of nature, still enjoying " the reign of picturesque beauty." Agriculture, like clothes, he believed, hid the form of nature. Wherever man appeared with his tools, deformity followed his steps. He reprimanded Dr. Johnson for his sentence on the Scottish scene, where the sage observed that " the appearance is that of matter, incapable of form or usefulness, dismissed by nature from her care and left in its original elemental state." " It is true," replied Gilpin, " that an eye like Doctor Johnson's, which he himself acknowledged was accustomed only to see the beauties of landscape in ' flowery pastures ' and ' waving harvests,' cannot be attracted by the great and sublime in nature. As for a Scotch mountain being incapable of form, he can only mean that it cannot be formed into meadows. Its form as a mountain is grand and sublime in the highest degree." In this he was not fair to Johnson. The Doctor was far from insusceptible to Scottish scenery, though he naturally viewed it with a poetic rather than pictorial eye. He was prepared to find " wild objects—mountains, waterfalls—peculiar manners." He condescended to be amused by grottoes, and felt to the full " the terrific grandeur of the tempestuous ocean." When the Doctor went to Wales, in the more sympathetic company of the Thrales, he caught their enthusiasm. He experienced a fearful joy at Sir Rowland Hill's—"a region abounding with striking scenes and terrifick grandeur." He commented upon " the extent of its prospects, the awfulness of its shades, the horror of its precipices, the verdure of its hollows and the loftiness of its rocks; the ideas which it forces on the mind are the sublime, the dreadful and the vast." He refrained, on this occasion, from adding, as he had before similar scenes in Scotland, that nevertheless " terror without danger is only one of the sports of fancy, a voluntary agitation of the mind, that is permitted no longer than it pleases." In Wales at least he relaxed his will to be stirred or not, at pleasure. The ideas of the sublime, the terrible, and the vast were allowed to take possession of his mind unchallenged and uncriticized.

Gilpin, the romantic, believed nature could do no wrong. She was the Ideal. Only man had deformed her. To the classical Johnson the process was the exact reverse. Nature in her primitive state was chaotic. Only with the assistance of art and intellect could she be made beautiful, regular, fruitful. In practice, however, Gilpin could not throw off the aesthetic habit of his age. Though wild nature " is always great in design," she is " unequal in composition." " She is an admirable colourist and can harmonize her tints with infinite variety and inimitable beauty: but is seldom so correct in composition as to produce a harmonious whole. . . . The case is, the immensity of nature is beyond human comprehension. She works on a *vast scale*; and, no doubt, harmoniously, if her scheme could be comprehended. The artist, in the mean time, is confined to *space*. He lays down his little rules, therefore, which he calls the *principles of picturesque beauty*, merely to adapt such diminutive parts of nature's surfaces to his own eye, as comes within its scope." [1]

[1] *Tour of the Wye*, p. 18.

Had Gilpin been a poet, he might have consistently apprehended the existence of this mighty force, nature, and have united it to his own spirit. He saw her vastness, and knew that he could not comprehend it. But he was a painter, in mind if not in execution, and a painter trained in the same art principles as was Johnson.[1] He was thus involved in a perpetual compromise, adapting nature, which he understood only vaguely, to art, which he understood (in his generation) well. He tried to mould what he knew to be above reason, to a rational system. Thus we get perpetually the comical vision of the kindly parson, first abasing himself before nature as the source of all beauty and emotion; then getting up and giving her a lesson in deportment. He saw romantic scenery, and analysed and bottled it into the picturesque.

Gilpin's sketches, reproduced in his books in aquatint, exactly embody Johnson's requirements of pictures. They exhibit " the prominent and striking features " and " neglect the minute descriptions." In the *Tour to the Lakes* Gilpin explained their object. They made, he said, no attempt to be portraits, for " Mr. Farington's prints render any other portraits unnecessary." On the other hand they were intended " to illustrate and explain picturesque ideas—one of the most useful aids of the pencil," and to characterize the general face of the country which, as Johnson put it, " are alike obvious to attention and neglect." They were glimpses of the ideal—showing what nature would have liked to produce, according to man's idea of picturesque beauty.

[1] "The business of a poet is to examine not the individual, but the species—to remark general and large appearances. He does not number the streaks of the tulip, nor describe the different shades of the forest. He is to exhibit in his portraits of nature such prominent and striking features as recall the original to every mind, and must neglect those minute descriptions which one may have remarked and the other neglected, for those characteristics which are alike obvious to attention and neglect " (*Rasselas*).

They generalized in order, as Reynolds would have said, to express the particular. " Exact copies," Gilpin felt, " can scarcely ever be entirely beautiful, whilst he who works from imagination, culling a distance here, and there a foreground, will probably make a much better landscape."

Nevertheless he laid down certain bounds beyond which the imagination should not pass. Since only the picturesque features in any scene were admired, the artist might be allowed some liberty with the ground he stood upon. Trees might be moved or altered; withered stumps be substituted for spreading oaks and *vice versa*. But the insertion of a magnificent castle or a river in a scene was forbidden. The artist might, however, break an ill-formed hillock, or pull up an awkward piece of paling, or throw down a cottage, and alter the line of a road or river a few yards. Such events might, in fact, take place to-morrow.

There is something of the same beauty in Gilpin's little plates, as aquatinted, that is usually confined to Chinese landscape painting. Both illustrate, not an actual scene but an idea, everything unessential to which is eliminated. Gilpin gives us the essence of picturesque beauty. It is thus to mistake their intention to look for detail, and to call them " poor in character." [1] Most of his plates, some of which he engraved himself, have a tinted ground, generally of yellow ochre. He considered that a yellowish or reddish stain took off the glare of the paper and added also " a degree of harmony to the rawness of black and white."

The picturesque method of composing a landscape by selecting and combining objects necessitated clear ideas as to what was and was not picturesque. So in his *Tour to the Lakes* Gilpin made an *Analysis of Romantic* Scenery or, in other words, a collector's list of features suitable for inclusion in a picture. For this purpose he divided

[1] S. T. Prideaux, *Aquatint Engraving*, p. 259.

every view into three parts: *Background*, containing
Mountains and Lakes; *Off-skip*, comprising Valleys,
Woods, Rivers; *Foreground*, comprising Rocks, Cascades, Broken Ground, and Ruins. Of the whole
collection of these objects only certain specimens were
picturesque—adapted to form part of a picture. In the
case of mountains, for instance, " the pyramidical shape
and easy flow of an irregular line will be found the truest
source of beauty." The majority of mountains erred
one way or another into ugliness of outline—saddlebacks,
alps, and all such forms, suggested lumpishness, heaviness, and were disgusting. Gilpin was happier when
he was appreciating, not attempting to criticize. Thus,
in writing of the colours on a distant mountain side he
anticipated to some extent the vision of Turner:

They are rarely permanent; but seem to be a sort of floating
silky colours—alway in motion—always in harmony—and playing with a thousand changeable varieties into each other. They
are literally colours dipped in heaven.

The picturesque function of mountain and lake was to
provide the background and middle distance. Gilpin
then went on to analyse the most fitting kinds of foregrounds, which consisted in broken ground, trees, rocks,
cascades, and valleys. Whereas the ruling character
of the distance was tenderness, in the foreground this
must give way " to what the painter calls force and
richness, variety of parts and glowing tints." " The
painter will easily find broken ground, a rough knoll,
the sloping corner of a hill, perhaps worn by a mountain
torrent, or a rugged road winding through the chasm
of a rifted promontory—or some other part of nature
equally grand and picturesque." A true remark, for
the painters of the time were singularly apt at discovering such appropriate foregrounds. Then, too, we may
" call for an ancient oak to give the foreground grandeur
when we want the magnificence of its shadowing form

Plate XIV. REV. WILLIAM GILPIN. Lake District Scenery

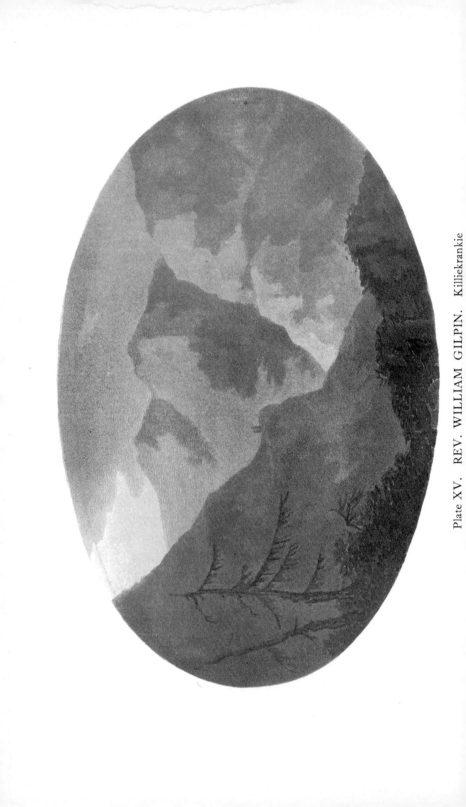

Plate XV.   REV. WILLIAM GILPIN.   Killiekrankie

to mantle over a vacant corner of a landscape, or to scatter a few loose branches over some ill-shaped line." How many sketchers, professional and amateur, have successfully " called on " this invaluable tree! Rocks, too, were well adapted to receiving " smart catching light," but " happy the pencil that can seize the spirit, agitation, and brilliancy of a broken cascade."

So closely did he consider rivers to be associated with the picturesque that he recommended the student to place before him a map of England and to settle in his head the course of all the chief rivers, making of them the " great directing lines of his excursions. On their banks he would be sure, not only to find the most beautiful views; but also obtain a compleat system of every kind of landscape."

Valleys were particularly valuable to the picturesque artist, as providing ready-made " side screens " for his compositions, and Gilpin's sketches make copious use of them.

Ruins, an integral part of landscape, came excellently into foregrounds. His view of them was naturally not architectural. At Tintern he found that to the beauty of the architecture

are superadded the ornaments of Time. Ivy, in masses uncommonly large, has taken possession of many parts of the walls; and gives a happy contrast to the grey-coloured stone. . . . Nor is this undecorated. Mosses of various hues, with lychens, maiden hair, penny-leaf, and other humble plants, overspread the surface . . . all together they give those full-blown tints which add the richest finishing to a ruin.

An even richer finishing, of grouted concrete, has now " overspread the surface " of many parts of Tintern.

Figures were, of course, invaluable in carrying out the " idea " of a scene. Between Grasmere and Rydal he found a view " entirely of the horrid kind, not a tree appearing to add cheerfulness. With regard to the adorning of such a scene with figures nothing could suit it better than a group of banditti. Of all scenes I ever saw, this was the most adapted to the perpetration of some dreadful deed."

The subject of figures involved him in a difficulty. " Moral and picturesque ideas do not always coincide."

In a moral view, the industrious mechanic is a more pleasing object than the loitering peasant. But in a picturesque light, it is otherwise. The arts of industry are rejected; and even idleness, if I may so speak, adds dignity to a character. Thus the lazy cowherd resting on his pole; or the peasant lolling on a rock, may be allowed in the grandest scenes. . . .

The characters that are most *suited to these scenes* of grandeur, are such as impress us with some idea of greatness, wildness or ferocity; all which touch on the sublime.

Figures in long, folding draperies; gypsies; banditti; and soldiers—not in modern regimentals; but as Virgil paints them.—

—longis adnixi hastis, et scuta tenentes

are all marked with one or other of these characters, and mixing with the magnificence, wildness or horror of the place, they properly coalesce.[1]

In corroboration he appealed to Salvator Rosa, " who seems to have thoroughly studied propriety in figures . . . his grand scenes being inhabited chiefly by banditti." He also referred to his book of figures. Many years later W. H. Pyne took a different view of the function of " figures." In his great collection of suitable groups [2] only one page of " banditti " was given, as against several

[1] *Tour to the Lakes*, vol. ii, pp. 44 *et seq.*

[2] W. H. Pyne, *Picturesque Groups for the Embellishment of Landscape*. Above 1000 subjects . . . An Encyclopaedia of Illustration. Aquatinted by J. Hill. Explanations, etc., by C. Gray. M. A. Nattali (1845). Among the contents of vol. i are: Army, Banditti, Brickmakers, Butchers, Camp Scenes, Carts, Ferry boats, Fire Engines, Games, Gypsies, Gleaners, Gravel Diggers, Grinders. In vol. ii appear Postchaises, Racing, Ropemakers, Rustics, Smugglers, Statuary, Threshing, Timber Waggons, Toll-gates, Travellers reposing, Trucks, Wheelwrights, and Woodmen.

devoted to such avocations as Rustics, Travellers, and Brickmakers. The reason was that sublimity had gone out of fashion and the picturesque had become respectable, responsible. The " encyclopaedia," it was hoped, " opens a new field to the student of the picturesque. It may be useful even to the advanced artist." Note the distinction.

From human figures Gilpin went on to consider animals. " In a picturesque light no ornament is more adapted to a mountainous or rocky country than an animal.... The actions of a goat are still more pleasing than the shagginess of his coat." Then, in a remark reminiscent of the goat that petrified Gray, " it would add new terror to a scene, to see an animal browsing on the steep of a perpendicular rock." The lines of the cow are more picturesque than those of the horse, her lines being varied here and there by a squareness which is very picturesque. The tints of cows he would have us know, are broken and warm, and that " cows are commonly the most picturesque in the months of April and May, when the old hair is coming off."

So Sidney Smith[1] summed up the difference between the two great categories: " The Vicar's horse is *beautiful*, the Curate's *picturesque*."

From the picturesque point of view the grouping of figures and animals was at least as important as the animals themselves. Various directions are given, one of the more important of which is that two cows will not group well. " With three you are sure of a good group, except indeed they all stand in the same attitude at equal distances." Presumably the gentleman mentioned by Price was a disciple of Gilpin, who, when his economical wife suggested that for their domestic needs two of their three cows would suffice, answered, " Lord, my dear, *two* cows you know can never group."

In the accounts of his excursions, it is evident that

[1] Lockhart's *Life of Scott*, ch. xxv.

Gilpin made every effort to approach each " scene " in an appropriate frame of mind. He saw clearly the necessity of the mind's being educated to appreciate scenery, or else that would be called picturesque which in reality was merely fruitful or pleasant. Similarly wild, natural country repelled the generality of people who could not view it abstractly.

The spectator should investigate the *sources of beauty*, and evince that a scene, though replete with every circumstance of *horror*, may be very picturesque. I have an instance at hand to my purpose. One of the voyagers in the Northern seas [Captain King, who succeeded Captain Cook] in sailing up a river thus describes the scene :—

"The country," says he, "on each side was very romantic, but unvaried ; the river running between mountains of the most craggy and barren aspect, where there was nothing to diversify the scene, but now and then the sight of a bear, or a flight of wild fowl. So uninteresting a passage leaves me nothing further to add."

It is hardly possible, in so few words, to present more picturesque ideas of the horrid and savage kind. We have a river running up a country broken on both sides with wild romantic rocks, which we know nature never constructs in a uniform manner. We naturally conclude, therefore, that they ran out in some parts into vast diagonal strata, on the ledges of which a bear or two appeared, sitting on their hams or howling at the boat. In other parts, the rocks would form lofty promontories, hanging over the river and inhabited by numerous wildfowl screaming round them. This is copied from Captain King's sketch, and yet he has no idea that a scene so savage could present any other ideas than such as were disgusting.[1]

This instructive passage, in which we see a sketch worked up into a picture by what Gilpin called " high colouring," shows the essential contribution of the picturesque to literature, and appreciation. " It is the aim of picturesque description," he says, " to bring the images of nature as forcibly and as closely to the eye as

[1] *Forest Scenery*, vol. ii, p. 166.

it can, by high colouring." This process " is not a
string of rapturous epithets, but *an attempt to analyse the
views of nature,* and to express all the detail in terms as
appropriate and vivid as possible."

This was the task he set himself in his books. They
were to be preparations for the ceremony of visiting
the scenes themselves. But not only was the visitor to
be prepared for appreciating. His critical faculty was
to be stimulated and instructed as well. In the *Tour
to the Lakes* Gilpin rarely finds a prospect entirely
free from some defect or other. Even the fall of
Lodore, " a noble object both in itself and as an ornament to the lake," lost for him some of its grandeur by
being seen over a tongue of low ground.

He did not offer primroses and violets on the picturesque path. It led along the brinks of precipices, it
climbed mountains, and threaded gorges.

He who is in quest of the picturesque scenes of the lake
must travel along the rough side-screens that adorn it; and catch
its beauties as they arise—its little bays, winding shores, deep
recesses and hanging promontories, its garnished rock and distant
mountain. These are, in general the picturesque scenes which
it affords.[1]

There is a *gusto*, a fullness, about his descriptions,
that is dramatic, even powerful, as in his relation of the
pursuit of the Derwent:

Turning the first great promontory on the left, we found
ourselves in a vast recess of mountains. We had seen these at
a distance, from the northern extremity of the lake. They were
then objects of grandeur. But now they had assumed their full
majestic form; surrounding us on every side with their lofty
barriers; and shutting out in appearance every idea of escape.
Wild and various beyond conception were their shapes; but
they participated rather of the desolate than of the fantastic
idea. . . . The summits receded far behind; and we saw only

[1] *Op. cit.*, vol. i, p. 86.

the bursting rocks and bold protuberances with which the sides of these enormous masses of solid earth are charged.

Gilpin's *Forest Scenery* differs from his other publications in being, not the worked-up journal of a hurried tour, but the matured product of many years spent in the New Forest. It contains valuable hints on the picturesque handling of woodland, and considers each species of tree in a picturesque light. As a genus trees, he maintained, were the grandest and most beautiful of earth's products, because they were adapted so perfectly to grouping in landscape and for receiving light and shade. He maintained this attitude of admiring and understanding nature in so far as she approximated to seventeenth and eighteenth-century painting throughout the book. But whilst, in theory, " without form, lightness, and proper balance, no tree can have picturesque beauty," he repeatedly excepts, as in the case of figures, the products of injury and decay.

How many forests have we wherein you shall have for one living tree, twenty-four evil-thriving, rotten and dying trees; what rottenness! what hollowness! what dead arms! withered tops! curtailed trunks! What loads of mosses! dropping boughs and dying branches shall you see everywhere!

Yet " these are often the very capital sources of picturesque beauty." For hollow trunks are invaluable for foregrounds, withered tops are of great use when we wish to break the regularity of a continued line—witness the use put to them by Salvator. Then blasted trees:

When the dreary heath is spread before the eye, and ideas of wildness and desolation are required, what more suitable accompaniment can be imagined than the blasted oak, ragged, scathed and leafless, shooting its peeled white branches athwart the gathering blackness of some rising storm?

Even while admitting the mischievousness of ivy, he insisted on its capacity to adorn and enrich. Heaving roots, the more tortuous and knobbly they were, the firmer they established the grip of the tree upon the earth, and the more dignity that tree consequently assumed.

It was a relief to him that the Oak was as useful as picturesque. Of all trees it best fulfilled the character of any scene, adding new dignity to the ruined tower, new grandeur to the pastoral scene. The Ash, though equally useful, was less picturesque, the lightness of its foliage being its only redeeming feature. The Elm was far better adapted to receiving the grand masses of light and shade that were vital to picturesque effect. The Beech, he thought, a heavy tree, made up of littleness, and he oddly enough failed to notice how the Hornbeam beyond all other trees grows gnarled with age. For Poplars he had nothing good to say—for Daubigny and Sisley had not yet revealed them. The Chestnut, on the other hand, was Salvator's tree, and the stem of Birch was particularly picturesque. One has only to look at the backgrounds of Reynolds's portraits to see how invaluable " nature's beau," as Fielding called the birch, was to the generalizing painter.

Of evergreens, the Cedar of Lebanon held preeminence, if only " on account of the respectable mention that is everywhere made of it in scripture." The Stone Pine always suggested ideas of broken porticoes, Ionic pillars, and fragments of temples—a most valuable association. Unfortunately, well as it might do in English pictures, it would not do in English woods. Here the Scots fir must be used instead. Gilpin was one of the first to admire " Scotch." In perfection he recognized it to be a very picturesque tree. It was its hardiness that caused it to be put to servile uses, in screens or mixtures. He considered this an ignominious treatment, and tried, successfully, to " rescue it from disgrace and establish it as a picturesque tree."

In dealing with " forest scenery on canvas," Gilpin made an important point that marks exactly how far he had moved towards the colour-vision that Knight subsequently attained, and how strictly he nevertheless observed the conventions of eighteenth-century painting. He is speaking of the effects of atmosphere on the colour of woodlands.

When there is a north wind, blue and purple clouds will be lowering over the horizon, and the forest, overspread with a deep blue and purple reflection, will present a very picturesque appearance. But he strongly urges the painter to be cautious in setting down the full strength of these colours if he observes them.

The appearance of blue and purple trees, unless in the remote distance, offends, and though the artist may have authority from nature for his practice, yet the spectator, not versed in such effects, may be displeased. Painting, like poetry, is intended to excite pleasure: and though the painter with this view should avoid such images as are trite and vulgar ; yet he should *seize only those which are easy and intelligible.* Neither poetry or painting is a proper vehicle of learning. The painter will do well to avoid every uncommon appearance in nature.

It is as remarkable to find a man fully alive to the impressionistic view of nature in 1791 as disappointing that he should not have the courage to insist on artistic truth. To do so, however, needed more explosive force than Gilpin possessed. A revolution was required before the basic dogma, "Paint what you think," as accepted by all artists at this time, was overthrown by the impressionists' gospel of "Paint what you see." Picturesque theory eventually achieved this liberty. But not through Gilpin. It was Constable and Turner who were the liberators, even though Payne Knight anticipated them in theory.

Knight himself did not attain the abstract view till late in life. In his diary [1] of the tour to Sicily that he

[1] Knight's journal is preserved only in the translation of it that Goethe included in his biography of Hackert. Goethe's *Werke* (1891), vol. xlvi, pp. 151 *et seq.*

undertook with Philipp Hackert, the German painter, and Charles Gore in 1777, Burke is the origin of his sensibility.

The culmination of the tour was the ascent of Etna to see the sunrise. The adventurers camped for the evening in a cave at the edge of the lava fields. Then at midnight they rode eight miles on mules till the steepness compelled them to dismount. Knight's faculties were keyed up to appreciate the sublimity.

A complete stillness lay over all, broken only from time to time by the thunder of the mountain like waves breaking in a storm. The crater could be discerned by a lurid red light which pierced the black clouds of smoke rolling from it. The scene was the most truely sublime that I have ever beheld and is surely incomparable.

After two hours' climbing they reached the crater:

The prospect that here presents itself is beyond all description and imagination. The whole of Sicily, Malta, Calabria and the Lipari Islands extend at your feet as on a map. Details were lost in the azure tints of dawn and the world appeared sunk in silence and repose.

When the sun rose, Knight observed that Etna "formed the gnomon of a vast sundial of which the shadow stretched far beyond the visible horizon." He began to use his glass, which it is interesting to find was furnished by a firm still with us:

I even thought that I could see the coast of Apulia with Dollond's pocket spy glass; but the cold was so great that I could not keep my attention fixed on it . . . [consequently] I could not study these marvels of nature with the thoroughness that I should have preferred.

Nevertheless, he was determined to look into the crater before turning homewards.

Our guide had a good deal to say of the danger of attempting to do so, and of the frequency with which the overhanging lava

THE PICTURESQUE

cliffs crumble away. But after some discussion and much calling
upon the holy Agatha, he led me to a spot where it was the
custom for foolhardy foreigners to stand. Hence I gazed on the
dreadful abyss of fire, and saw the clouds of smoke rolling out
between the huge crags, over which a dismal flickering light
was playing; I could observe no bottom; but the heaving
billows of molten matter produced sufficient sound to raise in
me some idea of the floods and whirlwinds of tempestuous
flame that raged below.

If Knight, thirty years later, ridiculed Burke's notion
of sublimity, as a young man of twenty-seven he shows
himself to have been as apt a disciple as ever was Price.
But by the end of the century the fact is that rapture
was beginning to be commonplace. The astonishment
was lacking that was requisite to sublime emotions.
The Picturesque was already becoming a little obvious.
The Lakes, for instance, were beginning to be exploited.
The *Monthly Magazine* in 1778 expressed the opinion
that " To *make the Tour* of the Lakes, to speak in fashionable terms, is the *ton* of the present hour." A *Guide*
published by Thomas West in 1778 had reached a
seventh edition by 1799; and was so arranged that the
tourist was conducted " from the delicate touches of
Claude, verified on *Coniston* Lake, to the noble scenes of
Poussin, exhibited on *Windermere*-water, and from there
to the stupendous romantic ideas of *Salvator Rosa,*
realized in the Lake of *Derwent.*" A *Survey of the Lakes*
by James Clarke was published in 1787, *A Fortnight's
Ramble to the Lakes* in 1792, and so on. The numbers
of painters who visited them increased yearly.

Other parts of England were scarcely less favoured,
though the books describing them tended to unite the
picturesque with archaeology and architecture. The
Antiquities of Captain Grose, the tours and histories of
William Bray, Britton, Lysons, and numerous others,
whose works can be found on the shelves of any topographical library, were illustrated with engravings after

the water-colours of a host of artists, by now steeped in the principles of the picturesque.

The finest minds had no need of the picturesque medium in their communing with nature. Professor Manwaring quotes the disappointing experience of a Dr. Adar who, with certain ladies, visited Caldron Linn with Burns. " I am surprised that none of these scenes should have called forth an exertion of Burns' muse," observed the Doctor, " but I doubt if he had much taste for the picturesque." The ladies were desolated " at his not expressing in more glowing fervid language his impressions of the scene, certainly highly sublime, and somewhat horrible."

Coleridge, on the other hand, who took a walking tour in Wales in 1794, found the scenery " most wild and romantic." He spent two hours of a luminous evening among the ruins of Denbigh Castle " feeding on melancholy." When two other travellers entered and one, like Sir Oran Hauton of famous memory, produced a flute, observing " it will have a romantic effect," Coleridge settled down for a feast of sensibility.

He sate down amid the most awful part of the ruins; the moon just began to make her rays predominant over the lingering day-light; I pre-attuned my feelings to emotion; and the romantic youth instantly struck up the sadly pleasing tunes of *Miss Carey*, *The British Lion is my Sign* and *A roaring trade I drive*.

Cowper found no need of the picturesque, and Wordsworth[1] congratulated himself on his immunity from its influence:

> . . . for this
> Although a strong infection of the age
> Was never much my habit,—giving way
> To a comparison of scene with scene,
> Bent overmuch on superficial things,
> Pampering myself with meagre novelties
> Of colour and proportion.

---

[1] *The Prelude*, Book XII. See also p. 49 *supra*.

CHAPTER V

GARDEN SCENES

§ I

THE FERME ORNÉE

Le Pittoresque nous vient d'Angleterre; un beau paysage fait partie de la religion comme de l'aristocratie d'un Anglais; chez lui c'est l'object d'un sentiment sincère.—Stendahl, *Mémoires d'un Touriste.*

IN the creative arts that were decisively affected by the picturesque, Vanbrugh stands out as the original innovator. It is Uvedale Price who credits him with the dictum, when consulted upon the lay-out at Blenheim, " You must send for a landscape painter." His application to architecture of the principles of picturesque composition was observed by both Robert Adam and Sir Joshua Reynolds. Hitherto William Kent has usually been recognized as the originator of landscape gardening, on the strength of Walpole's sentence, " Kent first leaped the fence and saw all nature was a garden." It was the substitution by Vanbrugh of a ha-ha for a fence that enabled Kent to leap it. At Castle Howard, at Eastbury, at Claremont, to take but the largest of Vanbrugh's schemes, enough of his work survives to prove that it was he who first conceived the approximation of gardens to painted landscape, with lakes, vistas, temples, and woods worked into a composed whole.

The results of this revolution in gardening were far-reaching. " Why may not a whole Estate," asked Addison in 1712,[1] " be thrown into a kind of garden by frequent Plantations. A man might make a pretty Landskip of his own Possessions." He was taken at

[1] *Spectator*, No. 414.

his word. The whole kingdom was gardened by the landowners of the eighteenth century. Only the other day Mr. Belloc gave as, in his view, the only contribution of the landowners to society, " the landscape of rural England, the character of the paradise and especially the preservation of old trees." There is no denying that the gradual disappearance of this class is resulting in the blighting of the countryside. The woods, the downs, the fields that we have come to take for granted, are now seen to have been but parts of a vast created landscape, natural enough to our eyes, but in reality managed as much for picturesque appearance as for economic returns. The landscaping of gardens in the eighteenth century deprived their owners of many a delicious pleasaunce. But the gardening of landscapes gave the nation its countryside.

Vanbrugh's experiments are echoed in the literature of the time not only by Addison. Shaftesbury (1711) resolved that rocks, caverns, cascades, and grottoes, even " the horrid graces of the wilderness itself," as representing nature more, were preferable to the " mockery of princely gardens." Hutcheson (1725) observed that regularity was beginning to be abandoned " to obtain imitation of Nature," and Pope proclaimed that " All gardening is painting." Bridgeman, instructed by Vanbrugh, and Switzer were the fashionable practitioners of this new conception. The latter[1] urged patrons to quit their tulips and observe " the sweet meanders and precipitate falls of a river." Their works, however, fell short of their professions. Even Pope's garden at Twickenham, though it comprised a grotto and a grove, was a very rectangular affair. As yet Vanbrugh's painter had not presented himself. In William Kent he appeared—a fashionable portrait and ceiling painter besides an architect, who began his London career in 1719-20. Quite possibly, as Joseph Warton believed,

[1] *Ichnographica Rustica* (1718).

the addition of gardening to his repertory was owing to his acquaintance, through Lord Burlington, with Pope. In any case Kensington Gardens, Gunnersbury, Euston, Holkham, and Rousham were put in his hands, and received clumps, winding paths, and serpentine rivers. Kensington even had dead trees planted in it to heighten the similarity to Salvator's landscapes, whilst Walpole found it difficult to conceive that Claude had not painted many of his pictures in the grounds of Stanstead, which Kent laid out for Lord Halifax.

Kent's principles were expressed in words by Batty Langley,[1] as " a continued series of new and delightful scenes at every step we take." His illustrations do not bear much resemblance to paintings or nature, the copying of which he advocated. Yet he was sufficiently imbued with a tendency to picturesqueness to include several designs for Roman and Gothic ruins " to close vistas."

The next step was to work the meadows and farms themselves into the picture. The invention of the *ferme ornée* is attributed to Philip Southcote of Wooburn Farm, near Chertsey, in whom Kent's " Elysian scenes excited the idea of improving his own domain." [2] His real discovery was evidently the " belt," which, with a path, he carried all round his farm, diversifying the circuit with a Gothic temple, a menagerie, and contriving for the visitor to feel himself still on a farm by getting glimpses of the meadows and arable fields in the centre of the ground.

His plan was adopted by Shenstone at the Leasowes in about 1745. Mr. Saintsbury has called Shenstone a master of " the artificial-natural style in poetry," and the Leasowes was his most elaborate poem. The principle of his garden lay-out was that when a building or other object had once been viewed from its *proper point,*

---

[1] *New Principles of Gardening* (1728).
[2] George Mason, *Essay on Design in Gardening* (1768).

the foot should never travel to it by the same path which the eye had travelled over before. " Lose the object and draw nigh obliquely."

He was the first to apply the term " Landskip garden " to " our present taste in gardening." " Any good painter of landskip appears to me," he wrote, " the most proper designer." Consequently, " a rural scene is never to me perfect without some kind of building," whether a " ruinated structure " or a cottage.[1]

The Leasowes were frequently described by admiring visitors, best by Richard Graves in his delightful novel *Columella, or The Distres't Anchoret* (1779), in which the plot is woven round the garden and a gently satirized presentment of its owner. As at Wooburn Farm, a winding walk led round the domain, diversified by a root house, irregular groups of trees, " fit for the pencil of Salvator Rosa," a seat in Gothic form, a Lovers' Walk leading to an assignation seat, and numerous urns and prospect seats. Having made the circuit the visitor then descended into the central area—" a beautiful gloomy scene called Virgil's Grove "—by a sloping path deeply shaded, below which murmured a rill, and beyond a splashing sound announced the proximity of the cascade. When Hortensius and Atticus visited Columella, the friends were approaching this, the sublime culmination of the circuit, called in the story " Arno's Vale," when their host's man Peter approached and told Columella that the farmer's heifers were got into the young plantation at the bottom of *Aaron's Well*.

"Aaron's Well! you blockhead," says Columella, "Arno's Vale, you mean." " Nay, nay," quoth Peter, "I know the right name of it is Tadpole Bottom."

Shenstone was himself a hermit, as Graves makes his counterpart observe in *Columella* to the professional

[1] Shenstone, *Unconnected Thoughts on Gardening* (1764).

[131]

applicant for the post. One day the friends were summoned to the door

where they beheld a very venerable figure, with a long white beard, a bald head, and dressed in a long brown cloak almost down to his ankles: he had two sticks nailed across in his hand, by way of a crucifix, and a string of issue peas for a rosary of beads.

The man repeated. . . that he had heard his honour wanted an hermit to live in his woods, and said that he should be very proud to serve him. . . . He said he had lived four years in that capacity with the late Sir Humphry Whimwham. But that when Sir Humphry died, his son had insisted on his doing a great deal more work than he had agreed to do with Sir Humphry; which was to keep his hermitage clean, and to sit at the door with a book in his hand when any company came.

It subsequently transpired that the hermit had been discharged for certain inappropriate relations with a dairy-maid, and for being more than once caught with a pipe and a jug of ale, instead of his book and his beads. A hermit actually had been employed by Charles Hamilton at Pains Hill.

The Leasowes was a shining example to the age of how well a small domain could be formed into a series of pictures. There are many descriptions in the literature of the time of how badly they could be dealt with. In *Columella*, Mr. Nonsuch, a neighbouring *nouveau riche*, had such a garden, confined by a wall and of less than an acre in area.

Within this compass, however, they had contrived to introduce every individual article of modern taste. Here was a large shrubbery, a small serpentine river over which was thrown a Chinese bridge of a considerable diameter; there was a Chinese pagoda, a Gothic temple, a grotto, a root house, a hermitage, a Cynic tub or two by the water side; at one corner of the garden was a summerhouse with a gilded ball which Mr. Nonsuch boasted could be seen twenty miles round, and at the opposite corner a barn-end converted into a gothic spire.

Plate XVI.   PAUL SANDBY.   A Picturesque Composition suggestive of Park Scenery

Fig. 1.   A Gothic pavilion, convertible into a greenhouse,
suitable for a Gothic mansion. From *Theory and Practice
of Landscape Gardening*, by H. Repton, 1803

Fig. 2.   A Ruin containing a Dairy.   From
Hints on Ornamental Gardening, by J. B. Papworth, 1823

Plate XVII

Mrs. Delany's " park " at Delville, which she was laying out about 1743, was decidedly of the *ferme ornée* description. It consisted of a shallow valley with a stream at the bottom, looking over Dublin harbour and " mountains." The floor of the valley was a meadow where was " one hay rick." One side rose into hanging woods, the end near the house was a bowling green, and on the other side was a terrace walk planted with flowering shrubs. Disposed about the grounds were " an old castle (as it were)," and underneath it a cave " that will make a very pretty grotto," a portico, and a " *beggar's hut*, which is a seat in a rock." " The fields are planted in a *wild way* with *forest trees and with bushes*, that look so naturally you would not imagine it the work of art " and " there are several prettinesses I can't explain to you." [1]

Shenstone's influence was most purely and strongly felt at Hagley. We have already had the poet Thomson's description of the view from the grounds that Lyttelton, with the help of his cousin William Pitt—a confirmed picturician, with his park at Holwood, near Keston—had formed. Its lawns and rills and verdure and prospects made Horace Walpole " quite forget my favourite Thames ":

and there is such a small lake, with cascades falling down such a Parnassus! With a circular temple on the distant eminence . . . and there is a hermitage, so exactly like those in Sadeler's prints, on the brow of a shady mountain . . . and there is such a pretty well under a wood, like the Samaritan woman's in a picture by Nicolo Poussin.[2]

Elsewhere was an artificial ruin by Sanderson Miller that Walpole declared " had the true rust of the Barons' Wars."

In some ways, the most remarkable landscape garden in England that still survives in its original condition,

[1] Mrs. Delany to Mrs. Dewes, 19th July 1744.
[2] To Bentley, 1753.

[133]

is that at Stourhead in Wiltshire. It was begun early in the eighteenth century in a far more pictorial style than was prevalent at that time. It occupies a number of converging valleys on the edge of Salisbury Plain, the floor of the main valley having been dammed up to form a large, irregular lake. On its skilfully planted shores various members of the Hoare family raised a succession of ornamental buildings which are arranged so as to be seen picturesquely down glades, beneath trees, or across the lake. A Pantheon, a Temple of Apollo, a magnificent grotto graced with lines specially written by Pope, a Gothic cottage, and a mill are among the incidents composing the various Claudian landscapes.

The later writers on the picturesque were most impressed by the more natural grounds at Pains Hill, Cobham, where Charles Hamilton laid out a glorified *ferme ornée* in the 'forties and 'fifties of the century. Hamilton's supreme merit, in the eyes of Price, was that he had " not only studied pictures, but had studied them for the express purpose of improving real landscape."

Hamilton preserved a certain formality about the house, with a grassy terrace on which are some of the finest urns and statues from Van Nost's workshop, and a number of magnificent cedars with the greater of which he designed to frame his landscapes. A large sheet of water was formed and picturesquely planted up, a temple of Bacchus set in a telling position, and a classic bridge constructed (ingeniously of timber) to cross the water at a picturesque point. But it was the walks through the woods that most impressed Price. He contrasted them to Kent or Brown's treatment of paths at neighbouring Claremont. At Pains Hill " we have enjoyed the dear delight of getting to some spot where there were no traces of art, and no other walk or communication than a sheep track." At Claremont an identical wood—

GARDEN SCENES

A wood with many old trees covered with ivy, mixed with thickets of hollies, yews and thorns,—a wood which Rousseau might have dedicated *à la rêverie*, is so intersected by walks and green alleys, all edged and bordered, that there is no escaping from them ; they act as flappers in Laputa, and instantly wake you from any dream of retirement.

§ 2

" CAPABILITY " BROWN

Born to grace Nature, and her works complete ;
With all that's beautiful, sublime and great !
For him each Muse enwreathes the Laurel Crown,
And consecrates to Fame immortal Brown.
—*The Rise and Progress of the Present Taste* . . . 1767.

Nature did her best to protect herself, by arranging that her wooer-to-be should be born with the name of Brown. " At least," she said, " if he does come and plague me, nobody will be foolish enough to think him one of those inspired artists—not with a name like that." At his christening the fairies were divided upon what other name he should be given. But finally the romantic ones prevailed, and he was called Lancelot. " For," they said, " he will fill the land with beautiful lakes, so we will name him after the Knight of the Lake." " Very well, then," said the minority, who wanted to call him Dick, or Tom, or Harry, " Lancelot be it." But a powerful fairy, the Queen of Water Fairies and Laughing Moorland Streams, arose among the Opposition members and said, " You have given him his baptismal name. But we will give him a name by which all who come after shall know him. Your name will be given him at his birth and will be a token of his intentions. But our name will be given him when he dies, and will sum up his achievements."

[135]

And so it came about that after a long and immensely successful career, during which thousands of square miles had been made far more Ideal and Beautiful than they had been before, poor Mr. Brown lost his splendid name Lancelot, and was known ever after as Capability. For it had so happened that whenever the Knight of the Artificial Lake was called in by a distressed land-owner, he had always said, " Well, my lord, I observe that your park has *great capabilities*." As Mr. Brown was also a very capable, honest, and cheerful gentleman, he was invariably allowed to " improve " people's parks and make them romantic and picturesque. But when his work came to maturity, alas! people saw that Brown had only been a very capable gardener and not the flashing champion of nature after all. So everybody called him, as the fairy had prophesied, after his achieve-ments—Capability.

He was born in Northumberland in 1715, and after serving as a gardener near Woodstock, was given command of the kitchen garden at Stowe, later becoming bailiff. Whether or no he himself assisted in the exten-sion of the grounds at Stowe from the original twenty-eight acres into the three hundred that they covered by the middle of the century, he certainly formed his ideas largely on Lord Cobham's garden. In 1751 Horace Walpole noted that grounds at Warwick had been " well laid out by one Brown who has set up on a few ideas of Kent and Mr. Southcote," from the latter of whom he borrowed the " belt." At about this date he undertook important works at Blenheim, set up independently as an " improver," and was appointed royal gardener at Richmond.

Though Brown's system of treating grounds was considered, by those who came after him, as the anti-thesis of the picturesque, it was closely connected with the theory of painting as then accepted. He was unsuccessful, if he ever tried his hand, at turning country sides into pictures. What he did attempt was to create landscapes that should arouse emotions, by means of the recipes for beauty evolved by Hogarth and Burke. Like nature, as Kent considered her, he " abhorred a straight line "; on Hogarth's principle, he formed all his walks, lakes, and belts of trees in serpentine lines and gave to the surface of the grounds he improved gentle undulations, such as aroused in Burke the sensations of beauty. The circular clumps, with which he dotted the landscape, had the " sublimity " of " rotund forms," and anything in the shape of formal gardens, terraces, yew hedges, or of utilitarian objects such as kitchen gardens, stables, and even back-door approaches were swept away or concealed, lest they should interfere with the " beautiful ideas " aroused by gently flowing lines and undulating turf.

He was, in fact, that most dangerous phenomenon, a practical man inspired by a theory. By a theory, moreover, that, although derived from visual qualities, had become intellectual and standardized. Mrs. Elizabeth Montagu, whose grounds at Sandleford turned under his direction into " sweet pastorals and elegant elegiacs " was on the track of his foible when she said that, besides being " an agreeable, pleasant companion, and a great genius, in his profession," she " considered him as a great poet." [1] Hannah More gives further evidence of Brown's literary, as contrasted with pictorial, bent. During a " very agreeable two hours " that he spent with her

he promised to give me taste by innoculation. I am sure he has a very charming one, and he illustrates everything he says about gardening with some literary or grammatical allusion. He told me he compared his art to literary composition. Now there, said he, pointing his finger, I make a comma, and there, point-ing to another part (where an interruption is desirable to break

---

[1] Mrs. Montagu, *Queen of the Blues,* ed. Blunt, 1924, vol. ii, p. 123.

the view) a parenthesis—now a full stop, and then I begin another subject.[1]

We have seen how a literary way of considering landscape arose out of the poetry of Thomson, Dyer, and their followers. And how the resulting literary conception of what landscape should look like, was carried into practice by a poet-gardener like Shenstone or a dilettante like Lord Lyttelton. Brown formed his system on their experiments. As he happened not to be a poet, but only a man of few ideas, albeit fashionable ideas, the result was apt to be unsatisfactory if viewed with other considerations than his own amalgam of pictorial-poetic-grammatical principles.

Nevertheless, many intelligent men, whose view of painting was literary, regarded him as a great painter. If one considers that a Claude or Poussin merely took so many symbols of ideas, such as rocks for wildness, groves for solitude, a stream for coolness, waving lines for beauty and so on, and combined them into a landscape that consequently aroused all these ideas, then Brown was indeed a great painter on such principles. Joseph Warton was right when he thought it " neither exaggeration nor affectation to call Mr. Brown a great painter; for he has realized

> What'er Lorraine light-touched with softening hue,
> Or savage Rosa dash'd, or learned Poussin drew."

The anonymous author of *The Rise and Progress of the Present Taste in Planting Parks, Pleasure Grounds, Gardens, etc. from Henry the Eighth to King George III* in 1767 compared Brown to the giants of two arts.

> At Blenheim, Croome and Caversham we trace
> Salvator's wildness, Claude's enlivening grace,
> Cascades and Lakes as fine as Risdale drew,
> While Nature's vary'd in each charming view.

---

[1] *Memoirs*, ed. Roberts (1834), vol. i, p. 267.

To paint his works wou'd Poussin's Powers require,
Milton's sublimity and Dryden's fire.

But if we can see more in ideal landscape than literary symbolism, as the students of the Picturesque succeeded in doing, and recognize the high pictorial skill of these painters in composing their masses and massing their colours, then we can observe Brown's shortcomings.

The worst of these was a cut and dried system that he applied, on principle, to every scene that he was called upon to improve. Price summed up this system acidly when he exclaimed:

Few persons have been so lucky as never to have seen or heard the true *proser*; smiling, and distinctly uttering his flowing commonplace nothings, with the same placid countenance, the the same even-toned voice—he is the very emblem of serpentine walks, belts and rivers, and all Mr. Brown's works—like him they are smooth, flowing, even and distinct—and like him they wear one's soul out.[1]

On one occasion Owen Cambridge remarked, " I wish I may die before you, Mr. Brown." " Why so ? " inquired the puzzled but flattered Brown. " Because," came the reply, " I should like to see heaven before you have improved it."

In *The English Garden*, published between the years 1771 and 1781, William Mason set out to criticize Brown's methods, but actually wrote a panegyric. He described Brown's principles as based on utility. Taste, inspired by Truth, exalts her voice:

> Beauty scorns to dwell
> Where Use is exiled. At the awful sound
> The terrace sinks spontaneous; on the green,
> Broidered with crisped knots, the tonsile yews
> Wither and fall; the fountain dares no more
> To fling its wasted crystals through the sky,

---

[1] *Op. cit.*, p. 233.

> But pours salubrious o'er the parched lawn
> Rills of fertility.—Oh! best of Arts
> That works this happy change!

No doubt an undulating expanse of grass *looked* more useful than a series of parterres and walls, even though the latter produced vegetables and fruit. Again, Brown's passion for removing kitchen gardens, stables, even whole villages to places where they could not be seen, could scarcely be supported on grounds of convenience, any more than the indeterminate line taken by his approach roads. But agricultural reform was in the air, and the improver of grounds liked to think that he was also benefitting husbandry. The true purpose of Brown's schemes was to suggest ideas of " simplicity " and " naturalness." These, if not useful in themselves, gave an impression of being so.

Mason's fallacy was thinking that a thing is more useful if it is more natural. A fountain is not natural, therefore it is not useful (though the water must go somewhere), therefore it is not beautiful. Even Uvedale Price, in advocating a return to a formal Italian style of gardening, was still sufficiently obsessed by the need for a " natural " sanction, to adduce geysers as a natural counterpart to fountains.

Having removed the old formal surroundings of the house, Brown would then remodel the grounds. His eye would light upon the avenue.

> Pity, sure,
> Will spare the long cathedral aisle of shade . . .
> The axe must do its office. Cruel task,
> Yet needful. Trust me, though I bid thee strike,
> Reluctantly I bid thee; for my soul
> Holds dear an antient oak, nothing more dear;
> It is an antient friend. Stay then thy hand;
> And try by saplings tall, discreetly placed,
> Before, between, behind, in scattered groups,

To break th'obdurate *line*. So may'st thou save
A chosen few. . . .
                              parted now,
Each tree becomes the father of a tribe.[1]

The remnants of an avenue, that is, could be formed into clumps. In place of the avenue, Brown would trace a " line of beauty " by way of a road—

                    that peculiar curve
Alike averse to crooked and to straight,
Where sweet Simplicity resides . . .
'Tis Nature's curve, instinctively she bids
Her tribes of Being trace it.[2]

" This fellow," said a friend to Price, " crawls like a snail all over the grounds and leaves his cursed slime wherever he goes." Not only did the roads and paths wind; so did the lake; and so did the " belts " with which Brown surrounded a park. In these his favourite mixture was beech and Scots fir.

" Clumps " were so celebrated in connection with Brown, that when he was High Sheriff of London, some wag shouted after him, as he went in procession, " clump your javelin men."

One can usually tell a park that has been made by Brown, by the numbers of small plantations of trees dotted about the surface. Many have now been thinned out into dignified groups, but since in Price's time they were circular bulbous excrescences his " indignation was very justly excited." In extenuation of Brown, it may be urged that he fully intended this thinning-out to take place, when the selected trees were sufficiently well grown. Price, however, found that although " Mr. Brown frequently repeated his visits, as far as I have observed, the trees in his plantations bear no mark of his attention—indeed, his clumps strongly prove his love of compactness."

[1] W. Mason, *op. cit.*, bk. i.   [2] *Ibid.*

" Thames, Thames, you will never forgive me,"
Brown is reported to have exclaimed, on viewing one of
his " artificial rivers." In every one of his schemes,
where possible, a long and slightly winding lake is to
be found, dammed up at the lower end, but without
bordering trees. He was not, as a rule, very happy in
his treatment of lakes. " What makes their sweep
much more formal, is their extreme nakedness," said
Price, and he very soundly insisted that large portions
of such waters should be wooded to their brim, and their
ends be lost to view among trees.

Many of Brown's landscapes have in the process of
time acquired charm. But his treatment of the immediate surroundings of houses can never again be justified.
His aim was to make it appear that a house was planted
slap down in its park, the grass coming up to the walls
on all four sides. To realize this, it was desirable to
eliminate the back door and service region, which he
sometimes succeeded in doing by means of a subterranean approach to the tradesman's entry. At Claremont you reach the back door by a tunnel under lawns.
At Harleyford, where the arrangement remains un-
altered, Mrs. Lybbe Powys found in 1767 " the whole
of the offices so contrived in a pit as to be perfectly
invisible—a great addition to the looks of any place,"
a reflection with which few mistresses of households
would agree to-day. Sweeping lawns, then, surrounded
a house, intersected with serpentine paths.

There must be a ha-ha, so that if there are sheep

> the dubious eye
> Decides not if they crop the mead or lawn.[1]

Mason even suggested that there need not even be
a ha-ha. The children of neighbouring paupers might,
he recommended, be suitably dressed, and employed
to form a living fence. Such an arrangement would,

[1] W. Mason, *op. cit.*, bk. iii.

moreover, be truly benevolent. The distance would, of course, be treated

> As best befits the Genius of the Scene.

He is a despotic monarch, and must be humoured:

> Stands he in blank and desolated state,
> Where yawning crags disjointed, sharp, uncouth,
> Involve him with pale horror?

—He must be planted up till he is " awful still, but not austere." On some such precept as this a disciple of Brown recommended the blowing up of the hanging terraces that clothe the rock on which Powis Castle stands, and the smoothing of the escarpment into a green slope. Or if the Genius of the Place is not in a sublime mood:

> On some plain
> Of tedious length, say, are his flat limbs laid?
> Thy hands shall lift him from his dreary couch,
> Pillowing his head with swelling hillocks green,
> While all around, a forest curtain spreads
> Its waving folds.

The monotonous mellifluence of Mason's verse is nicely adapted to describe the works of Brown. Payne Knight, in a celebrated passage in *The Landscape* [1] attacked the principles described in the last few extracts in the light of picturesque doctrine.

> Hence let us learn in *real* scenes to trace
> The true ingredients of the painter's grace.
> To lop redundant parts, the coarse refine,
> Open the crowded and the scanty join.
> But ah! in vain—see yon fantastic band,
> With charts, pedometers and rules in hand.
> T' improve, adorn and polish they profess;
> But shave the goddess whom they come to dress. . . .

---

[1] *The Landscape.* A Didactic Poem, addressed to Uvedale Price, Esq., 1794.

Wrapt all o'er in everlasting green
Makes one dull vapid smooth and tranquil scene.
Shav'd to the brink, our brooks are taught to flow
Where no obtruding leaves or branches grow ;
While clumps of shrubs bespot each winding vale . . .
Each secret haunt and deep recess display'd
And *intricacy* banished with its shade.

Hence, hence ! thou haggard fiend, however called,
Thin meagre genius of the bare and bald.
Thy spade and mattock here at length lay down,
And follow to the tomb thy fav'rite Brown:
Thy fav'rite Brown, whose innovating hand
First dealt thy curses o'er this fertile land.

The relation of architecture and gardening to country life during the Brown epoch is amusingly illustrated by the fourth book of William Mason's *English Garden*.[1] In this Mason, in view of the fact that ten years had elapsed since the publication of the earlier books, abandoned the " strain didactic," and wrote " a romantic tragedy " of landscape gardening, with " a complete Improver " as the hero and " an already improved Country Seat as the setting." It is the apotheosis of Mason's poetry. The very union of " instruction with amusement," is typical, on a large scale, of his passion for circumlocution. Had he not given, earlier in the poem, this excuse for his efforts to avoid the " vulgar " names of things ?—

Ungrateful sure,
When such the theme, becomes the poet's task :
Yet must he **try** by modulation meet
Of varied cadence and selected phrase,
Exact yet free, without inflation bold
To dignify that theme.

" Modulation meet " nevertheless produced such monsters of " inflation " as this description of an ice-house:

[1] Not published till 1781.

GARDEN SCENES

—the structure rude where Winter pounds
In conic pits his congelations hoar,
That summer may his tepid beverage cool
With the chill luxury.

In the 4th Book modulation meet is carried to a sublime pitch.

Alcander, the hero, is discovered in manhood's prime, possessed of a fair domain which his father had improved:

      each line destroy'd
Which Belgic dullness planned. . . .
Crowning a gradual hill his mansion rose
In antient English grandeur . . .
Coeval with those rich cathedral fanes
(Gothic ill-named) where harmony results
From disunited parts and shapes minute.
     . . . No modern art
Had marr'd with misplaced symmetry the pile.

Alcander inherited the paternal love of improvement, and contemplated a cow-house in the baronial style.

    "Draw round yon knowl,"
Alcander cried, "in stately Norman mode,
A wall embattled, and within its sward
Let every structure needful for a farm
Arise in castle-semblance ; the huge barn
Shall with a mock portcullis arm the gate
   . . . and every buttress broad
Whose proud projection seems a mass of stone
Give space to stall the heifer and the steed.
So shall each part, though turn'd to rural use,
Deceive the eye with those bold feudal forms
That Fancy loves to gaze on."

Then he managed to make his bailiff understand, in the words already quoted, that he wanted an ice-house. And then for a dairy,

He builds of old disjointed moss-grown stone
A time-struck abbey. An impending grove
Screens it behind with reverential shade.

THE PICTURESQUE

The Alcandrian seat was next the sea, of which it commanded a view down a dell. In the dell was a rill, which, in due course, fell down a grotto, " of conchs and spars, petrified with branching corallines." One " vernal morn " when he and his swains were hard at work, a storm rushed impending upon them and drove a ship ashore. The working party hurried to the beach, but not a soul was rescued, except

> One tender maid, sav'd by Alcander's arm.

This lady turned out to be

> As poets picture Hebe, or the Spring,
> Graceful withal . . . th' impassioned youth
> Felt more than pity.

He loved. Enraptured he led her through his groves " where ancient beech their awful foliage flung." The lady had unusual ideas about gardening. Almost alone among the critics of her age,

> "Tell me," she cry'd,
> " Why on these forest features all intent,
> Forbears my friend some scene distinct to give
> To Flora and her fragrance ? . . .
>   Turn thy taste
> E'en in this grassy circle where we stand,
> To form the plots; there weave a woodbine bower
> And call that bower Nerina's. . . ."
>   Love with Art
> Uniting, soon produced the finish'd whole.

The place they stood in was indeed exquisite.

> Wand'ring lines
> Of shaven turf twisted to the path,
> Leading the eye to many a sculptured bust
> Or shapely pedestal of sage or bard.
> Many an urn there too had place.

But Nerina's bower, in the hands of one who was both artist and lover, took on a more worthy semblance.

> Her lover's genius form'd
> A glittering fane, where rare and alien plants
> Might safely flourish. . . .
> High on Ionic shafts he bad it tower
> A proud rotunda; to its sides conjoin'd
> Two broad piazzas in theatric curve,
> Ending in equal porticos sublime.
> Glass roofed the whole, and sidelong to the south
> Twixt every fluted column, lightly reared
> Its wall pellucid.

Clearly a conservatory.[1]   And beneath the dome stood a statue of classic origin, to which Alcander ingeniously added a head having the features of Nerina. Alas! this tribute of affection did not arouse the blushing approval it was intended to, Nerina being unaccountably disappointed.

> "Why," she cried,
> "Why would my best preserver here erect
> With all the fond idolatry of love
> A wretch's images whom his pride should scorn
> (For so his country bids him)? Drive me hence!
> Transport me quick to Gallia's hostile shore,
> Hostile to thee, yet not, alas! to me!"

And so it transpires that Nerina is an alien enemy. Later we discover that she is an American, rendered homeless by the War of Independence then raging, who believes her father to be in France.   In a flood of tears and humiliation she cries:

> I only begged a little woodbine bower
> Where I might sit and weep, while all around
> The lilies and the bluebells hung their heads
> In seeming sympathy.

---

[1] Mason's description corresponds to the conservatory at Stowe, one of the first of its kind.

Alcander was not a little mortified, and cruel suspicions were awakened by her disapproval. The scene, she considered

> "Too strongly paints the passion which stern Fate
> Forbids me to return." "Dost thou then love
> Some happier youth?" "No; tell thy generous soul
> Indeed I do not"—More she would have said,
> But gushing grief prevented.

A year elapsed. Nerina, consumed by secret sorrow, peeked and pined. In vain Alcander tried "with scenes of novel charm her grief to calm." Noticing that she was fond of feeding birds, he resolved

> To give her feathered favourites space of land
> And lake appropriate.

An aviary was constructed on a grand scale, replete with exotic birds. So assiduous was the anxious Alcander at creating "scenes of novel charm," that "no scene remained unpolished," and his rapidly extending grounds acquired wide celebrity. Men came from far and near

> With envious eyes to censure or admire.
> . . . Oft he himself
> With courteous greeting will the critic hail
> And join him in the circuit.

All was now prepared for the crisis. Landscape gardening had been utilized to an unprecedented extent, the stage was bustling with a chorus of tourists. Then one day "a youth of mild yet manly mien" appeared, who "seemed to taste the beauties he surveyed." Alcander was gratified and waxed modest, apologizing, as he showed the visitor round, for lack of "Vitruvian art" where "all is home-bred Fancy." At this the mild youth was all the more delighted.

> "Ornament," he observed,
> "When foreign or fantastic, never charmed

Fig. 1. T. GAINSBOROUGH. A Garden of Idea

Fig. 2. T. HEARNE
A rude bridge in the grounds of Downton Castle

Plate XVIII

Fig. 1

Fig. 2
Plate XIX   HUMPHRY REPTON
Original condition and proposed treatment of the
ground at Bayham Abbey, Kent.   From *Theory
and Practice of Landscape Gardening*, 1803

My judgement; here I tread on British ground;
Some Yorkist or Lancastrian baron bold (pointing to the cow-
  house)
Yon massy bulwark built; on yonder pile (indicating the dairy)
In beauteous ruin, I distinctly mark
The ruthless traces of stern Henry's hand."

Alcander simpered with delight, and, warming to his guest, explained how, whilst classic rules were suitable for houses,

> shun we here
> By these to form our ruins. Much we own
> They please, when by Pannini's pencil drawn,
> Or darkly graved by Piranesi's hand.

But the builder of classic ruins in England

> builds but a splendid lie.

Thus deep in assenting controversy they approached the domed conservatory, where the mild youth suddenly came face to face with the statue with Nerina's face on it.

> "Heav'ns! Just Heav'ns!"
> He cry'd, "Tis my Nerina." "*Thine*, mad youth?
> Forego the word." Alcander said, and paused;
> His utterance failed—

he fainted away at the base of the statue, " a lifeless load of being."

> Worse.
> Nerina's self appears; the furthest aisle
> She, fate-directed, treads. Does she too faint?
> Would Heav'n she could! It were a happy swoon
> Might soften her fix'd form.

With a cry the mild youth clasps her in his arms. But the lady remains struck so, till Alcander revives. Nerina then finds her tongue and requests that they will carry her to the woodbine bower.

> For there indeed I wish to breathe my last. . . .
> Her languid limbs they decently composed.

She assures both the unhappy gentlemen of her love and esteem, commends them to one another, and expires.

Then the youth, whose name we are told is Cleon, reveals that he too is an American—a forerunner, as we see, of those tourists for whom English gardens happily still possess an appeal. He reveals how he is a fugitive, and the bearer of the worst of news in regard to Nerina's father—

> a venerable sage
> Whom Boston, when with peace and safety blest,
> In rapture heard pour from his hallow'd tongue
> Religion's purest dictates.

Cleon, at an early stage of " our civil broils " had saved the reverend gentleman's life and been promised Nerina's hand. Then she was sent to France, her father intending to follow. But unfortunately he was confined to bed by a disorder.

> There was he burnt!
> Burnt by thy countrymen! To ashes burnt!
> Vengeance and Glory call me.

Exit Cleon. As for Alcander, for many weeks he was quite unmanned. Scarcely did his groves, his grot, or any portion of his grounds console him, save such as Nerina had never, in his recollection, visited. At length his eye encountered the church, and his ancestors' sabbath path thereto, " wandering through a grove of sable yew." Long had their boughs forgot the shears; the spire, the holy ground, all they banished by their umbrage. In his grief the Genius of the Place approached him with words of comfort, whispering suggestions for opening a vista which should reveal the fane set off by a few other solemn shades, such as cypress, bay, and pensive birch. Alcander revived as if by magic. He was his old enthusiastic self again:

> " Yes, yes," he cry'd, " why not behold it all ?
> That bough removed shows me the very vault
> Where my Nerina sleeps."

The " hinds " were summoned,

> Joyful to see, as witless of the cause,
> Their much-loved lord his sylvan arts renew.

Having cleared a vista, he constructed, in one of its recesses, a hermit's cell of ozier and wattle—

> The place where he and Melancholy mean
> To fix Nerina's bust, her genuine bust,
> The model of the marble.

At morn and eve he visited the bust, the genuine bust, and, by this ingenious piece of planning, could simultaneously command the vault. The poem closes with some striking references to Rapine and Corruption waving their banners in high places, and a prayer to old England's genius to arise and save

> Her throne, her altars, and her laureat bowers.

—Church, State, and Landscape Garden.

§ 3

THE GARDEN OF IDEA

If we have the seeds of a Claude or Gaspar among us, he must come forth. If wood, water, valleys, glades can inspire a poet or a painter, this is the age to produce them.—Horace Walpole, *Essay on Modern Gardening* (written 1770).

When Brown was at the height of his reputation, during the 'sixties and 'seventies of the century, complacency prevailed among the critics and hierarchs. The literarily composed landscapes of Brown aroused the required " ideas " in the minds of spectators, because everyone knew the game; knew what emotions were represented by which counters. By far the most acute interpreter of Brown's system was Thomas

Whately, member of Parliament and Shakespearean critic (of a sort), whose *Observations on Modern Gardening* appeared in 1770, and had soon run through many editions, being translated into French the year following its publication. It was the text-book of gardening till 1794, when the Picturesque group manifested itself. Whately dealt with gardening—landscape gardening, of course—in the curious blend of abstract and practical that the style required. The gardener had five materials: ground, wood, water, rocks, and buildings. He was conscious that his " art " was " as superior to landscape painting as reality to imitation." He stood with a spade in one hand, and Burke *On the Sublime and Beautiful* in the other. He delved and grubbed to raise, not flowers or trees, but " great ideas," or " ideas of beauty or variety."

Thus the function of water was, in the shape of a lake, to be spacious, for " the mind, always pleased to expand itself on great ideas, delights even in its vastness." With ruins, too, Whately was far more interested in the ideas, historical, moral, etc., aroused by them than in their visual appearance. There is nothing in Whately evidencing such a picturesque vision as even William Mason possessed for similar objects:

> Happy art thou, if thou canst call thine own
> Such scenes as these: where Nature and where Time
> Have worked congenial; where a scattered host
> Of antique oaks darken thy sidelong hills;
> While rushing through their branches, rifted cliffs
> Dart their white heads and glitter through the gloom.
> More happy still, if one superior rock
> Bear on its brow the shivered fragments huge
> Of some old Norman fortress; happier far,
> Ah! then most happy, if thy vale below
> Wash, with the crystal coolness of its rills
> Some mouldering abbey's ivy vested wall.[1]

---

[1] *The English Garden*, bk. i.

Paintings, he maintained, should be used only as studies, never be copied. A thing was not admirable simply because it had been painted; but if it had been painted it *might* be worthy the attention of a gardener. At best, painting was a limited art, but gardening was not. Whately rarely let his visual faculties take charge, to delight in colour or light for their own sakes. If he was careful about the planting of trees so as to produce colour effects, it was only that the *idea* conveyed might be gay or gloomy as the case might be. He aimed at intellectual appeal. He was concerned in rousing ideas.

Horace Walpole, though Gothicism and gloom were little more than an intellectual diversion to him, admitted a far closer connection between painting and gardening. He included his *Essay on Modern Gardening* among his *Anecdotes of Painting*. As early as 1747 he had chosen " some Turkish sheep and two cows, all studied in their colours for becoming the view." [1] And he so far regarded painting and gardening as one art to use " picture " and " planting " synonymously: " there is another bit of picture of which I am fond, and that is a larch or spruce fir planted behind a weeping willow." [2] He constantly compares scenes to Albano, Claude, and Poussin, and often seems to be seeing himself and his companions as if in pictures. There is that delightful description of the fête given by Miss Pelham at Esher: [3]

The day was delightful; the scene transporting; the trees, lawns, concaves, all in the perfection in which the ghost of Kent would joy to see them. At twelve we made the tour of the farm in eight chaises and calashes, horsemen and footmen, setting out like a picture of Wouverman's. My lot fell in the lap of Mrs. Anne Pitt, which I could have excused, as she was not at all in the style of the day—romantic, but political. . . . We walked to the Belvedere on the summit of the hill, where

---

[1] To Mann, 5th June 1747.
[2] To Montagu, 8th Nov. 1755.
[3] To Montagu, 19th May 1763.

a theatrical storm only served to heighten the beauty of the landscape, a rainbow on a dark cloud falling precisely behind the tower of a neighbouring church, and the building at Claremont. . . . From thence we passed into the wood, and the ladies formed a circle on chairs before the mouth of a cave, which was overhung to a vast height with woodbines, lilacs and laburnums, and dignified by tall shapely cypresses. On the descent of the hill were placed French horns; the abigails, servants and neighbours wandering below by the river; in short, it was Parnassus, as Watteau would have painted it.

Another attempt at a Watteau *pastorale* at Stowe was unsuccessful owing to cold and wet weather and the infirmity of the guests. In describing the fiasco Walpole put his finger on one of the weak spots in the ideal phase of picturesque theory:

Our poets learnt their trade of the Romans, and so adopted the terms of their masters. They talk of shady groves, purling streams and cooling breezes, and we get sore throats and agues with attempting to realise these visions. Zephyr is a north-east wind, that makes Damon button up to the chin, and pinches Chloe's nose till it is red and blue. We ruin ourselves with inviting over foreign trees and make our houses clamber up hills to look at prospects. How our ancestors would laugh at us, who knew there was no being comfortable unless you had a high hill before your nose, and a thick warm wood at your back! Taste is too freezing a commodity for us, and depend upon it, will go out of fashion again.[1]

To a certain extent " taste " did go out of fashion, but only to that of substituting for Arcadian scenes those of Ruysdael and Hobbema; of forgoing the French horns and satins in favour of top-boots, broadcloth, and sandy lanes. The reaction was stimulated from two sources: Rousseau and China. The works of Rousseau contained numerous landscapes of a wild and thrilling order, and in 1777 his protector at Ermenonville, the Comte de Girardin, published *De la Composition des Paysages, ou les moyens d'embellir la Nature autour*

[1] To Montagu, 15th June 1768.

des Habitations, en joignant l'agréable à l'utile, translated
in 1783 by Malthus (not the Malthus of the theory of
population). The translator gave the keynote of
Girardin's theory in the sentence: " Many of our most
celebrated gardens have been found to make very indifferent pictures, this from a real want of picturesque
principles in their composition." Girardin was wholly
picturesque in his attitude to gardens, contending that
no scene in nature should be attempted till it had first
been painted. His own garden had as a principal
feature the Tomb of Rousseau on an island, surrounded
by poplars, which was at once the envy and the despair
of the many English who visited the grounds. There
are appropriate references through the book to contemporary landscape painters, such as Gessner and
Pillement, whose works are held up as models for wild
gardens. But before the Rousseau cult came over here
in the guise of the picturesque, the same spirit manifested
itself in the so-called Chinese style of gardening.

" Whatever," said Owen Cambridge, " may have
been reported, whether truly or falsely, of the Chinese
garden, it is certain that we are the first of the Europeans
who have founded their taste." [1] De Ligne, writing in
1781,[2] acknowledged the priority of the English in the
Chinese field.

Les Français auraient pu les avoir avant les Anglais: mais
leurs Missionaires pensaient trop aux consciences et au commerce. Ils ont dédaigné des remarques plus intéressantes. . . .
Les Anglais en avait saisi jusqu'aux meubles, et en simplicité en
délicatesse et propreté, c'est encore une très bonne acquisition
qu'ils ont faite.

Long before the end of the century *le jardin Anglais*
and *le jardin Chinois* were indistinguishable. De Ligne
admitted that when he said " jardin Anglais " he meant

[1] *The World,* No. 118, 1756.
[2] *Coup d'Œil sur Belœil,* ed. de Ganay, 1922.

more accurately *jardin Chinois*. Superficial though the Chinese influence on English design may have been, the cult did contribute to the evolution of the picturesque. As Shaftesbury had seen no difference between the " deformity " of Gothick and Chinese taste, so did the minds of mid-century confound them. Both were bizarre, yet significant.

The eighteenth-century mind, as it cultivated idealism in landscape, dimly perceived that the Chinese, both in gardening and painting, had succeeded exquisitely in doing what Europeans were clumsily fumbling for: painting a landscape of idea, whence everything inessential to that idea was eliminated. In their gardens they had evolved, and the Japanese retain, a rigid symbolism. Different ideas attached to every species of rock, plant, and combination of objects, to an extent far more intricate than English admirers of Claude or Salvator ever envisaged in their ideal classical reproductions.

In practice, *chinoiserie* consisted in a rearrangement of conventional lines in furniture design, and a slightly exaggerated baldness and wriggliness in gardens, where more shrubberies and ornamental contraptions were introduced even than in Brown's gardens.

The fact is that " Chinese " was the label given to the wave of fashion that succeeded Brown's first triumph. We have seen how each improver—Kent, Langley, Shenstone, Brown—claimed to have at last freed nature from the deformities of " accident " and the false taste of his predecessor so that she could flourish ideally. Now came William Chambers—ambitious, pushing, an able architect but with few convictions— talking of his sojourn as supercargo in China. By a stroke of luck Carr of York suggested him to Lord Bute as an agreeable young man suitable to fill the double post of gardener to the Princess of Wales at Kew and of drawing master to her son the future George III.

Thus he was suddenly thrown into the most fashionable coterie where, as in all fashionable coteries, novelty is beyond all else required of an artist. He might do anything at Kew except copy Brown, the gardener to the rival royal faction at Richmond. Accordingly he elaborated a system of gardening which, he assured society, was the genuine Chinese style. Had he not been there? Had not he himself made drawings of pagodas on the spot? There was nobody to contradict him, save a missionary or two who had never heard of Kew. He was thus free to put over any kind of grotesquery that entered his head, so long as it was not obviously reminiscent of Brown. It was no use saying that the Chinese " imitated rural nature." That had been said before by every gardener since Kent. No. The Chinese, he insisted, range their gardens " in three separate classes: the pleasing, the terrible, and the surprising." Unlike England, where " it matters not who are the gardeners; whether a peasant or Poussin," in China, and " wherever a better style is attempted, gardeners must be men of genius, experience, and judgment; quick in perception, rich in expedients, fertile in imagination, and thoroughly versed in all the affections of the human mind." Men very like Mr. Chambers, in fact, but very different from Mr. Brown.

In place of the " ideas " that Brown set himself to arouse in his scenes, Chambers set out to " agitate the mind by a variety of opposing passions." The Chinese garden advocated by him was the garden of idea raised to a higher power. From pleasing scenes, " where all the gayest products of the vegetable world " were in China " disposed in all the picturesque forms that art or Nature can suggest," the visitor was hurried to the terrible or surprising, which derived in reality from Salvator Rosa rather than from anything in China:

Their scenes of terror are composed of gloomy, deep valleys, inaccessible to the sun, impending barren rocks, dark caverns and impetuous cataracts. The trees are ill-formed, forced out of their natural directions and seemingly torn to pieces by the violence of tempests . . . the buildings are in ruins, or half-consumed by fire, or swept away by the fury of the waters; nothing remains entire but a few venerable huts dispersed in the mountains. Bats, owls, vultures and every bird of prey flutter in the groves; wolves, tigers, jackals howl in the forest; gibbets, crosses, wheels, and the whole apparatus of torture are seen from the roads; and in the most dismal recesses of the woods, where the ways are rugged and overgrown with poisonous weeds, are temples dedicated to the King of Vengeance, deep caverns in the rocks and descents to gloomy subterranean habitations, are overgrown with brushwood and brambles; near which are inscribed, on pillars of stone, pathetic descriptions of many horrid acts of cruelty perpetrated by robbers of former times.[1]

There are ruins of castles, palaces, temples, and religious houses, or half-buried triumphal arches (odd in China) among which " faithful old servants of the family spend the remains of their life amidst the tombs of their predecessors," probably, we may opine, a period mercifully brief. In addition, there is " whatever else may serve to indicate the debility, the disappointments, and the desolation of humanity; which, by co-operating with the dreary aspect of autumnal nature, and the inclement temperature of the air, fill the mind with melancholy, and incline it to serious reflections."

Still more extraordinary, there were men in England who tried to fashion " gardens " on these Salvator Rosa-Chinese lines. There is a description in the *Scots Magazine* of 1767 of the " pleasure " grounds belonging to Mr. Tyers, proprietor of Vauxhall. This gentleman, well versed in the construction of what we call " side shows," made a garden at Denbies, near Dorking, whither he could retire from the gaudy scenes of his business, where the very walks were proper emblems of human life " in some parts easy, smooth and level, in

[1] Sir W. Chambers, *Dissertation on Oriental Gardening*, 1772.

others rugged and uneven "; decked with flags inscribed with moral sentiments. There was a " Valley of the Shadow of Death " containing latter ends of saints and sinners, with coffins instead of columns, and skulls agreeably scattered about.

Incredible as these extravagances may be, they were logical in the Garden of Idea. If a garden was to arouse emotions, by suggestion and not by pictorial effect, the result inevitably would be an " amusement park " in the exhibition sense of the word. Such places were " gardens," as Vauxhall was a " garden," and as the grounds at Kew were a garden until taken over for horticulture. The only respect in which Chambers brought any originality to garden design was through his architectural feeling—attributed, of course, to the Chinese—that regularity should be observed around the house, where geometrical gardens were in place. For the rest, Kew only differed from the Leasowes or Claremont in being flat and " insipid," and in having rather more buildings to the acre. There is, of course, the Pagoda, erected 1761-2. But besides there were numerous classic buildings, a " House of Confucius," a " Mosque " with two minarets, a " Gothic Cathedral "—by J. H. Muntz, borrowed from Batty Langley and Bentley—and a half-buried triumphal arch, straight out of Batty Langley's *New Principles of Gardening*, published thirty years previously. The latter alone served any practical purpose—the carrying of carts over one of the principal walks.

Walpole and his circle were fertile in gibes at the *Dissertation* and the *Designs for Kew Gardens*. William Mason embodied them in his *Heroic Epistle to Sir William Chambers* (1774), referring in the opening line to the Swedish knighthood that King George permitted him to use:

> Knight of the Polar Star! by Fortune plac'd
> To shine the Cynosure of British taste; . . .

O, let the Muse attend thy march sublime,
And with thy prose, caparison her rhyme;
Teach her, like thee, to gild her splendid song
With scenes of Yven-Ming and sayings of Li-Tsong;
Like thee to scorn Dame Nature's simple fence,
Leap each Ha Ha of truth and common sense.

But if Chambers had no direct influence on English gardening he exerted a very strong influence on the Continent,[1] and, indirectly, his " emotional " view of gardening was largely adopted by Payne Knight.

§ 4

THE IMPRESSIONISTS OF '94

The picturesque view of nature led towards the abstract appreciation of colour and light that in painting marks the work of Turner and Constable. In gardening the writings of Uvedale Price and Payne Knight urged a similar impressionistic preoccupation with the visual qualities of plants, quite apart from their botanical rarity or the " ideas " that their combination might produce. The impressionist garden that they visualized was a reaction from the garden of idea contemplated by Brown, Whately, and Chambers. But whereas Constable and Turner were able to see for themselves, Price and Knight still relied on old landscape paintings for the picturesque qualities that gardeners were to aim at displaying. A gardener who studied pictures, they explained, would get away from the " ideal " conception of nature and learn to love colour, light, shade, intricacy, apart from the objects that produced them.

[1] See Le Rouge, *Jardins Anglais et Chinois*, 1776-1788. Many plates show how Chambers's most extravagant ideas were carried out in France, Germany, and Austria. Plates from London and Wise, Chambers, Switzer, Colin Campbell, and Halfpenny are reproduced.

This culmination of the picturesque handling of gardens took place in the year 1794-5, when Price published the *Essays on the Picturesque*, Knight *The Landscape*, and Humphry Repton *Sketches and Hints on Landscape Gardening*. Repton was an impressionist of a different kind. While Price and Knight made impressionist effects a chief end in gardening, Repton made his effects grow out of his first impression of the "true character" of the place he was called upon to improve. His impressionism was an intellectual, not a visual, process; an attempt to arrive at the "ideal" by a mental snapshot. After the first few minutes he would set about developing the snapshot into a practicable and reasonable garden, of a kind not very different from Brown's.

All three acknowledged the value of pictures to gardeners, but in differing degrees. Repton admitted that he had discovered in practice that there was less connection than he had at one time believed between painting and gardening. The only real use that he made of old landscape paintings was in forming his ideas of what the "true character" of a place might be supposed to be. Having got that impression, he strove to bring his improved ground up to it, as nearly as was consistent with the other necessities of a garden, as he conceived it: elegance, convenience, impressiveness, and, to a certain extent, horticulture. Knight, though later in life he modified his attitude, was at first the exact opposite to Repton—with whom he kept up a wordy warfare for ten years. Gardens should reproduce as fully as possible the qualities that made the pictures of Salvator or Hobbema delightful. Consequently they must consist in similar scenes—wild woods, gorges, hovels, and cascades. Price occupied an intermediate position. While he differed from Repton in making the formation of scenes like pictures his ultimate object, he did not go so far as Knight in his pursuit of visual qualities. Where Knight wanted rampant neglect that should provide rich refractions of light, Price admitted the necessity for producing the effect more cleanly.

The controversy led to a revival of the formal garden round the house. Price and Knight felt the need for it on aesthetic grounds, Repton on those of convenience. Judged by its results—the restoration of the formal garden, the perfection of natural planting, and the preparation of the English garden to receive the galaxy of new plants the introduction of which is the characteristic of nineteenth-century gardening—we are entitled to regard these three " impressionists " as the greatest artists in their craft that the country has produced.

Humphry Repton came of respectable parents in Bury St. Edmunds, where he was born in 1752. After attempts at commerce and speculation he was reduced to the verge of ruin in 1788, and then conceived the idea of making an original use of his personal assets. These were a considerable circle of influential friends, an engaging personality, some experience of landscape gardening obtained when he had a little place of his own, and very real talent for painting in water-colours. One sleepless night he resolved to press these advantages into use and to set up as a " landscape gardener "—a title " of no mean pretension " that he was the first to adopt. In after years he thanked heaven that he was blessed with a poet's feelings and a painter's eye. "When I look back," he wrote, " to the many hundreds of evenings passed in the circle of my own family—drawing and representing to others what I saw in my own imagination, I may reckon this art among the most delightful of my joys." There is no doubt of his charming skill as a water-colourist. But this sentence does suggest his cardinal failing. He was rather a prig, and a humble prig at that. I have before me a curious volume consisting of pencil notes by William Beckford

of Fonthill, some of them original criticisms, more of
them extracts from the reviews, perhaps used by him as
an armoury whence to draw brilliant remarks for the
dinner-table. I find this:

Repton's odd whims. . . .
Among these odd whims the author's wonderful humility is
not the least.

His profession necessitated acquaintance with " the
great." He was complimented by Burke and Pitt,
and no doubt retailed the praises of the famous to his
prospective clients. To these he would write with a
devastating mixture of servile pomposity, urging them,
if wealthy, to make no bones about it in their improvements:

Ornaments by their number and excellence distinguish the
taste, wealth, and *dignity* of their possessors. In England there
is no reason to conceal these marks of grandeur. Rank and
affluence are not crimes in England.

It was his business to talk like that. But the publication of such observations is a blemish on an otherwise
attractive personality. Then, as to his " poet's mind."
Here is a specimen of his verse, urging the redecoration
of a room:

No more the *Cedar Parlour's* formal gloom
With dullness chills, 'tis now the *Living Room*;
Where guests, to whim, or taste, or fancy true,
Scatter'd in groups their different plans pursue . . .
Here, books of poetry, and books of prints
Furnish aspiring artists with new hints;
While discords twanging from the half-tuned harp
Make dullness cheerful, changing flat to sharp.
Here, 'midst exotic plants, the curious maid
Of Greek and Latin seems no more afraid;
Silent midst crowds the doctor here looks big,
Wrapp'd in his own importance, and his wig.

Amusing album stuff, but scarcely warranting the author to claim the possession of a " poet's mind."

Having conceived the idea of launching out as a landscape gardener, he circularized his friends and acquaintances, and received his first commission from Jeremiah Ives of Gunton in Norfolk, his second at Holkham. In 1789 came a summons from Welbeck, where the Duke of Portland's clearly expressed requirements and encouraging manner dispelled, as Repton afterwards recorded, his diffidence.

I had then had little practical experience, and felt a painful degree of anxiety at every new concern; afraid of committing myself, and doubting my own powers to suggest new ideas.

This he soon lost, and by 1794 had been employed in fifty places. His engaging personality and lively sense of humour recommended him to the country gentry, if it earned the sentence of " coxcomb " from the aged Horace Walpole and the King.[1] It was during these years that he made the acquaintance of the west country theorists, Uvedale Price and Payne Knight. When engaged at Ferney Hall, near Ludlow, he politely courted the advice of Knight. It was this action, combined with an admiration for his drawings, that led Price to seek his acquaintance. Apparently Price and he formed a friendship, and took a picturesque tour of the river Wye together. The friendship, however, was strained by Repton lightly treating Price's suggestion that hints could be taken from such a fine natural river for the formation of artificial ones. And Price began to think that, charming as his friend's drawings were, they might have been better if he had studied " the higher artists." [2]

The publication of *Sketches and Hints of Landscape Gardening*, in 1795,[3] gave a further impetus to his

1 *Farington Diary*, vol. i (February 1794).
2 Price, Letter to Humphry Repton, Esq., 1794.
3 Repton's other publications were: *Observations on the Theory and Practice of Landscape Gardening* (1803); *An Inquiry into the Changes*

Fig. 1. T. HEARNE. The Gorge of the Teme at Downton

Fig. 2. WILLIAM OWEN. The Bath house at Downton

Plate XX. From a set of water-colours made for
R. Payne Knight and preserved at Downton Castle

Plate XXI.　Scotney Castle, Kent
The view looking over the Quarry

practice. The book, like all his subsequent works, was a collection of extracts from the individual " Red Books " that he prepared for each " job." These, so called from their being bound in red morocco, consisted in a number of water-colours of places as they would be when improved, over which flaps, or " slides," as they were called, fitted, showing them as they actually were. These " before and afters " were accompanied by manuscript disquisitions on the principles of taste involved. In book form many of the water-colours are reproduced in exquisite aquatints which convey, better than any words, the clean and neat ideal that Repton had before him in his schemes.

For the architectural side of his practice Repton formed an informal partnership with John Nash, which in 1798 Farington heard consisted in Repton's receiving two and a half per cent. out of Nash's seven per cent. earned in jobs done on Repton's recommendation. It was, then, a bitter irony of fate that made of Nash, who " in early life had participated in his bright visions of future fame," his supplanter as architect of the Pavilion for the Regent. Repton's designs for this building were published in 1808, after the scheme had been dropped for lack of funds. Much of Nash's work is a crib, and not always a very good one, of Repton's ideas. Its oriental character is in a large degree ascribable to Repton, who was convinced that the " revolution in taste " that he felt to be imminent, would introduce Indian architecture, as the Renaissance had introduced Italian, to England. Actually, in the battle of the styles, Gothic outstripped not only the Indian, but the Swiss, Italian, and Egyptian modes. Otherwise Repton might have become an Indian Pugin.

of Taste in Landscape Gardening ; To which are added some Observations on its Theory and Practice (1806); *Designs for the Pavilion, Brighton* (1808); *Fragments on the Theory and Practice of Landscape Gardening* (with the assistance of John Adey Repton) (1816).

The collapse of the Pavilion scheme was the crowning disappointment of Repton's life. In spite of the extent of his practice—200 red books are recorded—few of his schemes, he complained, had been carried out in such a way that he wished to own to them. He increasingly looked upon his books and drawings as his real achievement. If his recognizable work is often evil—as, for instance, the replacement of the descending brick terraces at Burley-on-the-Hill by sloping lawns and a revetment like a railway viaduct—his rejected recommendations are often worse. Among the apostles of the domestic Gothic revival he occupies, by his books, an unenviable eminence. He did continue the tradition of Capability Brown, on occasion defending him against hostile critics, and several of Repton's parks which are known to me certainly merit everything Price, Knight, and J. C. Loudon [1] said about them. Yet his influence on the whole was beneficial, and since his death, in 1818, landscape gardening on a large scale has changed little in its aims. In America, where more parks were laid out during last century than in this country, men like Olmsted formed their practice closely on Repton, and judging by a modern book [2] on him, he is considered in the United States as one of the apostles of Romanticism. We have in London not only his gardens in Cadogan Place much as he left them. But in Regent's Park, laid out by Fordyce, the Surveyor-General, in 1812, and St. James's Park, by Eyton in 1827, we possess typically Reptonian grounds.

Knight, in common with both his competitors, based his conception of gardening on harmonious composition:

> Tis just congruity of parts combin'd
> To please the sense and satisfy the mind.

---

[1] *A Treatise on Forming, Improving and Managing Country Residences.* By J. C. Loudon. 2 vols. 1806.

[2] *The Art of Landscape Gardening, by Humphry Repton, Esq.* Edited by John Nolen. Houghton Mifflin, 1907.

But in *The Landscape* he was biassed by his success at Downton in producing Salvatorial scenes, and obviously in agreement with Girardin. In endeavouring to

> Learn to cure or kill that strange disease
> That gives deformity the power to please,

he laid undue stress on the importance of " counterfeit neglect." He invited ridicule from the first by advocating that the foreground, in place of Brown's shaven lawn and gravel path, should be modelled on the foregrounds of pictures: for

> Nature's genuine charms we there descry . . .
> No leaf of fern, low weed, or creeping thorn,
> But, near the eye, the landscape may adorn ;
> Either when tufted o'er the moss-grown stone,
> Or down the slope in loose disorder thrown.

The improver swept away formal gardens and wild patches. But Knight bade the " Rural Nymphs "

> Teach him to place and not remove the stone
> On yonder bank with moss and fern o'ergrown.
> To cherish, not mow down, the weeds that creep,
> To break, not level, the surrounding sweep.

The rest of the landscape was to be modelled with equal faithfulness to pictures, and the " three distances " to be as rigidly observed as in painting. In pictures

> Three marked divisions we shall always find:
> Not more, where Claude extends the prospect wide . . .
> Nor where . . .
> Meek Hobbima presents the village mill
> Not more where great Salvator's mountains rise, . . .
> Than in the ivy'd cottage of Ostade,
> Waterlo's copse or Ruysdael's low cascade.

These distances should be filled in as landscape painters had taught.

Whatever foremost glitters to the eye
Should near the middle of the landscape lie.

Water made the best centre for the middle distance;

To show the clear reflection of the day
And dart through hanging trees the refluent ray,
And semi-lights and semi-shadows join
And quiv'ring play in harmony divine.

The beauty of this kind of lake was, in his view, almost entirely impressionist. Any shrub or mouldering bank that caught the dancing reflected light gave to him more pleasure than flowers or terraces. Buildings were by no means tabooed, so long as they served some practical as well as aesthetic purpose.

The cover'd seat that shelters from the storm
May oft a feature of the landscape form;
Whether, composed of native stumps and roots,
It spreads the creeper's rich fantastic shoots;
Or, rais'd with stones, irregularly piled,
It seems some cavern desolate and wild.
Let clust'ring ivy o'er its sides be spread,
And moss and weeds grow scattered o'er its head.

Natural features could, and should, be turned to picturesque purpose:

The quarry, long neglected and o'ergrown
With thorns, that hang o'er mouldering beds of stone,
May oft the place of nat'ral rocks supply.

But, better than any artificial or manipulated features, were such as time had ready disposed, and Ossian and William Mason approved by their verse:

Bless'd is the man, in whose sequestered glade
Some ancient abbey's walls diffuse their shade;
With mould'ring windows pierc'd, and turrets crown'd,
And pinnacles with clinging ivy bound.

Bless'd too is he, who, 'midst his tufted trees,
Some ruin'd castle's lofty towers sees,
Imbosom'd high upon the mountain's brow,
Or nodding o'er the stream that glides below.
Nor yet unenvied, to whose humbler lot
Falls the retired, antiquated cot :—
Its roof with weeds and mosses cover'd o'er,
And honey-suckles climbing round the door;
While mantling vines along its walls are spread,
And clust'ring ivy decks the chimney's head . . .
Still happier he (if conscious of his prize)
Who sees some Temple's broken columns rise,
'Midst sculptured fragments, broken by their fall,
And tottering remnants of its marble wall.

But there must be no neat miniatures of great classic buildings—.

No poor Baalbec dwindled to the eye
And Paestum's fanes with columns six feet high.
Such buildings English nature must reject,
And claim from art th' appearance of neglect.

There is more than a little in this of Chambers's landscapes of horror—where the convenience, even the life, of the visitor, is of no account against the arousing of emotions.   Knight, however, hotly repudiated any connection with either Chambers or Chinoiserie.

Repton quoted Knight's passage about the ancient abbey and antiquated cot with enthusiasm.   A mind was insensible that could not appreciate such scenes—precious relics that required utmost care and preservation.   But no one, he contended, would suggest that an eighteenth-century gentleman should live in one.   He was moved to defend Brown :

It is evident that the only source of disgust excited in this gentleman's mind, on viewing scenes improved by Mr. Brown, proceeds from their not being fit objects for the representation of the pencil.[1]

_____

[1] *Sketches and Hints*, chap. vii.

He maintained that it was impossible to plant a landscape in imitation of a picture. He quoted Gilpin as having shown that no good picture is an exact copy of nature. Then how and why make nature copy something that is not herself? Moreover, the gardener's and the painter's " three distances " were anything but the same. Whilst admitting the importance of intricacy and entanglement in satisfying the imagination, he pointed out that the " three distances " of the gardener were:

1. The scene that it is in his power to improve.
2. That which he can prevent being injured.
3. That beyond his control.

Fundamentally a garden, he was convinced, must be useful and practical. Such other qualities as it had must be produced by art, and art he believed with Burke to consist in " deception." He quoted the passage from *The Sublime and Beautiful*:

No work of art can be great but as it deceives. To be otherwise is the prerogative of nature only.

Burke seems to have meant by deception, suggestion, in distinction to literal representation. In painting and poetry, to which Burke was referring, we can often admire the rendering, the " deception," apart from the subject. But Repton did not realize the inapplicability of the sentence to landscape gardening, which, after all, *is* nature. The advocates of the picturesque knew very well what they wanted nature to be. But Repton, dispensing with pictures, had nothing to aim at. He idealized without knowing what the ideal was to look like. Half his time he was trying to produce visual impressions of non-visual ideas.

One of his favourite impressions or deceptions was that of " greatness." It was the subject of the most entertaining altercation between Knight and Repton, and was later immortalized by Peacock in *Headlong*

Hall. In the " red book " for Tatton Park, Knutsford, Repton went into the matter of approaches. After many sound remarks on the proper course to be taken by approach roads, he passed on to speak of their function of preparing the visitor for the house, as the hall does for the rooms. Somehow the approach must give the idea of " united and uninterrupted property." The church, inn, and village might be so built as to correspond to that of the mansion, and so form an overture. And milestones might bear the arms of the local family, as public houses often did.

Knight, the Whig, seized on the suggestion of armorial milestones with frenzy:

> Why not rather, at the porter's gate,
> Hang up a map of all my lord's estate?

Trivial as the incident was, it stuck in the minds of contemporaries, and it is as Marmaduke Milestone, Esq., that a person made up of the characteristics of Brown and Repton appears in *Headlong Hall* (1816). We see him in the drawing-room after dinner explaining to his host and two ladies his " red book " for Lord Little-brain's park:

MR. MILESTONE: This you perceive is the natural state of one part of the grounds. Here is a wood, never touched by the finger of taste; thick, intricate and gloomy. Here is a little stream, dashing from stone to stone, and over-shadowed by these untrimmed boughs.

MISS TENORINA: The sweet romantic spot! How beautifully the birds must sing there on a summer evening!

MISS GRAZIOSA: Dear sister! how can you endure the horrid thicket?

MR. MILESTONE: You are right, Miss Graziosa; your taste is correct. Now here is the same place corrected—trimmed—polished—decorated—adorned. Here sweeps a plantation, in that beautiful regular curve; there winds a gravel walk; here are parts of the old wood, left in these majestic circular clumps, disposed at equal distances with wonderful symmetry; there are some single shrubs, scattered in elegant profusion; here a Portugal laurel, there a juniper; here a laurustinus, there a spruce fir; here a larch, there a lilac; here a rhododendron, there an arbutus. The stream, you see, is become a canal; the banks are perfectly smooth and green, sloping to the water's edge; and there is Lord Littlebrain, rowing in an elegant boat.

Squire Headlong: Magical, faith!

Though this is far from being a true representation of Repton's views, it is not far wide of his results. He observed that " there are a thousand beauties in nature besides those which may be copied as pictures "; though none of them " picturesque," yet all well adapted for introduction to a garden. Picturesque features, indeed, he considered were better left in the gipsy's hovel and the sunken lane.[1]

Knight replied to such heresy with fervour.[2] Repton, he remarked, called himself a landscape gardener, but confessed that his art was not intended to produce landscapes, so much as " some kind of *neat, simple and elegant effects*, or nondescript beauties which have not yet been named or classed." Such were, in Repton's words, " the comforts of a gravel walk and the delicious fragrance of a shrubbery."

The point was that paths and shrubberies, and green turf, flowering shrubs, and bright lakes, though gratifying other senses, did not gratify the eye. They were not visual beauties, with which the art of landscape was solely concerned. Repton was welcome to make what use of them he liked.

All I beg of him is, that if he takes any *professional* title, it may be one really descriptive of his profession, such as that of *walk-maker, shrub-planter, turf-cleaner,* or *rural perfumer*; for if *landscapes* are not what he means to produce, that of *landscape gardener* is not only of *no mean*, but of *no true pretension.*

---

[1] An open letter to Uvedale Price from Humphry Repton, 1794. Printed in later editions of Price's *Essays.*

[2] A Note. Prefixed to the second edition of *The Landscape.*

Price summed up his attitude to gardening in a sentence: " All types of garden must be judged by the universal principles of painting." Gardening was not, as he conceived Knight to believe, the copying of actual pictures. Nor was it concerned with the reproduction of ideas and objects derived from pictures, as Kent, Brown, and their followers had preached. Price had early lost his faith in Brown's system, when he had swept away the old formal gardens at Foxley. His chief occupation for the rest of his life was remedying his initial mistake, and preventing others from making it. Instead of grounds being doctored in accordance with jejune ideas and whimsical theories, he bade men look at pictures, grasp the underlying principles of composition, derive from paintings a feeling for colour, light, and shade, and arrange their parks accordingly.

The quality that he put first among the necessities of a scene, whether painted or planted, was " breadth "— that massing of shadows and colours which twilight produces. He wanted no glaring oppositions of colour in his landscape, and no shapes that leaped to the eye. The outline against the sky must be " broad," consisting of sweeps of hill or wood, broken only with discretion. Flowers, as a means of decoration, he was inclined to pass over, not only because painters had made little use of them in landscapes, but because horticulture and gardening, by the end of the eighteenth century, had practically become separate arts. In the formal garden which, as we shall see, Price, Knight, and Repton were instrumental in reviving, the use of flowers is obvious. But outside it, gardeners, as apart from horticulturalists, have now gone back to an attitude differing only slightly from Price's. Unless flowers can be massed, or strewn in natural profusion through glades or on banks, they are better away. The dreadful compromise made during last century of " bedding out "—heaving odd-shaped beds on lawns where disconsolate conifers dodge winding paths—was exactly what Price was attacking. Even in the use of flowers such experienced practitioners as Miss Jekyll and Miss Wilmott, Mr. William Robinson and Mr. Avray Tipping, have gone back to the " principles of painting."

Our rock and water gardens derive directly from Price. Lucky man, he was spared the sight of rockeries and the cult of the " alpine." But he was the first to reveal the possibilities of what was then known as " ugliness." According to Burke, ugliness was angularity. With this he disagreed. It was want of form. The ugliest ground was that with neither beauty nor picturesqueness; which was neither smooth nor boldly broken, but unfinished, weedy, and slimy. Excessive deformity, on the other hand—as in a quarry or gravel-pit—was not only not ugly, but picturesque in itself and full of opportunities for the gardener:

> I have often thought that if a gravel pit with clean water were near a house, the banks of it might, with great propriety and effect, be dressed with kalmeas, rhododendrons, azaleas and andromedas etc. without any shrub too large for its scale ; and that so a beautiful lake in miniature might be made, . . . to represent no bad image of what one might suppose a full sized lake in Lilliput.[1]

A good example of this conception put into practice, combined with Knight's " Quarry long neglected and o'ergrown," is to be found at Scotney Castle, Kent, where my grandfather, Edward Hussey, " improved " the grounds about 1837. That he was well acquainted with Price's book there is little doubt, since I came upon a copy of it in the library at Scotney. The old castle of Scotney lies at the bottom of a valley surrounded by a moat. My grandfather decided to abandon it, owing to the cold and damp, and to build a new house overlooking

[1] *Essay on Artificial Water*, "Sir Uvedale Price on the Picturesque," ed. Dick Lauder (1842), p. 285.

it from above. He partly ruined the old house to form a picturesque object, and quarried the stone for the new one in the hill-side between the new and the old. This, planted with azaleas, andromedas, and rhododendrons, forms a rich foreground to the view down to the old castle, which is also skilfully framed by a cliff, pines, and other trees which were already full grown. Beyond, the opposite slope of the valley rises to a " broadly " wooded skyline.

Thus at Scotney my grandfather put into practice the advice of " improvers " from Mason's time onwards. He might have quoted Mason's lines:

> Happy art thou . . .
> Ah! then most happy, if thy vale below,
> Wash with the crystal coolness of its rills
> Some mouldering abbey's ivy-vested wall.[1]

Or Knight:

> Bless'd too is he who, midst his tufted trees,
> Some ruin'd castle's lofty towers sees,
> Nodding o'er the stream that glides below.

Price's later essays [2] are admirable practical guides to gardening, excepting for the narrow range of plants referred to. Yet of such recent introductions as had already been made he quickly availed himself, and urged their planting on rough banks or the rugged sides of lakes. Others, hitherto confined to borders and walls, might similarly be planted wild:

We see what rich mixtures are formed on rocky banks, by common heaths and furze alone, or with the addition of wild roses and woodbines; what new combinations might then be made with the Virginia creeper, periploca, trailing arbutus etc.... Many of the choice American plants of low growth, and

---

[1] *The English Garden*, bk. i.
[2] *On Artificial Water. On Decorations near the House.* 1798.

which love shade, such as kalmeas, and rhododendrons, by having the mould they most delight in, placed to the north, on that sort of shelf which is often seen between a lower and an upper ledge of rocks, would be as likely to flourish as in a garden. . . . When plants are placed in new situations . . . they assume so new a character, such novelty and brilliancy, as can hardly be conceived by those who only see them in a shrubbery or a botanical garden. . . . Bignonias, passion flowers etc. might often grow luxuriantly amidst similar accompaniments; those who have always seen them nailed against walls, can have little idea of their effect, or even of that of vines and jessamines when loosely hanging over rocks and stones, or over the dark coves which might be made among them.[1]

Price was also the first defender of avenues since Capability Brown. Burke had said something in their favour, as tending to suggest infinity and thence the sublime. Price felt their analogy to the twilight of Gothic aisles. He tells us of one that he attempted, in vain, to preserve, and of how he was approaching by moonlight " a venerable castle-like mansion, built in the beginning of the fifteenth century ":[2]

A few gleams had pierced the deep gloom of the avenue— a large massive tower at the end of it, seen through a long perspective, and half lighted by the uncertain beams of the moon, had a grand mysterious effect. Suddenly a light appeared in this tower—then as suddenly vanished—and only the quiet silvery rays of the moon prevailed ; again, more lights quickly shifted to different parts of the building, and the whole scene most forcibly brought to my fancy the times of fairies and chivalry. I was much hurt to learn from the master of the place, that I might take my leave of the avenue and all its romantic effects, for that a death-warrant was signed.

Price admits that in this case his sympathy was romantic, rather than picturesque. Yet, if the picturesque is visual romanticism, a professor of the one cannot escape references to the other.

[1] Price, *op. cit.*, p. 269.
[2] Probably Hampton Court, Leominster, which adjoins Foxley, and was at this time being restored by James Wyatt.

Repton, too, was sometimes partial to avenues, but not if they terminated in an obelisk or other " eye trap," for

the eye of taste or experience hates compulsion and turns away in disgust from every artificial means of attracting it ; for this reason an avenue is most pleasing, which, like that at Langley Park, climbs up a hill and, passing over the summit, leaves the fancy to conceive its termination.[1]

A good example, this, of the blending of romanticism with its opposite, typical of Repton's mentality and of that of his contemporaries. While he found the avenue speak to him of order and unity, at the same time he yearned for the indefinite; for distance, not for anything that it offered, but *qua* distance. It is a practical instance of that sentiment of Campbell's, about distance lending enchantment to the view. It typifies the eternal conflict of the romance of the known past, with the romance of the unknown future. How are they to be combined? Repton had no doubts. " Break the avenue," he cried. While the view down it was often sublime, it acted as a curtain, cutting the park in two and concealing diagonal views. Breaking could often, he said, be effected without being noticeable from either end. Unsatisfactory as this method may be, it was at least an advance upon Brown and Mason's disgusting habit of converting the remains of avenues into clumps.

But the reaction against Brown was most effectively shown in the revival of the formal garden round the house. Knight was the first to revert to its desirability. He did so timidly, as a hyperbole induced by disgust:

> Oft when I've seen some lonely mansion stand
> Fresh from th' improver's desolating hand,
> 'Midst shaven lawns that far around it creep
> In one eternal undulating sweep . . .
> Tired with th' extensive scene, so dull and bare,
> To Heav'n devoutly I've addressed my prayer:

---

[1] *Sketches and Hints*, chap. iii.

Again the moss grown terraces to raise,
And spread the labyrinth's perplexing maze—
Replace in even lines the ductile yew,
And plant again the ancient avenue.[1]

But his reason for so revolutionary a proposal was the exact opposite to that which inspired the architectural gardeners of the next, and this, century, who use the formal garden as a foreground for the house. Knight saw in them a satisfactory foreground to prospects from the house:

But better are these distant scenes display'd
From the high terrace, or rich balustrade—
'Midst sculptured founts and vases, that diffuse
In shapes fantastic, their concordant hues.

That is how the Picturesque, which began by sweeping away all formality, ended by reinstating it. Up till then improvers had been trying to create landscape by filling scenes with details from Italian pictures, as early renaissance architects strove to recreate classic architecture by the application of Roman capitals and friezes. The great lesson taught by Price to his contemporaries was the study of the principles, instead of the details, that produced picturesque scenes, chief among which was the quality of " richness " in colouring and texture. Whilst this love of broken surfaces had led the earlier improvers to build mock cataracts, ruins, grottoes, and root houses, and had led Knight to advocate a foreground of briars and rocks, Price realized that it was the effect, not the presence, of these objects that gave what was needed to a scene. Their quality of " intricacy " must be interpreted into art. His quarrel with Brown was that his parts were never massed, and that he banished art from the very part of the garden where it ought most to be employed.

1 *The Landscape* (1794), bk. ii.

GARDEN SCENES

All Price's contemporaries admired the ruins of antiquity, grouped with pines and acanthus. He bade them recall the no less magnificent gardens of the Roman villas.

I remember the rich and magnificent effect of balustrades, fountains, marble basons and statues, blocks of ancient ruins, the whole mixed with pines and cypresses. I remember also their effect, both as accompaniments to the architecture and as a foreground to the distance.[1]

He recalled the gardens of the Villa Negroni, already destroyed since his visit: " The more broken, weather-stained, and decayed the stone and brickwork, the more the plants and creepers seemed to have fastened and rooted in between their joints, the more picturesque these gardens become; and in that respect they have to the painter's eye an immense advantage over modern gardens, from which all present decoration, and all future picturesqueness, are equally banished."

Not for a moment did he advocate the building of ruined gardens. It was the principle that must be observed: the partial concealment of the regularity by vines, shrubs, and ivy; the contrast of stone with vegetation, the richness of the lights and shades. These were essentials of the picturesque, and an architectural garden alone could supply them with the formality demanded by vicinity to a house. There must be balustrades, urns, steps, paving—" finished, determined forms," over which a light cloak of climbing plants might be thrown. But he could not go quite so far as to advocate a revival of the Dutch garden. He feared that the prejudice against topiary was still so strong that to praise it might extend that prejudice to the Italian forms which he was advocating. In such gardens, too, there might even be fountains. They had been banished by Brown as " unnatural." The need of a sanction from

---

[1] *Op. cit.*, p. 299.

nature for all ornaments was still sufficiently strong to lead Price to point to the geysers of Iceland as natural fountains. But even so, he pursued, did a Bernini, when he devised fountains for the piazza of St. Peter's, to be seen in conjunction with his colonnades and statues, bother himself about natural sanctions? No. He saw that fountains could display water at its grandest—sparkling, fresh, transparent, and foaming. In his enthusiasm for broken light Price at last got away from the sophistries of the century. Art in gardens was *not* to conceal itself. Shenstone had been talking through his hat when he had written: " Art should never be allowed to set foot in the province of nature, otherwise than clandestinely." Repton was on a wrong track in perpetually making what was artificial appear natural and *vice versa*. " In the old Gardens art was meant to be apparent, and to challenge admiration on its own account, not under the disguise of nature. Richness, effect, and agreement with the surrounding artificial objects were what the planners and decorators of those gardens aimed at." In the last sentence of the essay [1] he summed up the achievement of the Picturesque in garden design:

The difficulties in gardening, as in other arts, do not lie in forming the separate parts, in making upright terraces and fountains, or serpentine walks, plantations and rivers, but in producing a variety of compositions and effects by means of those parts, and in combining them, whatever they may be, or however mixed, into one striking and well connected whole.

That surely is the ultimate criterion of all gardens. It is certainly that of modern gardens, of which to that extent Uvedale Price is the originator, and the Picturesque the underlying principle.

Once the tendency back to formality had been begun by Price's sane advocacy, its progress was sure if slow.

[1] *On Decorations near the House.*

Plate XXII.   JOHN NASH: Cottages at Blaise Castle, Glos.

Fig. 1.   Design for a Parsonage House

From *An Essay on British Cottage Architecture*, by
James Malton, 2nd edition, 1798

Fig. 2.   Design for a Castle on a Picturesque Site

From *Designs for Rural Retreats*, by James Malton, 1802

Plate XXIII

Repton, who had begun by attacking all symmetrical dispositions, before the end of his career was laying out knot gardens, the patterns of which he copied from the backgrounds of old portraits, the beds planted with the flowers shown in the nosegays of ancestors. Even in the *Sketches and Hints*, published in 1795, he admitted symmetry, " where it was useful," though in practice he at first found it useful nowhere except near the front of regular buildings. He would, however, allow small formal lay-outs in secluded parts of a garden where they would not be seen, but were suitable for herbs and roses. In the *Theory and Practice*, published 1803, after Price's *Essay on Decorations near the House*, he expostulated against " the error of *excessive* lack of formality round the house " and urged that where ornament was used it should be really, and not only apparently, costly, or it would be valued by no one;—his version, perhaps, of Price's " richness."

Then in 1805 came Knight's *Inquiry*, expanding the views on formal gardens already suggested in *The Landscape*. By now he had changed his stand. Whereas in *The Landscape* he had looked upon the architectural garden as a foreground for views seen from the house, in the *Inquiry* he resolved that " few persons ever look for compositions when within doors. It is in walks or rides through parks, gardens or pleasure grounds that they are allowed to and become subjects of conversation." Consequently the seating of the house in the landscape became more important than the framing of the landscape from the house. To make a house a picturesque adjunct to a scene became the chief object of architecture and gardening. He instanced Vanbrugh as the only architect who had studied this relation in the design and siting of his buildings. Price had similarly picked out Vanbrugh [1] as the only architect who had given his buildings architectural foregrounds. But in

[1] *Essay on Decorations near the House.*

place of this wedding of house to surroundings, and the grouping of the main block with subsidiary masses, whether wings, or outhouses, offices, stables, and forecourts, what did he find? The exact opposite; a fashion for " entirely hiding the offices behind masses of plantation, and leaving the wretched square solitary mansion house to exhibit its pert bald front between dwarf shrubberies, which seem like whiskers added to the portico or entrance." [1] Sometimes indeed the office buildings, instead of being strikingly grouped round the house, and varied by trees, were actually sunk underground—" the improver generally picking out the most retired, intricate, and beautiful spot to be found near the house to bury them in." This last remark he made probably with an eye on Claremont.

When this had happened, " I know of no remedy," he said, " but the hanging terraces of the Italian gardens. . . . They not only enrich the foreground, but serve as a basement for the house to stand on, which at once gives it importance and accompaniments." He approved, though more temperately than Price, " the terraces and borders intermixed with vines and flowers " of old Italian gardens, and even of old English gardens, where " the mixture of splendor, richness, and neatness, was beautiful and pleasing in the highest degree." Such decorations, he admitted, were " now rather old fashioned; but another revolution in taste, which is probably at no great distance, will make them new again."

Whilst Repton thought that the " revolution in taste " would be towards Indian gardens and architecture, he met Price and Knight, in his *Inquiry into the Changes of Taste in Landscape Gardening* (1806), on their own ground—the Italian terrace—demonstrating rather pathetically against the latter's persistent misunderstanding of him. He agreed as heartily as they,

[1] Knight, *On Taste*, p. 214.

he said, on the value of terraces and characteristically showed that, as they could be made to contain pantries, cellars, and sculleries, they were also justified by utility. So far from having ever buried offices himself, he instanced the case of a house where the architect had given the kitchen a copper roof, and he had been called in to plant trees on the top of it—which he had declined to do on Knight's very principles. Before the end of his life he even found himself observing " with peculiar satisfaction some few venerable gardens belonging to parsonage or old manor houses, where still may be traced the former grass-walks and box-edged bowers with thick and lofty hedges of holly, quickset and other topiary plants which, like the yew or ivy, seem to display a peculiar satisfaction in yielding a fence at once secure, neat and opaquely trim." [1]

In *An Inquiry* he described one of his latest lay-outs, at Woburn, which he designated a " modern garden." Its composition shows how far landscape and gardening, whether by Price's agency or no, had become divorced. How the picturesque, indeed, was becoming romantic in its aping of Tudor methods. There were to be a terrace and parterre near the house, a private garden only used by the family, a rosary or dressed flower garden in front of the greenhouse, an American garden for plants from that country only, a Chinese garden surrounding a pool in front of the Chinese pavilion, a botanic garden, an animated garden or menagerie, and the English garden, or shrubbery walk, connecting the whole.

Later still [2] he described the gardens at Ashridge, " the youngest favourite, the child of my age and declining powers," which he was called in to deal with apart from the park, and contrived into no less than

[1] *Fragments on the Theory and Practice of Landscape Gardening* (1816). Frag. VIII.
[2] *Ibid.*

fifteen different kinds of garden. They included a paved terrace, an embroidered parterre, a "broad sanctuary and holy well," a mount garden and a rosarium and fountain. At this, the last, part of his life, he confessed that fashion had frequently misled taste, and while the scenery of nature, called landscape, had been his main concern through life, the garden itself should contain the most beautiful contrivances of art undisguised.

For a time the revival of the architectural garden was delayed by the introduction of hundreds of new plants for the display of which the bedding-out system came into vogue. The most vigorous champion of Price and Knight was John Claudius Loudon, from whom a stream of books proceeded for forty years after 1800, dealing with landscape gardening, architecture, farming, and forestry. Then, with the 'forties, a group of men came to the fore, of whom Nesfield, Sir Charles Barry, and Paxton were the chief. By them the flower garden was taken in hand and formalized according to Price's method. Architectural gardens, with shaped beds, and box or yew edges, were created at Woburn, Worsley, Eaton, Trentham, Castle Howard, Harewood, Blicking, Stoke Edith, Arley, and Shrubland. In many of them elaborate knots or yew hedges were laid out, in others terraces, balustrades, and fountains. The invention of the mowing machine increased the formality of lawns. The formalists seemed to have gained permanent control of the garden when, in 1881, Mr. William Robinson published the *Wild Garden* and two years later that great book, *The English Flower Garden*, in which the principles of Uvedale Price, brought up to date to accord with the vastly increased resources of the horticulturalist, were again preached, with the vigour and enthusiasm customary with apostles of the Picturesque. A few years later *The Formal Garden in England*, by Mr. Inigo Thomas and Sir Reginald Blomfield, gave battle, the authors taking the Dutch garden as revived by Sedding as their theme. In a series of prefaces that recalls the " Notes " and " Letters " of Price, Knight, and Repton, the worthy antagonists slanged one another. But while the formal garden has been carried to great heights by architects such as Sir Edwin Lutyens, and to great depths by the amateurs of " crazy paving " and the like, two ladies—Miss Jekyll and Miss Wilmott—have carried natural gardening to the utmost beauty of which it is capable.

Has not this been said before? . . . I have my suspicions that the admirers of Kent, Southcote, Shenstone, Brown, said exactly the same. One wonders what Kent or Shenstone, if they found themselves at Munstead or Warley, would say. There is no doubt how Price or Knight would take those gardens. They would agree that, with far greater " richness " than they could conceive of, these two artists had succeeded " in producing a variety of compositions and in combining them into one striking and connected whole."

CHAPTER VI

ARCHITECTURE

§ I

THE PAINTER-ARCHITECT

*Variety and intricacy are beauties and excellences in
every other of the arts which address the imagination:
and why not in architecture ?*—Sir Joshua Reynolds,
13th Discourse, 1786.

BLENHEIM is picturesque. So is the modern
speculating builder's six-roomed house, with its
sham half-timbering, unbalanced fenestration, bay
window, and terra-cotta dragon on the gable. Both
exhibit the "variety and intricacy" that Reynolds
urged architects to adopt from painters. But whilst
Blenheim, leaving its size and classic garb out of the
question, is moulded to produce a varied and intricate
impression on the eye, by masses of light and shade,
and a dramatic outline built up like an apotheosis of
Rubens, the modern "dwelling" is given features that
appeal to the common mind as being in themselves
picturesque. To trace how the one is descended from
the other would be to write the history of two centuries
of architecture. Without going to such lengths, we
may, however, follow the effect on architecture of the
picturesque point of view, noticing how first it required
"movement," then contrast, then irregularity, mystery,
"romance," then texture, and at last was contented by
a symbol of all these qualities—a terra-cotta dragon on
the gable.

If the influence of the picturesque on architecture was
only a descent from the sublime to the ridiculous, it
would not be worth the tracing. The picturesque point
of view is responsible for many of the finest, and much

[186]

of what is good in the worst, buildings since 1800. The best as well as the worst rural domestic architecture of the present day is ultimately picturesque in intention. Town and village planning, the preservation of cottages and of rural England, the proper as opposed to the scientific care of ancient monuments, are results of the impulses and theories that we have been tracing from their seventeenth-century Italian origins. Just as the picturesque is a mode of vision, so picturesque architecture can be defined as building and design conceived in relation to landscape, whether as a setting, or as the source of certain qualities and features reflected in the architecture.

Broadly speaking, the effect of the picturesque on architecture was to set up irregularity in place of regularity as the essential of design. A desire for symmetry in buildings is inherent in the human mind. Man, with his symmetrical body, has instinctively reproduced the same balance in his three-dimensional arts since the first moment when art was added to necessity as a motive for making things. Gothic architecture, in its complete expressions, is as symmetrical as any other kind. The assymmetry of a large proportion of Gothic buildings, chiefly domestic, arises from their never having been intended to be works of art. Their function was utilitarian. Design, as we understand the word, did not enter into their fashioning, but when religion raised building on to the aesthetic plane.

This point has to be grasped before the magnitude of the revolution in design produced by the picturesque point of view can be appreciated. Irregularity is not inherent in Gothic, as the revivers of the style considered. Their enthusiasm for irregularity was picturesque in its origin, and was caught from men who saw with a painter's eye, such as Reynolds and Uvedale Price.

When symmetry was extended from ecclesiastical to domestic architecture, beginning in England during the early fifteenth century, the tendency of design set towards immobility. As knowledge of classic architecture increased, buildings increasingly became static, " dignified," " quiet." The picturesque point of view substituted for this immobility, proper to forms actually stationary and made of stone, a desire for the quality that distinguishes living forms and graphic art: movement. This " movement " was not the equipoise of thrusts and strains that Gothic engineering achieved. It was turbulent. It is the *baroque*. It reached England at the same time that the picturesque point of view was forming in this country, through that enigmatic genius John Vanbrugh. In him it was fused with a number of other non-architectural qualities; with a dramatist's sense of climax, an opera-producer's sense of the sublime, with a romanticist's affection for ruins, gothic, and landscape.

The importance of Vanbrugh in the formation of a picturesque view of architecture lies in the effect his buildings had on artists half a century after his death. Robert Adam, Reynolds, and Uvedale Price evolved from them a picturesque theory of architecture which is still prevalent. It is therefore with the effects, more than with the causes, of Vanbrugh's achievements that we are here concerned.

For fifty years after his death picturesque development was arrested in architecture, but made immense headway in literature, gardening, painting, and popular interest generally. When Robert Adam wrote a *Survey of the Arts in England*[1] in 1778, a picturesque point of view had come into existence, and had suddenly been redirected to architecture by the work of an artist of genius—G. B. Piranesi (1720-1778). His engravings

[1] Quoted by A. T. Bolton, " Robert and James Adam," *Country Life*, 1922.

[188]

vividly brought out the qualities in architecture that Vanbrugh had had in view, that the preachers of the picturesque were to popularize, but which were usually lacking in contemporary English architecture of the Palladian type. Piranesi seized on the picturesque qualities—what Reynolds called " intricacy and variety "—soaring, irregular masses, crumbling sur- faces, masses of shadow, and prodigious " movement."

Through Piranesi, Adam was the first Englishman of that generation to recognize that these had also been Vanbrugh's objectives, although, in Adam's opinion, he had failed through lack of educated taste to achieve "the truly elegant, simple and sublime." At first sight it would be difficult to imagine two architects with less in common than Vanbrugh and Adam. Mr. Bolton has shown how nearly allied the two in reality were. Adam, particularly in his youth, made a practice of composing gigantic conceptions very similar to those of Vanbrugh, which he gradually refined and pruned till they attained the elegant simplicity of his characteristic work. The real affinity between the two men lay in Vanbrugh's genius for expressing the quality that Adam considered essential to great architecture: " the magnitude and movement of parts."

" Movement " was precisely what the theorists of the picturesque sought to inculcate into architecture. Adam's definition of the quality,[1] and his subsequent panegyric of Vanbrugh, marks the beginning of the picturesque phase of English architecture. His words were drawn upon by both Reynolds and Price for their subsequent comments on the subject:

Movement is meant to express the rise and fall, the advance and recess with other diversity of form, in the different parts of a building, so as to add greatly to the picturesqueness of the composition, for the rising and falling, advancing and receding,

---

[1] R. Adam, *Works*, Introduction to Part I (1773).

with the convexity and concavity and other forms of the great parts, have the same effect in architecture that hill and dale, foreground and distance, swelling and sinking, have in landscape ; that is, they serve to produce an agreeable and diversified contour that groups and contrasts like a picture, and creates a variety of light and shade which gives great spirit, beauty and effect to the composition.

In this passage Adam clearly states the relation that was beginning to be recognized not only between pictorial composition and architecture, but between a building and its surroundings. He was himself a landscape painter of the most picturesque type. Not only are many of his designs given surroundings that breathe the sentiment of Gainsborough, but there are in the Soane Museum some forty semi-architectural landscapes and compositions of buildings and scenery— ruins, cataracts, blasted trees, fractured vaults, and so on, besides many rough sketches of picturesque glimpses made when he was in Italy (Plate XIII, fig. 1). After the passage defining movement, he definitely associated Vanbrugh with the quality, and paid him the highest tribute in his power:

Sir John Vanbrugh's genius was of the first class, and in particular of movement, novelty and ingenuity his works have not been exceeded by anything in modern [*i.e.*, since classic] times.

Unfortunately, he considered Vanbrugh's " taste kept no pace with his genius," and all the grand movement in his buildings was " so crowded with barbarisms and absurdities, and so borne down by their preposterous weight, that none but the discerning can separate their merits from their defects." However,

In the hands of the ingenious artist, who knows how to polish and refine and bring them into use, we have always regarded his productions as rough jewels of inestimable value.

ARCHITECTURE

Vanbrugh's architecture was a rough jewel in Adam's eyes just as landscape itself was a rough jewel till polished by the discriminating artist. His defect was lack of study of the great masters, and too much natural vigour in his composition. Unlike the painter, the architect could not find " an immediate standard in nature to which he can always refer." Architecture needed to be " informed and improved by a correct taste," [1] just as Mason considered that the countryside must be improved by Mr. Brown before it could be considered beautiful.

The enfranchisement of all styles, of which Adam's own work is an example, brought about the fall of the classic tradition. Stuart and Revett's *Antiquities of Athens* (1762) and the increasing popularity of Gothic forced men to recognize that architecture was not simply the art of building like the Romans. The collapse left critics without a clear body of principles whereby to estimate excellence. In 1786 Reynolds delivered his 13th Discourse, eight years after Adam's " survey."

The time was ripe for some fresh standard of visual appreciation. The Gothic revival was fast becoming literary and romantic in its aims, appealing to the intellect rather than to the senses. The Grecian style, in spite of Adam's personal admiration of " movement," was lapsing into excessive elegance and debility. In an effort to renew visual appreciation of architecture Reynolds went back to Vanbrugh. But whereas Adam had gone to the root of Vanbrugh's method and revealed his architectural quality of " movement," Reynolds popularized a more superficial but, as it turned out, more acceptable aspect of his merits.

In the 13th Discourse he urged the fuller use by artists of their imagination. Architects, too, he considered could find additional means of appealing to the spectator's imagination. Either by an association of ideas, with the castles of the barons, such as Vanbrugh

---

[1] Adam, *Works*, Part II (1774), Preface.

[191]

had contrived. Or by some striking novelty of effect. In reaction to the moribund tradition of symmetry, Reynolds turned to that " irregularity " which the picturesque writers were to raise to the potency of a principle. Architects, no less than painters, should avail themselves, he thought, of " accidents "—" to follow where they lead, and to improve them, rather than always to trust to a regular plan." He instanced old houses composed of additions made in various times and styles. " As such buildings depart from regularity they now and then acquire something of scenery, which I should think might not unsuccessfully be adopted by an architect." Then followed the passage that I have set at the head of this chapter, about variety and intricacy being able to address the imagination as well in architecture as in other arts. To appreciate the revolutionary character of Reynolds's suggestion, it must be remembered that no important building had been completed since the time of Queen Elizabeth that was not symmetrical in itself, and that no architect had imagined a serious design in which one-half did not reflect the other. His pronouncement must have come with all the shock that an advocacy of Herr Mendlesohn's Einstein Tower at Berlin would produce, coming from the lips of the present President of the Royal Academy.

Picturesque effect was exactly what Reynolds meant by " something of scenery." Intermittently for forty years this lead was to be followed, till G. L. Meason in 1827 published *Italian Landscape Architecture*, in which the conglomerate buildings shown in backgrounds by painters, from Giotto onward, were reproduced for the benefit of architects.

Reynolds concluded his suggestions on architecture with a further panegyric of the architect whose work had originally inspired them:

To speak, then, of Vanbrugh in the language of a painter, he had originality of invention, he understood light and shadow, and had great skill in composition. To support his principal object, he produced his second and third groups or masses; he perfectly understood in his art what is most difficult in ours, the conduct of the background ; by which the design and invention is set off to the greatest advantage. What the background is in painting, in architecture is the real ground on which the building is erected ; and no architect took greater care than he that his work should not appear crude and hard ; that is, it did not abruptly start out of the ground, without expectation or preparation.

The earlier protest made by Adam against the ignorant ridicule of Vanbrugh no doubt emboldened Reynolds to make his stirring apology. But the basis of his appreciation is his own. It is the picturesque conception of architecture that gives to dramatic massing, the handling of light and shade, and the wedding of a building to its landscape by the architectural treatment of the foreground, greater importance than to clear logic of design or nicety of detail; the point of view that, in a sentence, regards a building not as a form complete in itself, but as the background of a picture. Once the architect got into the habit of regarding his designs as it were from a distance, and as a mere part of a picture, he was only too apt to scamp the " close up." General effect was everything. Materials, excellence of mouldings and details, convenience of plan, the constructive use of orders or other structural members, were of subsidiary account. In reaction against the long reign of symmetry irregularity became an end in itself.

At first this quality was confined to the revival of Gothic, a movement that runs parallel to the development of picturesque architecture, as romanticism to the picturesque point of view. Both the architectural movements were begun by Vanbrugh and Hawksmoor, but then they separated and were not again associated till Reynolds's, Gilpin's, and Young's allusions to the picturesque nature of Gothic had been expanded by Price and Knight into a theory of architectural values.

Then Gothic, having been revived by antiquaries who enjoyed its associations with gloom and superstition, was found to provide just that intricacy and irregularity which the picturesque required. Generally speaking, Gothic was built after 1795 primarily with picturesque motives till Augustus Welby Pugin published his *Contrasts* in 1836 which, with his subsequent publications, led to a more architectural appreciation of the style.

The transition from an antiquarian and sentimental to a picturesque attitude to Gothic was largely brought about by Gilpin and Arthur Young's " criticisms " of ruins. To some extent an eye for colour and texture had been formed by the poetry of Gray and the Wartons. Thomas Warton's *Pleasures of Melancholy* (1747) refers to ruins in terms of colour as well as in terms of romantic sentiment:

> O lead me, Queen Sublime, to solemn glooms
> Congenial with my soul; to cheerless shades,
> To ruin'd seats, to twilight cells and bowers, . . .
> Beneath yon ruin'd abbeys moss grown piles
> Oft let me sit at twilight hour of eve,
> When through some western window the pale moon
> Pours her long-levelled rule of streaming light.

In the same year Horace Walpole got possession of the farm at Twickenham that was to become Strawberry Hill. But in spite of his " glooms " and his picturesque sheep and his passion for prospects, Walpole's Gothic was not described even by its admirers as picturesque. Its appeal was intellectual, not visual.

Gilpin approached ruins, like all other scenery, with a critical eye. He allowed neither sentiment nor antiquarianism to bias his judgment of whether or no a ruin was effective. Thus in 1770 he could write of Tintern, after acknowledging the delicious tranquillity of the scene as a whole:

Though the parts are beautiful, the whole is ill-shaped. No

ruins of the tower are left, which might give form and contrast
to the walls and buttresses, and other inferior parts. Instead of
this, a number of gable-ends hurt the eye with their regularity,
and disgust it by the vulgarity of their shape. A mallet judi-
ciously used (but who durst use it?) might be of service in
fracturing some of them.[1]

In the same year Young paid a visit to Fountains,
at that time in process of being tidied up and landscaped
by Brown. Both he and subsequently Gilpin made their
visits an occasion for laying down certain general
principles derived partly from Burke and partly from
painting, for the treatment of ruins—which might well
be taken to heart by more enlightened but less picturesque experts to-day.

Young[2] felt the romantic melancholy of retired,
neglected ruins. But he decided that they

generally appear best at a distance ; if you approach them the
effect is weakened unless the access is somewhat difficult. And
as to penetrating every part by means of artificial paths, it is a
question whether the more you see by such means does not
proportionately lessen the general idea of the whole. Looking
as it were stealthily through passages that cannot be passed,
heaps of rubbish stopping you in one place, broken steps preventing both ascent and descent in another ; in a word, some
parts that cannot be seen at all, others that are half seen, and
those fully viewed broken, rugged, terrible. In such the imagination has a free space to range in, and sketches ruins in idea
far beyond the boldest strokes of reality.

He did not wish to know of a ruin's style or details.
To him a ruin was a mighty picture in three dimensions.
Gilpin was highly indignant at the " vain ostentation of
expense " he found at Fountains:

The time came [which every lover of picturesque beauty
must lament] when the legal possession of this beautiful scene
was yielded to the owner of Studley ; and his busy hands were
let loose upon it. .·. . He has pared away all the bold roughness

---

[1] *Tour of the Wye.*   [2] *Northern Tour.*

and freedom of the scene and given every part a trim polish. . . .
In the room of detached fragments [*proper* because they account
for what is defaced, *picturesque* because they unite the principal
pile with the ground] a gaudy Temple is erected.

He went so far as to question the right of a proprietor
to behave in this way—a right which, alas, we are still
questioning:

A legal right the proprietor unquestionably has to deform his
ruin as he pleases.   But though he fear no King's indictment,
he must expect a very severe prosecution in the court of Taste.
The refined code of this court does not consider an elegant ruin
as a man's property, on which he may exercise the irregular
sallies of a wanton imagination; but as a deposit of which he is
only the guardian, for the amusement and advantage of posterity.
A ruin is a sacred thing.   Rooted for ages in the soil, assimilated
to it; we consider it rather as a work of nature than of art.   Art
cannot reach it.   A Gothic window, a fretted arch, some trivial
peculiarity may be aimed at with success ; but the magnificence
of ruin was never attained by any modern attempt.

A Goth may deform ; but it exceeds the power of art to
amend.[1]

Both Gilpin and Young frequently refer to the artificial ruins that had become popular as features in the
landscape garden.

Mention has already been made of the " eligible
ruin " at Hagley built by Sanderson Miller in 1748
which, according to Walpole, exhibited " the true rust
of the Barons' Wars."   The desire for such objects in a
landscape was of course based on their presence in the
pictures of Claude and Salvator, and the preference for
Gothic, as opposed to Classic, ruins, upon the greater
probability of the former—as William Mason explained
in *The English Garden*.   Miller received several com-

[1] *Tour of Cumberland and Westmorland.*   As a matter of fact, Gilpin's strictures made such an impression that the Fountains ruins
were soon afterwards restored to something like their original and
present beautiful condition.

Plate XXIV.   DUNGLASS, HADDINGTONSHIRE.

Designed by Richard Crichton and Alexander Nasmyth, 1807-13
in the style of Vanbrugh

Fig. 1.   Design for a Picturesque Village
From *Village Architecture*, by P. F. Robinson, 1830

Fig. 2.   A Mansion from a Landscape by Claude
From G. L. Meason's *Landscape Architecture*, 1827

Plate XXV

missions on the strength of his Hagley work. William Pitt got him to make a design " for a very considerable Gothick Object which is to stand in a very fine situation on the hills near Bath " in the grounds of his friend Allen—where it still stands. Lord Chancellor Hardwicke also wrote for one which still stands at Wimpole. It was not, like Lord Lyttelton's, to contain a keeper's house, but was to represent " mearly the walls and semblance of an old castle to make an object from the house." [1]

James Wyatt, the first important architect of the Gothic revival, brought considerable knowledge to the restoring of Salisbury Cathedral (1782) and the building of Fonthill (1796-1807) and Ashridge (1807-1814). Their complete absence of picturesque effect is owing to Wyatt's blindness to picturesque architecture, even when confronted with it. A passage in the *Farington Diary* [2] shows how Wyatt, whilst he felt the effects of the picturesque, was ignorant of it as an architectural quality:

Wyatt acknowledged that he never passed the road through the gate which leads from Woodstock to Blenheim without being exceedingly struck with the general effect ; and had often stood to consider to what cause it could be owing. It was not the buildings, or the grounds, or the woods or the walls singly, since none of these constituent parts were such as his judgment would approve entirely. Yet the whole together makes a forcible impression.

---

[1] Designs for ruins are to be found in Charles Middleton's *Decorations of Parks and Gardens* (1800), in J. Plaw's publications, and in W. Wright's *Grotesque Architecture* (1767).
[2] 22nd January 1798.

THE PICTURESQUE

§ 2

THE CULT OF THE COLOSSAL

Mr. Burke observes, that the sublime in building requires solidity, and even massiness; and in my own idea, no single cause acts so powerfully, and can so little be dispensed with as massiness; but as massiness is so nearly allied to heaviness, it is—in this age especially—by no means a popular quality.—Uvedale Price, *Essay on Architecture.*

In the same year that Wyatt was puzzled to account for the powerful effect of Blenheim, Uvedale Price repeated, still more explicitly, the reason as already suggested by Adam and Reynolds:

His [Vanbrugh's] first point seems to have been massiness, as the foundation of grandeur. Then to prevent that mass from being a lump, he has made various bold projections of various heights which from different points serve as the foregrounds to the main building. And, lastly, having probably been struck with the variety of outline against the sky in many Gothic buildings, he raised on the top a number of decorations of various characters.[1]

But what really impressed Price were the distant views of the palace. He admired in particular one from across the lake. " The house, the lake, and the rich bank of the garden may be so grouped with some of the trees that stand near the water and hang over it, and so framed amid their branches and stems, as to exclude all but the choicest objects; and whoever catches that view towards the close of the evening, when the sun strikes the golden balls and pours his beams through the open parts, gilding every rich and brilliant ornament, will think he sees some enchanted palace." No other

[1] *Essay on Architecture* (1798).

great house, he maintained—not even Fonthill or Kedleston—could so recall Alcina and Armida.

The essentially *fribble* nature (to use Lord Lyttelton's expressive word) of much of the architecture of the late eighteenth and early nineteenth centuries, against which Price inveighed, cannot be laid at the door of the picturesque. The latter tended, it is true, to set effect before construction. But amorphous design and bad construction were endemic in "Gothistic" design. Adam himself, or at any rate his host of imitators, by the excessive refinement of their designs, cannot be absolved from the charge of encouraging slightness in every branch of design. So far from trumperiness being the result of picturesque theory, that monumental, almost megalomaniac, phase through which architecture passed during the first quarter of the century is foreshadowed, and in part accounted for, by the picturesque. Hardwicke's portal at Euston, Smirke's British Museum, Elmes' St. George's Hall, Liverpool, are instances of the gigantic in English architecture.

The tendency towards the gigantic was foreshadowed by Burke's making it a quality of the Sublime. Price justified it by appealing to the ruined temples of Sicily and Paestum, as illustrated by Piranesi, and took the step of comparing great architecture directly to " natural architecture," such as cliffs, with the comment that " the effects of art are never so well illustrated as by similar effects in nature." [1] The passage as a whole forcibly recalls Piranesi's conceptions.

In his engravings the structures seem to loom aloft with the grandeur of cliffs, their bases piled with fragments and vegetation, their surfaces scarred like a precipice. Taken in connection with his sanction of size, Price's analogy of nature and architecture clearly illustrates how the picturesque is related to the monumental by those famous engravings. M. Henry

[1] *Essay on Architecture.*

Lemonnier [1] has traced the same process in France. Piranesi " voit plus grand que nature; même les repro-ductions d'édifices étudiés de plus près prennent chez lui un aspect disproportionné . . . une sorte d'amplifica-tion épique." He points to Piranesi's reconstructions, where tombs and monuments of every style are grouped together, to his " salles à perte de vue, intérieurs mys-tèrieux et sombres de prisons," and to his habit of pour-ing together, as from a combined treasury, armoury, and museum the hoarded relics of an epoch. In France, Piranesi's influence was at its height from 1760 till 1770, at the very time when writers were beginning to celebrate the heroic if austere virtues of the Roman Republic, and artists to familiarize men with the primitive Doric of Paestum and the ruins of Egypt. Aesthetic and historical perspective was suddenly jogged. Political and dimensional grandeur became associated at the same moment that Rousseau and Diderot were beginning the subordination of reason to sensation, and literature was waxing grandiloquent.

Out of this combination of forces there arose in France a veritable cult of the gigantic, headed by Peyne, Gondoin (1737-1818), and Boullée (1728-1799), with Quatremere de Quincy as its apologist. " Nous ne craindrons pas de le répéter," he wrote [2] in 1816, " la grandeur physique est une des principales causes de la valeur et de l'effet de l'architecture." By this time Ledoux (1736-1806) had built (1782) the heavy but impressive *barrières*. And under the Empire the tend-ency found a political justification. Brongniart's Bourse, Poyet's façade of the Corps legislatif, the Madeleine, the Arc de Triomphe—designed in its main lines and proportions by Chalgrin—all are gigantic. Nor were these architects pure students of classic design.

1 *La Mégalomanie dans l'Architecture* (*L'Art Moderne* 1500-1800, *Essais et Esquisses*). Hachette, 1912.
2 *Eloge de l'architecte Chalgrin* (*Notices historiques,* vol. i, p. 18).

The majority of them were painters or engravers as well
—luckily for them, since the reputation of the earlier
among them rests on their superb, and huge, plates of
" projects." Gondoin's Ecoles de Chirurgerie (now the
Faculty of Medicine), begun under Louis XV and
finished under his successor, is in itself a memorial of
its architect, but his projects for the completed scheme [1]
far surpass it in extent and magnificence. Boullée, a
pupil of a painter as well as of an architect, according to
Quatremere, caught from Servandoni the habit " de
voir grand." " Il vit surtout colossal," adds M.
Lemonnier. An analogous character was Desprez,
architect, painter, and draughtsman. Sent to Rome in
1779 by a scholarship, he executed " prospects " of the
Temple of Isis at the moment of the eruption of Vesuvius,
and of the catacombs during the nocturnal confabula-
tions of early Christians. His representation of *Hannibal
burning Selinontis* shows a huge port jostling with vessels,
the moles encumbered with pylons and cenotaphs,
illumined by sinister gleams, flames roaring skywards,
the whole in the style less of Turner than of Martin.
In that bizarre character—John Martin [2] (1789-1852)—
whose gigantic canvasses once stirred the country as no
pictures have done before or since, the cult of the
gigantic found its English culmination. His *Belshazzar's
Feast* and the *Overwhelming of Sodom*, still to be found in
engravings in spare bedrooms and boarding-houses, are
the final embodiment of " sublimity induced by vastness
and obscurity."

This lust for the grand and dramatic made its way to
this country and appears, then, in Price's admiration of
Vanbrugh. An architect who produced such effects,
by whatever violations of rules, must, he was convinced,

---

[1] *Description des Ecoles de Chirurgerie* (1780).
[2] Martin was also a visionary engineer. He produced a scheme
for a Thames embankment, and for a new water supply for the
Metropolis.

be worthy of study, though not of imitation. Price, going further than Adam, recommended an architect

to make drawings of Blenheim, endeavouring to preserve the principle of light and shadow, the character of the architectural foreground, the effect of the raised decorations on the roof and the general grandeur and variety of the whole; but trying, at the same time, to give more lightness and purity of style to that whole, more elegance and congruity to the parts; observing as he proceeded how far he found it necessary to sacrifice these to preserve the effects which Vanbrugh has produced.

It is a matter for speculation whether Soane was an admirer of Vanbrugh as well as of Piranesi. The evidence of his work strongly suggests that he was, and much of it in any case has precisely those qualities that Price recommended an architect to combine with " more elegance and congruity." Some of his simpler designs, particularly those for the barracks at the Bank, and for metropolitan churches, recall Hawksmoor's handling of similar buildings. His careful concealment of his roofs, and the care given to sky-line features—often of a kind which interpret Vanbrugh's Roman into a more refined Greek guise—exemplify much that Price drew attention to. In his project for a royal palace a plan extremely like that of Blenheim was adopted, with a similar use of groups of sculpture and square pediments emphasizing the parts. The gateways and piers are frankly *baroque* of the kind employed by Vanbrugh, though in detail inspired more probably by Piranesi's profusions of classical ornaments. Be this as it may, Soane's architecture, in spite of its Grecian mode, appeals to essentially the same emotions as Vanbrugh's. There is in both the same massiveness, richness, and dramatic use of light and shade, entitling us to regard Soane as the greatest exponent of picturesque architecture in the Greek medium. A picturesque bias would certainly seem to account for much that is of doubtful origin in his compositions. One has but to see the series of Piranesi's

drawings of the ruins of Paestum, Clerisseau's ruins of
Thermae, and J. Gandy's *Bank of England in Ruins*,
that hang in his house, to be reminded at once of Price's
arguments on the picturesque character of the ruins of
once beautiful buildings. I am inclined to think that
the industrious Soane, besides designing buildings that
should be beautiful in their perfection, had an eye on
their picturesque character in decay.

Among the characteristics of Vanbrugh's architecture
that Price regarded as most picturesque, were his skylines, as contrasted with the lame treatment by other
architects of that part of a house, even when it was of the
most expensive kind. The turning of attention to the
roofs and chimneys of houses, largely ignored by the
Palladians, was an important result of picturesque study.
He remarked that the landscape painters were no more
helpful than Palladio in giving hints on the treatment
of chimneys, and suggested that turrets, urns, vases, and
obelisks might be employed for the purpose, as Vanbrugh had shown, but he forbade columns. Another
method used by Vanbrugh and approved by Price was
the linking of stacks by arches. This became a common
feature of picturesque architecture. On the whole he
preferred "old English chimneys" which had the
virtue of not pretending to be anything else than what
they were.

Interesting skylines were not to be confined to
country houses. If properly employed, Price considered,
they would enormously improve the appearance of towns,
particularly those such as Bath that were frequently
seen from above or on the side of a hill.

In situations of that kind, were an architect with a painter's
eye to have the planning of the whole, he would have an opportunity of producing the richest effects, by combining his art
with that of painting—by varying the characters of the buildings and particularly of their summits, according to the place
which they were to occupy.

§ 3

TOWN AND VILLAGE PLANNING

This led Price on to a brief consideration of picturesque town planning, in which he contrasted Tivoli and Bath. At Tivoli " the general outline of the town appears to yield and vary according to the shape of its foundations with now and then a counteracting line that gives a zest and spirit to the composition. Not a projecting rock or knoll but is occupied, the buildings advancing or retiring according to their situation, while the happy mixture of trees completes the whole." With Bath, on the other hand, he, like Catharine Morland, had been disappointed. " Whoever considers what are the forms of the summits, how little the buildings are made to yield to the ground, and how few trees are mixed with them, will account for my disappointment." Price was not visualizing the jagged skylines that architects of the eighteen-eighties loved to give to expensive streets, or jerry-builders of to-day to suburban rows, by means of endless gables, rustic roofs, and terra-cotta gryphons. He was visualizing such a town as Vanbrugh or Soane might have conceived, with cupolas, louvres, pediments, and sculpture enriching without tearing the skylines of the streets. Considering the unusually accidented site of Bath, it must be confessed that Wood and his successors took little advantage of the gradients. Indeed, they ignored them, and laid the town out as though it was on a plain. When a street goes up hill, the houses painfully mount it like a flight of steps. The treatment of a rising street is admittedly difficult. In some cases it can be made effective by placing two large masses at the bottom and contriving for the buildings to diminish in height as the gradient rises. More satisfactory is Price's implied suggestion that the street form should be abandoned and the houses be disposed in groups suggested by the contours. Many modern housing schemes have successfully adopted this method.

Now that town and village planning has received the attention it demands, Price's observations on the subject are, historically, of considerable interest. No branch of architecture is so closely connected with the picturesque, but it is only during the past five and twenty years that the principles that should govern lay-out have been rediscovered. Price devoted many pages of his essay to the subject for the benefit of landowners. He considered it necessary to apologize for the subject, and for the length of his treatment of it. He pleaded as his excuse

that there is no scene where such a variety of forms or embellishments may be introduced at so small an expense, and without anything fantastic or unnatural, as in a village ; and where the lover of painting and the lover of humanity may find so many sources of amusement and interest.

His interest in the subject had been aroused by his acquaintance with Gainsborough and Reynolds.

When Gainsborough lived at Bath I made frequent excursions with him into the country; he was a man of an eager, irritable mind, though warmly attached to those he loved ; and of a lively and playful imagination, yet at times severe and sarcastic. But when we came to cottage or village scenes, to groups of children, or any other objects of that kind which struck his fancy, I have often remarked in his countenance an expression of particular gentleness and complacency. I have too observed Sir Joshua Reynolds, when children have been playing before him—the most affectionate parent could not gaze at them with a look more expressive of kindness and interest. . . .

Thus attracted by picturesque and benevolent concern, Price turned to village improvement. He advised those who were thinking of rebuilding a village to consider it in relation to the landscape generally, and to that end to study Titian's method of grouping humble houses and villages in an attractive manner. Ornamental displays of wealth he condemned, but where a great house was situated close to a village " far from interfering they would add to each other's effect; and it may truly be said that there is no way in which wealth can produce such natural unaffected variety, and such interests, as by adorning a real village and promoting the comfort and enjoyments of its inhabitants." This he said with a memory of Chambers's description of sham villages made to divert the Emperor of China " in which the various incidents of real life are acted by Eunuchs." His aim was to show that the " ravages of wealthy pride " described by Goldsmith in *The Deserted Village* were also bad taste.

In rebuilding, or laying out a village, symmetry and " ribbon development " were to be avoided. " The characteristic beauties of a village are intricacy, variety and play of outline; whatever is done should be with a view to promote those objects." Inequality of ground, existing trees and bushes or old buildings were not only to be retained, but to suggest the character of the new buildings. The old buildings were particularly to be preserved; an improver who found such a one " in which not only the forms were of picturesque irregularity, but the tints were of that rich, mellow, harmonious kind so much enjoyed by painters," would not, if he had studied pictures, " suffer them to be destroyed by plaster or whitewash." On the other hand a nondescript plastered house would gain neatness and evenness of colour from a coat of whitewash. In cases where a new house was needed among many picturesque old ones, it should be perfectly simple, yet with well marked shadows such as are given by projecting roofs, porches, and well recessed windows. Attention, too, should be given to the form of the chimneys. A meagre pattern

would spoil a good house. He instanced a village otherwise well built by a gentleman—" but the chimneys are
all single, tall and thin . . . producing the most wretched
meagre outline I ever beheld. It is the more provoking,
as the village is beautifully backed with trees." Exceptionally massive chimneys, on the contrary, whilst
exceedingly picturesque, would scarcely be built save
by a lover of painting who found a massive object
necessary at that point in the composition.

Price is particularly sound on the union of trees with
village architecture. " Cottages appear to repose under
their shade, to be protected, sometimes even supported
by them." A landowner would be well advised to
introduce such exotics as acacia, pines, cedars, arbutus,
a cluster of lilac, into villages (as seems often to have
been done in suburban schemes). In a humble setting
they displayed their beauty better than in a crowded
shrubbery. Climbing plants, he emphatically urged,
should be introduced, particularly on the porches of
village houses, and in such other warm nooks as old
cottages present in abundance. A collector of such
plants might distribute his specimens round his village
and thus gain a double pleasure in his walks abroad.
Flower gardens and fruit trees were likewise to be
encouraged among villagers.

The church, as the centre of the village, should be
the object of the local landowner's particular attention,
both in its upkeep (and he implies restoration), and the
planting of its rood. Yew was, of course, the most
appropriate tree—no churchyard should be without one.
But whatever was planted should be of a dark colour,
for instance cedars or cypress. " In high romantic
situations particularly, where the churchyard is elevated
above the general level, a cedar, spreading its branches
downwards from that height, would have the most
picturesque and at the same time the most solemn
effect."

[207]

Every village was improved by a brook, or by water in any form. If a foot-bridge were needed, heavy flag-stones formed the simplest, most durable, and picturesque sort. Where stone was plentiful, washing stones could be disposed in picturesque positions on the bank.

One naturally finds more interest on Price's part in the appearance of villages, than in their sanitariness. There were no inspectors and Ministry of Health Regulations in his time. Nevertheless, the cult of the picturesque can be credited with a vast amount of decent building, on the whole ornamental and comfortable. The demand that there was for picturesque cottages during the first half of the nineteenth century is attested by the numerous books of architects' designs for " rural embellishments."

It may surprise some to find John Nash laying out a village. Yet Blaise, near Bath—that same Blaise where the sham castle was never visited by Catharine Morland —is by the architect of Regent's Street. It consists (Plate XXII) of thatched cottages picturesquely distributed round a green, on which a column-sundial combined with a pump is to be seen. The work was done for J. S. Harford in 1809, and is a very fair example of Price's type of village building. An earlier, and bad, example is Newnham Courtney, rebuilt by Lord Harcourt when William Mason was laying out the grounds. Though the cottages themselves are not unprepossessing —brick and timber—they are all identical, and line both sides of the main Oxford-London road at regular intervals. A more successful scheme was that of Milton Abbas, Dorset, with which Sir William Chambers was probably concerned in about 1775.

ARCHITECTURE

§ 4

IRREGULARITY

A. Theory

The best style for irregular and picturesque houses which can now be adopted, is that mixed style which characterizes the buildings of Claude and the Poussins.— Payne Knight, *On Taste*, 1805.

Some of the consequences, whether direct or indirect, of Reynolds's animadversions on architecture have now been traced, particularly his suggestions that Gothic and Vanbrugh might be studied, and the results be applied to classic forms. There remains his most important suggestion—" the use of accidents," the abandonment of the regular plan, and the consequent acquisition by the building of " something of scenery."

While irregularity for its own sake was aimed at by a few exponents of the Gothic revival, irrespective of either picturesque effect or convenience of plan, these latter considerations quickly asserted themselves, together with a third, particularly stressed by Payne Knight and Repton. This, called by Repton " characteristicness," was the germ of modern domestic architecture, in that it required a building, whatever its style, to proclaim above all its character. If it was intended for private residence, whether the style was castellated or monastic, classic or " mixed," the house must look like a *house*, not like a temple or castle or abbey. In the early days of the Gothic revival many bizarre solutions were offered of the difficult problem of adaptation. So long as any antique style was rigidly adhered to, the demands of the house—aspect, sash windows, convenient plan, drain-pipes, chimneys, etc.— were bound to conflict more or less acutely with the demands of the style. The problem was anything but new. The sudden recognition of its urgency at this juncture was consequent upon the collapse of the classic tradition, by which it had been largely ignored, and the rapid multiplication of eligible styles. If every house was *not* to look more or less like a temple, then equally it must not merely change its clothes and look like a castle or abbey or mosque. What had happened, in fact, was an awakening to the real nature of architecture. A realization that a classic portico or Gothic windows were not the be-all and end-all of architecture, joined itself with the elaboration of ways of living, forcing men to face fundamentals for themselves. And they didn't like them. Over a century has elapsed, and we are even now only beginning to agree upon the proper nature of a house. During all this time men have been only too glad to take a way of less resistance and adopt a " style." But throughout the complicated course of architectural development during last century one group of qualities has tended to remain constant, and can be found to have been adopted in all buildings that continue to give aesthetic satisfaction—namely, the qualities of picturesqueness. By this time the reader will not confound conscious eccentricity with picturesque principles. The treatment by Vulliamy of Dorchester House—the very choice of the Italian villa style—was picturesque. On the other hand, P. F. Robinson's Swiss Cottage (that has now given its name to a district abounding in minor picturesque architecture), whilst picturesque in intent, cannot be said to have had any principles beyond that of eccentricity. The qualities in architecture that the picturesque has caused to be most studied are relation to landscape, grouping or effective silhouette and modelling, texture, and the adoption of a plan that not only is convenient, but causative of effective modelling.

The study of texture—that is, of materials, mouldings, and wall planting—was reserved till comparatively recent years. But the other qualities were from the first given serious attention. Reynolds suggested the conformity of plan to the surface of the site. But, apart from him, Uvedale Price [1] was the earliest writer to suggest an alternative rationale to symmetry, namely planning for outlook. He instanced a site surrounded by picturesque views:

If the owner of such a spot, instead of making a regular front and sides, were to insist on having many of the windows turned towards the points where the objects were most happily arranged, the architect would be forced into the invention of a number of picturesque forms and combinations which otherwise might never have occurred to him; and would be obliged to do what so seldom has been done—accommodate his building to the scenery, not make that give way to his building.

Among the numerous advantages accruing from such a procedure, he considered that, first, " it is scarcely possible that a building so formed should not be an ornament to the landscape, from whatever point it might be viewed. Then the blank spaces that would be left where the aspect suddenly changed—which by admirers of strict regularity would be thought incurable blemishes —might, by means of trees and shrubs or of climbing plants be transformed into beauties." Then, the plan would at least be as convenient as in more uniform buildings. He was convinced, moreover, that even persons of an unpicturesque turn of mind would be charmed by the odd shapes of the rooms, " and even conceive an idea of comfort from it."

Repton to some extent adopted this procedure in his plan for Stanage,[2] where the wild and splendidly wooded park not only demanded a " gothic outline " for the house, but that the windows should command agreeable

---

[1] *Op. cit.* (1798), " Essay on Architecture," p. 368 (edition of 1842).

[2] *Fragments*, 1816.

prospects. He cited Payne Knight's neighbouring
" castle " at Downton for precedent.

It is to Knight, indeed, that we must turn for the most
vigorous championship of irregularity, not only in plan
but in the mixture of styles. Knight was all for impression, for effect, in externals, and cared nothing for
archaeological exactitude, or correspondence of interior
to exterior. The only curb he would put on " effect "
was the necessity of a country house being unmistak-
ably a country house. In his case it was primarily this
commendable intention that led him to give the least
commendable advice. Thus Downton, he maintained,
was primarily a house, although called a castle, and
" ornamented with what are called Gothic towers and
battlements without; with Grecian columns and en-
tablatures within " (with, in fact, some charming rooms
of Adam type). He was entirely satisfied with it,
" having at once the advantage of a picturesque object,
and of an elegant and convenient dwelling," and one
which could be added on to in any direction " without
injury to its genuine or original character." Nor, in
his opinion though scarcely in ours, was there " any
appearance of trick or affectation " in it. In fact, he
regarded building in a style from exactly the opposite
point of view to that which is usually ours. Mock
Gothic offends us because it is more mock than Gothic.
To Knight the " mockery " of Gothic principles constituted the only excuse for their employment. Only by
using a travesty of the style would the result avoid
being the copy of a castle or abbey, and be a " gentleman's house of the nineteenth century." It was useless to
try to get pure Gothic, since " there is no pure Gothic." [1]
Contrast was the true leading principle of Greek architecture, lightness of Gothic, wonderfully combined with
solemnity.[2] In Gothic, moreover, a small scale was
effectively employed. Whilst the use of a large scale in,

[1] Knight, *op. cit.*, p. 159.   [2] *Ibid.*, p. 172.

Fig. 2. A Hunting Lodge or Villa in the
Italian Style. From *Rural Architecture*, by
Francis Goodwin, 1835

Plate XXVI

National Gallery, Edinburgh

Plate XXVII.   REV. J. THOMSON OF DUDDINGSTON.   The Castle on the Rock

for example, St. Peter's only resulted in the vast building appearing smaller than it really was, a Gothic building seemed all the greater by reason of the minuteness of its parts. Thus he contrived to reverse Addison's and the Palladians' principle, that largeness of scale was the only source of great ideas.

Since Knight's aim was to provide a modern man with a Gothic, or more properly a " Gothistic," house, the copying of detail from originals was pointless, indeed harmful, for " the scale of its exactitude becomes that of its inconsistency." He put forward the suggestion that " gothic " houses should not be judged as copies but as original conceptions. We concede this right to Palladian buildings, but unfairly deny it to Gothistic.

A house may be adorned with towers and battlements, or pinnacles and flying buttresses ; but it should still maintain the character of a house of the age and country in which it was erected ; and not pretend to be a fortress or monastery of a remote period or distant country ; for such false pretensions never escape detection ; and, when detected, necessarily excite those sentiments which exposed imposture never fails to excite.[1]

The theory is ingenious. But it may be objected that the reasoning by which it was arrived at has the falsity inherent in the picturesque view of architecture when it is uninformed by knowledge and uncontrolled by architectural principles. A building designed solely to look well in a picture, I agree, is no more architecture than a building designed to look well in a house-agent's price-list or a manufacturer's poster. But that is not to say that a capable architect may not have these objects before his eyes. Nor is it to deny that, if judged by other than architectural standards, a picturesque building of this kind cannot be viewed with pleasure. On the contrary, if it is bad architecture, it should be with pleasurable surprise that we discover it to " compose "

---

[1] Knight, *op. cit.*, p. 218.

into picturesque scenes, just as the house-agent is delighted with a building full of "modern conveniences" and the manufacturer with works that are "posteresque."

The Gothic revival at this date would have been none the worse for just such a stimulus towards "effect" as Knight contrived to give it, had it not, like so many stimuli, been taken in excess. Wyatt raised Fonthill and Ashridge. But his imitators were tending to perpetuate the Strawberry Hill tradition, collecting details from all over the place and sticking them on to box-like structures. Repton deplored[1] that while attention was given to the details of Gothic, it was denied to that bold and irregular outline which constituted the real basis and beauty of the Gothic character.

Such opinions, united with those of Price on the merits of Vanbrugh and of the buildings painted by old masters, tended to form a picturesque standard capable of being applied to all styles, whether long established or freshly introduced. Knight, in fact, urged their mixture. Whilst pure Classic was as inappropriate as pure Gothic to modern times and, in the case of the former, to English climate and landscape, a blend of both styles could be as picturesque and convenient as was desired. The models he had in view were the buildings shown in the backgrounds of pictures by such men as Claude and Gaspar, in which Grecian and Gothic were mixed with the happiest effect.

No critic has ever yet objected to the incongruity of it: for, as the temples, tombs, and palaces of the Greeks and Romans in Italy were fortified with towers and battlements by the Goths and Lombards of the Middle Ages, such combinations have been naturalized in that country, and are therefore perfectly in harmony with the scenery; and so far from interrupting the chain of ideas, they lead it on and extend it.[2]

[1] *Fragments* (1816), Preface and Fragment VI.
[2] *Op. cit.*, p. 157.

In this country, he believed, we were becoming too great sticklers for purity, in rejecting the similar combinations (though reversed in order of date) of Gothic and Classic, as, for instance, in " the fortresses of our ancestors transformed into Italianized villas and decked with the porticos, ballustrades and terraces of Inigo Jones and Palladio." These afforded " in many instances, the most beautiful compositions, especially when mellowed by time and neglect, and harmonized by ivy, mosses and lichens." Buildings of this kind, now generally admired, he was one of the first to proclaim as picturesque—" That is (possessing) the beauty of various tints and forms happily blended without rule or symmetry, and rendered venerable by those imposing marks of antiquity which the successive modes of decoration, employed by successive ages, and each become obsolete in their turn, afford." [1]

§ 5

IRREGULARITY

B.   Practice.   1785-1845

An eye for picturesque composition and a knowledge of its principles must serve in lieu of the direct laws of symmetry and the guidance of the positive rules that in classic building used as much to help as fetter the architect.—Francis Goodwin, *Rural Architecture,* 1835.

These sixty years form a distinct phase in architectural design, during which picturesque effect tended to be the controlling factor in architecture. No style commanded sufficient acceptance to be deemed the only one suited to the needs of civilized men as was the

[1] *Op. cit.,* p. 158.

[215]

case both before and after. Instead, every style was subordinated either to its visual qualities or associated ideas. Subsequently the feeling for style revived. By 1845 it had made sufficient headway, and a sufficient number of styles had become familiar, whether the Gothic or the Tudor, the French *château* or the Italian villa, for one of them to be *de rigueur* for every building. They were all preferably used with picturesque effect. But as knowledge grew, picturesque qualities were increasingly subordinated to stylistic accuracy.

The first of the above dates is that of the publication of John Plaw's *Rural Architecture*. William Mason had published the Fourth Book of *The English Garden* four years previously, and Reynolds delivered his discourse on irregular architecture in the following year. Plaw's designs are simply " rustic," of a kind corresponding to Mason's verse or Wheatley's pictures. They are symmetrical, and of considerable charm; their chief materials plastered cob or brick, thatch, and tree trunks for supporting the thatch over verandas. The objects shown range from a " monastic farm," " American cottages," and a " Gothic fold yard " to a structure containing a convenience, but so designed that " it preserves the *equivoque* under the character and appearance of a wood pile." Plaw marks the appearance of the picturesque in architecture in its simplest form—the rustic. The second date quoted is more arbitrary. The picturesque in architecture is still with us, whether in the " plastic " houses designed by Mr. Oliver Hill, or the terra-cotta dragons in the building lots. But styles had by then emerged from the chaos that followed the collapse of classic tradition, and the acceptance of picturesque as equivalent to architectural qualities. In 1847 Ruskin published the *Seven Lamps of Architecture*, setting his seal on minute imitation. After that date a decreasing number of buildings were put up which can be said to be primarily picturesque in intention.

Picturesque architecture, then, is not, except in rare instances, a style, but a method of using and combining styles. In accordance with the three meanings of " picturesque," designs might be so described if they had objective qualities in themselves considered picturesque. Or if they aroused an association of ideas with Italian or classic landscape. Or if the character of the site required a certain style (*e.g.*, a fertile valley demanding monastic gothic) for the general effect to be picturesque. These three senses correspond roughly to the meanings given to the word respectively by Price, by Alison, and by Knight, Gilpin, and Repton.

The first sense is the only one that it is intended to pursue. The third is infinitely the most important, resulting, as it did, in the acceptance of the precept that the site should suggest and largely control the design of a building, whatever its particular style. To follow up this development is outside the scope of this work, and would be, in fact, to trace the development of the modern country house.

The second, Alisonian, sense will be no more than alluded to again, so may be briefly considered at once. Its contribution to architecture was important, since it presented in a favourable light to contemporaries the two classic styles that still continued in favour: the Greek and the Italian villa, the latter as used by Sir Charles Barry in, for instance, the Reform Club, or by Vulliamy in Dorchester House. The " classic " use of the Greek style was largely confined to towns. Claude's views of seaports full of palaces and temples were borne in mind by the designers of such works as Carlton House Terrace, Belgrave and Eaton Squares (1820-30). Piranesi begot the British Museum (1823-47). Burton's arches and screen at Hyde Park Corner (1828), and Thomas Hamilton's High School at Edinburgh (1829) —the latter recalling the Propyleia—are picturesque in effect as well as exquisite architecture, and were clearly associated with the ideal appearance of a "modern Athens." The Italian villa style had more obvious analogies in the prints and pictures of Italian cities which, by another link in the chain of ideas, were associated with the pleasure of seeing pictures in their palaces. In this sense the National Gallery, as erected from designs by William Wilkins, is admirably picturesque. Stored with pictures, it calls up at first glance ideas of classic landscape, basilicas, and Guardi to any visitor acquainted with Italy or Italian painting. Both the National Gallery and University College, Gower Street, however, are also good examples of an objectively picturesque quality being given to a Greek elevation, namely, variety of outline. Exquisite as was Wilkins' hellenism, he was a Goth at Cambridge, for instance, in the screen of King's College. With admirable results he accepted Price's advice that classic buildings should be given varied summits.

In both the preceding senses a building might be picturesque owing to the nature of the surrounding scenery or the mood of the observer. But design in itself picturesque made use of qualities which Reynolds, Price, and Knight deduced from Italian and, later, English landscape painting. Irregularity best summarizes these qualities. Irregularity of plan; the union of different styles in one building; irregularity of elevation—produced by breaking the skyline, variegating the windows, and contriving bastion-like projections and shady recesses; variation of colour and texture in surface whether by choice of materials or wall-planting;—these factors in design came to be regarded as ends in themselves. The whole building was to "compose" picturesquely into masses suggested by the buildings in the backgrounds of Italian pictures. In addition, picturesque architecture, in this sense, comprised the qualities required by the other senses in which the word was understood. It was to recall pictures generally. And was, above all, to harmonize with its setting.

Plaw's designs were picturesque in this latter sense alone, and so were Sir John Soane's *Sketches in Architecture*, published 1798, but prepared as early as 1793. In the latter work all the buildings are set in picturesque scenery; great use is made, in the designs, of light and shade, whilst such projects as a Castella d'Aqua for Wimpole, in a picturesque and sublime setting, and an ice-house in a gloomy wood over a pool, ally Soane with the ideal landscape painters as closely as Tyringham and the Bank of England connect him with Vanbrugh and Piranesi. Charles Middleton's *Picturesque and Architectural Views for Cottages, farm houses, villas, etc.*, published 1795, but prepared in 1790, contains neat, regular, verandahed houses similar to Plaw's.

Our phase, however, does not properly begin till 1798. In that year Price published the *Essay on Architecture*, and James Malton his *Essay on British Cottage Architecture*, both of which were constantly referred to by designers during the period. Malton was a charming topographical draughtsman, son of T. Malton *sen.*, and brother of T. Malton *jun.*, both well-known water-colourists. Several of James's drawings are in the Victoria and Albert Museum. His importance lies in the designs he made for cottages in a variety of traditional styles, under the direct influence of Price's *Essay on the Picturesque*, which he frequently quotes. He was dissatisfied with the existing books on cottage architecture, none of which, he said, answered his idea of it. Not all irregularity was necessarily picturesque. But " to combine irregularity into the picturesque is the excellence of cottage construction." To him the picturesque was based on Ruysdael and the Dutch landscapers, whilst he divided other scenery into the grand, as shown by Claude and Poussin, and the savage, as by Salvator Rosa and de Loutherbourg. Some of his three-roomed dwellings would produce a crisis if submitted to the Ministry of Health. But the majority are delightful and well planned, making use of such traditional materials as brick nogging, timber studding, thatch, weather board, and tiling. He had at first no bias towards Gothic, but rather introduced Georgian features such as Venetian windows in just that simple way which gives charm to so many old cottages (Plate XXIII, fig. 1). In a later book [1] the influence of Price is still more evident. Malton followed him in admiring Vanbrugh whose buildings, when placed amid woods, lawns, and waters, he considered finer than any Roman or Greek designs. His own designs exemplify irregularity. Their object, he pointed out, was to reject entirely the classical mode in favour of more picturesque forms and less expensive decoration. Thus there are strange triangular villas, stretching out domes at the end of curving wings, as though Nash's terraces in Regent's Park had been softened by heat and pulled about. Then alternatively there are castles in Gaspar Poussin's style (Plate XXIII, fig. 2).

Regular Grecian elevations with irregular plans are most characteristic of David Laing, the architect of the London Customs House, whose *Hints for Dwellings* appeared in 1801. They were picturesque in their eccentricity of plan and from several of them having been, as he tells us, " made for particular Situations, in which the Peculiarities of the surrounding Scenery have been attended to and the Style of the Building been made to correspond with its Situation." He quoted Price's remark that " the most painter-like effects may be produced by a mixture of the simplest things when properly combined with each other." A favourite plan of his was a rotunda or octagon with a pair of wings forming an angle of some 120 degrees on the front.

[1] *A Collection of Designs for Rural Retreats as Villas, principally in the Gothic and Castle styles* (1802).

Laing referred to the war as imposing economy and compactness. Picturesque architecture would undoubtedly have developed more fully, and left more frequent early examples had the country been at peace. On the other hand the lack of employment among architects encouraged some of them to publish books of designs, in which we can conveniently study the tendency of architecture. When the war ended there was a building fever, paralleled only by the activities of the last ten years which, after a pause, produced another crop of books of design, still more picturesque in character.

Richard Elsam's *Rural Architecture* (1803) protested against irregularity, whilst stressing the importance of picturesque effect. He contended that the charm of Morland's cottages arose from the *tout ensemble*, the group of cottagers before the door, the ass, the overhanging trees, rather than from any intrinsic merit in the building itself. In this, regularity was essential. He accordingly produced a variety of triangular and other eccentric plans which presented neat regular elevations, whether in the " modern elegant " or Gothic styles. Unlike Laing he stipulated that the plan should be settled first, the situation be found second.

In 1805 Knight's *Inquiry* appeared, with its encouragement of irregularity and picturesque grouping. In the following year a fresh recruit, who was to champion the picturesque both in architecture and gardening for forty years, appeared in the person of John Claudius Loudon, with the publication of *A Treatise on forming, improving and managing Country Residences*. He was an enthusiastic admirer of Price and Knight, and at first a violent opponent of Repton, particularly of his " deceptive " trick of fixing slides on his drawings of suggested improvements. He was objective in his definition of beauty, sublimity, and picturesqueness. The latter word he recognized had " been originally applied to such objects and scenes as were best suited to painting."

Now " it is applied more generally and is characterized by roughness, abruptness and irregularity, either in outline, form, disposition or colour." He held that one of the chief advantages to the architect of studying the principles of painting was that it enabled him to discriminate the " character " of any scene and then to intensify that character in his building. There was no better guide than pictures in the choice of a building's form, its composition, and relation to scenery. He had a high admiration of Vanbrugh's composition, but drew the conclusion that his work really showed " the Grecian " style to be unsuited to modern domestic needs. Of his own designs, a series in Gothic marvellously display the possibilities of irregularity, while one interesting plate shows " a house calculated for being decorated with Ivy and Creepers," with the comment: " This style would have a singular and very picturesque or perhaps romantic effect." He naturally insisted on the initial selection of the site—preferably on the margin of a lake or a rocky seashore. The style of the house could then be adapted to accentuate the character of the scene. The result should be such that no artist could resist painting it. A cardinal defect in the siting of Kedleston was that " no one would ever think of making a drawing of the scene."

From this date till after the end of the war there are no outstanding publications of designs.[1] The period, however, was partly occupied (1807-13) by Sir James Hall, Bt., of Dunglass, Haddingtonshire, a noted savant and author of a work on the origins of Gothic (1798; reprinted 1813), in rebuilding his house in a purely picturesque style that was clearly formed on the principles enunciated by Price and Loudon (Plate XXIV). The site

[1] The most notable are James Randall's *A Collection of Architectural Designs for Mansions, etc.* (1806) and W. F. Pocock's *Architectural Designs for Rustic Cottages, Picturesque Dwellings, Villas, etc., with appropriate scenery* (1807).

is on the edge of a deep ravine where the Lammermuirs come down to the sea. A few yards from the house stand the ruins of a priory church such as would have delighted William Mason or Knight. But in spite of his interest in Gothic, Hall was too keen a disciple of Price to build in that style. Entries in his accounts of payments to Alexander Nasmyth,[1] the landscape painter, "for a model of the house," suggests that he adopted Price's recommendation that an *architetto pittore* should decide the composition of the design and the treatment of the grounds. The design of the building makes it quite certain that he got the architect, Richard Crichton of Edinburgh, to study Blenheim or some other of Vanbrugh's buildings, in order to "preserve the principle of light and shadow, the effect of the raised decorations on the roof and the general grandeur and variety of the whole; but trying at the same time to give more lightness and purity of style to the whole, more elegance to the parts." Dunglass is an attempt to translate Vanbrugh into the neo-grec style of the early nineteenth century. Whilst the outline, with its octagonal tower above the ravine, was probably Nasmyth's idea, based on Claude or Gaspar, the details are an elegant version of Vanbrugh. The broken skyline of the building, set as it is on a cliff, further suggests a reading of Price's analogy between cliffs and architecture.

Contemporary with Dunglass, and of far greater influence on development, was Thomas Hope's building at Deepdene, near Dorking, of which P. Atkinson, a Gothic revivalist when left to himself, was architect. As a whole Deepdene is an Italian villa, with its campaniles, terraces, and loggias; the parent of Dorchester House and innumerable suburban villas. Hope, like Knight, was a Grecian, but no less an advocate of "irregularity" both in architecture and gardening. Loudon subsequently (1833) considered Deepdene a

[1] See Appendix, p. 266.

perfect example of grouping, massing, variety, and unity with situation. Atkinson's design for Garnons, Herefordshire, shows that he could work picturesquely in a manner derived from the fortified manor-houses of the Scottish border.

At the end of the war exhaustion gave place to an unprecedented building activity, fostered in cities and on their fringes by the industrial expansion, and in watering places by the newly recognized virtues of sea air. For the most part architects adopted the refined classicism of Nash, Wilkins, Papworth, Smirke, and young Decimus Burton, in effect setting a fashion in which Charles Barry, C. R. Cockerell, and Elmes were to make their names.

During the late 'twenties there was a remarkable revival of picturesque principles. A group of architects and writers discovered Price and Knight.[1] Of these the most conventional, but the most engaging, was J. Thomson (1800-1883). His book is illustrated with delightful coloured aquatints, each design introduced with a sententious preface, and the designs themselves extraordinarily ingenious. He called each after its dominating characteristic. Thus there is Grecian Cottage, Uniform Cottage, Family Villa, Corinthian Villa, and (perfect name for a residence), Irregular House (Plate XXVI, fig. 2). The latter is a masterpiece of compact eccentricity:

Each elevation differs from the rest. The Portico forms a striking object in the entrance front. A tower-like appearance

---

[1] The most important books are these: P. F. Robinson, *Rural Architecture* (1823), four editions; *Designs for Ornamental Villas* (1827); *Designs for Farm Buildings* (1830); *Village Architecture, being a Series of Designs illustrating the observations contained in the Essay on the Picturesque by Sir Uvedale Price* (1830); *Vitruvius Britannicus, including drawings of Hatfield, Hardwicke, and Castle Ashby* (1833-1844); *Domestic Architecture in the Tudor Style, selected from buildings erected after designs by P. F. Robinson* (1837). J. Thomson, *Retreats* (1827). T. F. Hunt, *Architettura Campestre* (1827). G. L. Meason, *On the Landscape Architecture of the Great Painters of Italy* (1827), 150 copies only printed.

is assumed on the west side. To the north, a colonnade presents itself, and the east end is relieved by a rotunda.

The object of irregular houses was that " they convey the appearance of greater magnitude than they actually possess, and create great variety of outline." This house was suitable to a bachelor who needed a private museum. Numerous villas in Thomson's style can be seen in the neighbourhood of Maida Vale and St. John's Wood.[1]

The main impulse of the other books published in 1827 was Italian domestic architecture. T. F. Hunt was one of the earliest architects to make practical recommendations for producing picturesque texture. He laid stress on " the new Italian style," and strongly recommended the adoption of Italian tiles as " a picturesque mode of roofing." Hunt is one of the earliest advocates of campaniles, many of which he introduced into his designs. He was considerate of those who drew their relish for the picturesque from literature, prefacing each description with a quotation from Shenstone, Mason, Cowper, and even Bacon. Burke's remark about designs that are vast only by their dimensions being the sign of common low imagination was prefixed to a design for a diminutive campanile containing a garden seat.

P. F. Robinson (1776-1858)[2] was an architect with a large practice and one of the first designers in the Tudor style (subsequently to be studied by Salvin), on which he wrote several books. His picturesque mind, however, turned for preference to older and stranger forms. He designed the original Swiss Cottage in St. John's Wood (1829-32) and Egyptian Hall in Piccadilly (1823).

[1] In 1827 he designed Cumberland Terrace and Place, Regent's Park, and subsequently laid out an estate at Notting Hill. In 1840 he read a paper to the R.I.B.A. on " Vanbrugh and Composition in Architecture."

[2] A pupil of Holland, Lancelot Brown's architect.

His *Designs for Farm Buildings* (1830) consist of beautifully lithographed pencil sketches showing how the same farmyard, carpenter's shop, or cow-house could be treated in the Swiss, Italian, or Old English manner. A similar method characterizes *Designs for Ornamental Villas* (1827); Swiss, Grecian, Palladian, Anglo-Norman, Elizabethan, Timber, and Tuscan designs succeeding one another. Their merit is largely dependent on the skill with which he presents them in scenic settings. He considered that such " scenic drawings " should invariably be made when a house was projected, and noted that the habit was not nearly prevalent enough. In his explanatory notes he constantly recommends a design as " peculiarly picturesque."

He quoted Price as the originator of the cottage or manor-house style, and his admiration of him led him, three years later, to work out his suggestions for a whole village. Various cottages, shops, almshouses, a workhouse, a parsonage were designed with commendable knowledge of timber architecture. The church and town hall were more fancifully Gothic. Our plate of the village street (Plate XXV) shows how sympathetically Price's lead was being followed by at least one well-known architect. And Robinson felt strongly the menace, still graver to-day, of

the London tall and unsightly brick house with the modern shop front [that] has usurped the place of the modest gable in the most distant parts of the country. . . . A little taste and feeling may stem the torrent, and, as many houses have recently been erected in the Old English style, it may be hoped that our Cottage Architecture may at length meet with some attention.

Almost exactly a hundred years later the Royal Society of Arts and the new Council for the Preservation of Rural England have taken up the cause of the picturesque almost in the same words.

As Robinson took Price as his source of ideas, Thomas Laing Meason, in a book that excited a remarkable influence in proportion to its restricted impression, went back to Knight. Meason was another of the amateur squires who played so prominent a part in the picturesque movement. His place was Lindertis, Forfar, a Gothic house by Archibald Elliot. He took as his text Knight's passage that I have put at the head of Section 4, asserting that the best style for irregular and picturesque houses was that which characterized the buildings in Claude's and the Poussins' pictures. His book consists of sixty drawings of buildings from Italian painted landscape, some of them alleged to be as early as Giotto, and ranging through Raphael, Titian, and Michael Angelo, to Giulio Romano and Solimena. He assumed that the buildings shown in the pictures were based on existing buildings, and that these had been originally Roman villas, partly ruined, and partly fortified by the Goths and Lombards; in some cases even adorned at the Renaissance. His object was to assist architects in the composition of irregular mansions. Great masses and " breadth " were the characteristics of picturesque building. Texture should be given by the use of rough stone, not ashlar, whereby modern architects had spoilt many potentially picturesque conceptions.

With Meason we come as close as we ever do to a picturesque style. But it was one thing to make pencil sketches of romantic castles, with dots and dashes for the windows, and another, as architects discovered, to make detailed drawings that avoided all known stylistic details. Still, the attempt was frequently made, as numerous mansions and villas testify, to which it is impossible to assign any style—buildings with round-headed windows, gables, campaniles. They are the products of the picturesque phase of architecture.

A good example, that incorporates most of these features in a grouping reminiscent of Vanbrugh and

[227]

paintings, is Francis Goodwin's (1784-1835)[1] " Hunting Lodge or Villa in the Italian Style " (Plate XXVI). Here he has let his eye for picturesque composition " serve in lieu " of classic or any other rules. His comments on his designs are curiously deprecatory. In this case he regretted that " there is little to be said on the exterior, beyond that it has a certain piquancy." However, a tower such as he had worked in enabled " ladies of the family to accompany the sportsmen in the chace with their eyes if not more amazonially on horseback; or with a telescope to observe the approach of the unbidden or undesired." He was more proud of a " rustic Greek " style that he evolved, in which columns were made of lengths of rough stone of different thickness, and lattice windows were combined with classical pediments. His designs for cottages were prefaced by the comment that they were " undoubtedly more in the style of such cottages as young ladies built in their dreams than of those which Gainsborough and Morland painted." That was precisely the difficulty that the picturesque approach to architecture encountered. It was far easier for architects to design buildings that were picturesque through sentiment or an association of ideas than in appearance.

This phase of architecture culminated, so far as books are concerned, in the prodigious *Encyclopaedia of Cottage, Farm and Villa Architecture and Furniture*, compiled by J. C. Loudon, published in 1833 (enlarged edition 1842), and containing upwards of 1300 pages. Numerous architects contributed designs and specifications which were printed together with Loudon's criticisms.

[1] *Rural Architecture. Designs for Rustic, Peasants' and Ornamental Cottages, Lodges and Villas*, by Francis Goodwin. 2 vols., 1835. Goodwin had a considerable practice in Lancashire and Staffordshire, where he built churches and town halls. The Town Hall, Manchester, his *chef-d'œuvre*, was begun in 1819. He died of apoplexy when working on competitive designs for the new Houses of Parliament. They were subsequently published.

In the collection of P. M. Turner, Esq.

Plate XXVIII.   JOHN HOPPNER, R.A.   A Landscape

Plate XXIX. JOHN CONSTABLE. The Cornfield

As final arbiter he appears to have employed Sir Charles Barry, who was responsible for the designs of " the Beau Ideal of an English Villa " in the Tudor style. Every class of country building and style was copiously represented, but Loudon's picturesque attitude to them all is illustrated by his asserting:

If there is one test rather than another by which the taste or no taste of an Architect can be detected with certainty (always supposing that he is master of the mechanical rules of the art), it is the degree of perfection which he has attained in sketching general scenery.

This really marks the beginning of the " sketchesque " phase of architecture, in which architects were encouraged to fill their sketch-books with picturesque details from foreign buildings to be incorporated in future designs. Loudon gave a number of details for porches and campaniles " from the portfolio of a young Architect lately returned from a professional tour through Italy." The chief drawback of this pleasant habit is that nothing short of a measured drawing can ensure the accurate reproduction of the " charming feature." Not the least cause of much vile architecture of last century is the inaccuracy of borrowed features.

Soon a greater force than Loudon, or Knight, or Reynolds was to arise. To Ruskin we owe the triumph, complete while it lasted, of Gothic over Classic. A Gothic, moreover, that based its claim to beauty not on its picturesque effect at a distance, but on its understanding and imitation of mediaeval forms, aspirations, and details. It is, however, from Ruskin's, and in a greater degree from Morris's, teaching on the value of sincerity and craftsmanship, that modern architects derive their ideals of form expressive of plan and purpose, and of harmonious texture. A country house by any of the hundreds of capable architects of to-day may seem a long way from Reynolds's *Discourses* and Thomson's

Seasons. But through Ruskin they derive from the obscure gentlemen whose works we have been glancing at; through them from Price, Knight, Malton, and Meason; and thence from Gainsborough and Morland, Claude, and Salvator Rosa.

Whatever Ruskin might write, moreover, the picturesque point of view had been sufficiently engrained in architects of his own age for Barry and Pugin to raise the Houses of Parliament, G. E. Street the Law Courts, Gilbert Scott St. Pancras Station and, under Palmerston's pressure, the renaissance Foreign Office. These buildings, however unattractive in detail, are picturesquely suited to their sites, and in the blue haze of London's winter have all the mystery of romance and the intricacy and variety that Reynolds desired. The view of the Foreign Office from the bridge in St. James's Park, in which architecture and landscape gardening are united, might have been sketched by a Claude, imagined by a Vanbrugh, and would undoubtedly have ravished a Price. It is the grandest of the nineteenth-century's conceptions of the Picturesque.

Chapter VII

LANDSCAPE, WITH FIGURES

§ 1

THE PICTURESQUE NOVEL

" *It is very true,*" *said Marianne,* " *that admiration of landscape scenery has become a mere jargon.   Everybody pretends to feel and tries to describe it with the taste and elegance of him who first defined what picturesque beauty was.*"

" *I like a fine prospect,*" *said Edward,* " *but not on picturesque principles.   I do not like crooked, twisted, blasted trees, I admire them much more if they are tall, straight and flourishing.   I am not fond of nettles or thistles or heath blossoms.*"

Marianne looked with amazement at Edward.

"Sense and Sensibility."

ANOTHER appearance of the picturesque that still remains to be noticed is in the novel. Following on Horace Walpole's *Castle of Otranto* came what Professor Elton calls " the novel of suspense," or, as the writers themselves sometimes called their works, the " gothic romance."   At first the mediaeval trappings monopolized the descriptive passages, but Charlotte Smith, a pupil of George Smith of Chichester, the painter, and Mrs. Ann Radcliffe described landscapes with gusto in the manners of Claude and Salvator. Neither had ever visited the Mediterranean lands in which the majority of their stories were set.   But prints and paintings obviously supplied the want of first-hand impressions.   Mrs. Radcliffe in particular visualized every scene as if it had been painted, exhibiting her figures through a picture frame.   Her popularity was not a little owing to the delight with which her readers beheld live people wandering, galloping, sailing, and having innumerable adventures, in pictures. She brought the " landscape with figures " to life.

This was something new to novel-readers. The writers of the Georgian epoch were not unappreciative of scenery. But such landscape as they mention is very uncertain and very much in the background. They paint portraits rather than prospects. Fielding, who had a relish for landscape gardening, occasionally described the settings of scenes in *Tom Jones*, and Smollett made Matthew Bramble a critic of painting and landscape. Graves is in a little class by himself with *Columella, or the Spiritual Quixote* (1773), painting, in the latter, numerous picturesque backgrounds. *The Life of John Buncle* (1750-66), by Thomas Amory, was the earliest novel in which picturesque description was allowed to hold up the narrative. But male writers tended to ridicule the sentiment for landscape. It was not till the lady novelists began to capture the romance-market that heroines went sketching and carried pocket volumes of Thomson to lonely cascades, or heroes were endued with the "taste and enthusiasm to enjoy" sublime prospects. Charlotte Smith's yearly novels[1] suggest a careful reading of Gilpin and considerable knowledge of engravings. But by 1795, when she published the second edition of *The Banished Man*, she was beginning to feel the powerful competition of Mrs. Radcliffe, and complained that

My ingenious contemporaries have so fully possessed themselves of every bastion and buttress, of every gallery and gateway, together with all their furniture of ivy mantles and mossy battlements, tapestry and old pictures, owls, bats and ravens, that I . . . have hardly a watch-tower, a Gothic arch, a cedar parlour, an illumined window left to help myself.

Later, in 1799 (*Letters of a Solitary Wanderer*), she

[1] Among them *Emmeline, the Orphan of the Castle* (1788), *Ethelinde, or the Recluse of the Lake* (1789), and *The Old Manor House* (1793).

assured her readers that "should I meet with either ghost or banditti, I will not fail to engage them to

> Deepen the horror of the falling floods,
> And breathe a browner horror on the woods,"

as well as in "any novel in the very newest taste." In *Rural Walks* (1800), "Dialogues intended for the use of young persons," she recommended an eye for the picturesque as enhancing the charms of nature, as warmly as ever did Marianne or Elinor Dashwood to Edward Ferrers in *Sense and Sensibility* (first draft 1797-8; published 1811). Charlotte Smith even more strongly approved of sketching which, besides providing a resource, might even be a solace in adversity.

This it actually had been to one of Mrs. Radcliffe's heroines—the hapless Emily in *The Mysteries of Udolpho* (1794). Though the novel is laid in the year 1584 Emily, after her attempted abduction and a duel fought over her person, "checked her propensity to anticipate evil; . . . took her instruments for drawing and placed herself at a window, to select into a landscape some of the features of the scenery without." Her thoughts doubtless flew back to that room which she had used to call her own, "adjoining the eastern side of the greenhouse" at her home among the Pyrenees, then remote indeed from this prison among the Apennines. There she had "her books, her drawings, her musical instruments with some favourite birds and plants." Most of Mrs. Radcliffe's young ladies, whatever costume they might wear, had been brought up in such houses, recalling the rural retreats of John Plaw or Soane, and had read their Gilpin and Thomson. The following "sunrise" out of *Udolpho* is a close transcription of Thomson's lines (quoted on p. 41) and has caught the secret of Claude's and Wilson's luminous glow:

The dawn, which softened the scenery with its peculiar gray :int, now dispersed, and Emily watched the progress of the day, first trembling on the tops of the highest cliffs, then touching them with splendid light, while their sides, and the vale below, were still wrapt in dewy mist. Meanwhile the sullen gray of the eastern clouds began to blush, then to redden, and then to glow with a thousand colours, till the golden light darted over all the air, touched the lower parts of the mountain's brow, and glanced in long sloping beams upon the valley and its stream. The spirit of St. Aubert was renovated. His heart was full ; he wept ; and his thoughts ascended to the Great Creator.

Among scenes of beauty Mrs. Radcliffe's folk were generally moved to think of " the Great Author of their being." Virtue, she made one of them explain, and taste are nearly the same; for virtue is little more than active taste; and the most delicate affections of each combine in real love. This is little different from Shaftesbury's attitude to beauty, yet the beauty was of the kind that painting had revealed. It is picturesque beauty merging into the romantic; it "softens the heart like the notes of sweet music and inspires that delicious melancholy which no person who has felt it once would resign for the gayest pleasures."

In contrast to Claudian beauty Mrs. Radcliffe wielded the dashing brush of Salvator. Occasionally she could not refrain from mentioning the source of her inspiration at the risk of an anachronism: " This was such a scene as Salvator would have chosen had he then existed, for his canvass." Such scenes repeatedly occur, as in this, of a gipsy encampment:

Emily looked with some degree of terror on the savage countenances of these people, shown by the fire, which heightened the romantic effect of the scenery as it threw a red dusky gleam upon the rocks and on the foliage of the trees. . . . The whole formed a picture highly grotesque. The travellers plainly saw their danger.

As the romance proceeds, and Emily enters the

clutches of the villain Montoni, who carries her from Venice to Udolpho, the sublime and terrible become more frequent. The very approach is dark with foreboding, for Mrs. Radcliffe saw Gothic picturesquely:

"There," said Montoni, speaking for the first time in several hours, "is Udolpho."

Emily gazed with melancholy awe upon the castle, for though it was lighted up by the setting sun, the Gothic greatness of its features, and its mouldering walls of dark gray stone, rendered it a gloomy and sublime object.

Once within its walls we move through labyrinths of vaults " dropping with unwholesome dews," barred by iron gates, and replete with hollow groans and things suspiciously like corpses. Udolpho takes on the appearance of a Piranesian *carcere*:

As they crossed the first court, the light showed the black walls around them, fringed with long grass and dark weeds that found a scanty soil among the mouldering stones, the heavy buttresses, with here and there between them a narrow grate, the massy iron gates of the castle, whose clustering turrets appeared above, opposite the huge towers of the portal itself.

The rooms we peer into are heavily panelled, with high, antiquated casements, furniture of ancient date, beds of blue damask, and arras worked in grotesque legend. Whole wings in castles are deserted and entice the footsteps of adventurous heroines.

A Sicilian Romance (1790), the earliest of Mrs. Radcliffe's picturesque romances, following the Ossianic *Castles of Athlin and Dunbayne* (1789), contains many of the most vigorous paintings, and foreshadows the procedure adopted in its successors.[1] The labyrinthine vaults, halls, staircases, and galleries, haunted by groans

[1] *The Romance of the Forest* (1791), *Udolpho* (1794), *The Italian* (1797), *Gaston de Blondeville* (posthumous, 1826).

and echoes, that riddle her castles, are all explored at midnight by the light of a flickering lamp. The "supernatural machinery" advocated by Bishop Hurd [1] is put to its fullest use, although Mrs. Radcliffe was careful to reveal, seriatim, that the groans and spectres had rational explanations. One section of this particular work is the nearest approach to the cinematograph-picturesque towards which Mrs. Radcliffe's method was always moving. She systematically flickered paintings before her readers' eyes, the characters making their way from canvas to canvas. In *A Sicilian Romance* there is a *pursuit*, and the pictures melt into one another without interruption. The wicked Duke, pursuing an eloping couple, gallops all over the island, through interminable forests, dismal plains, ghastly mountains. Each night finds him and his men in the midst of terrific desolation, whether on heaths or among crags. One night he stumbles for shelter into a banditti's cavern— and finds his long-lost son their captain; next night he discovers a " large and gloomy " monastery by a burst of moonlight; penetrates it; is told the monks are all at prayer, but discovers them actually occupied in a bacchanalian scene in the refectory, that recalls Magnasco's monastic revels. On the following night his shelter is a vast and gloomy deserted mansion, but next morning he comes into " a beautifully romantic country " in the style of Wilson. Reaching " the summit of some wild cliffs," he pauses to view the picturesque imagery of the scene below. " A shadowy sequestered dell appeared buried deep among the rocks, and in the bottom was seen a lake whose clear bosom reflected the impending cliffs and the beautiful luxuriance of the overhanging shades." The " figures " in the scene were partaking of a repast, and were, he concluded, the objects of his pursuit.

There is a series of monastic pictures, gloomy and

1 *Letters on Chivalry and Romance* (1762).

glittering with stained glass, and plenty of clearly visualized landscapes:

There appeared on a point of rock impending over the valley the reliques of a palace, whose beauty time had impaired only to heighten its sublimity. An arch of singular magnificence remained almost entire, beyond which appeared wild cliffs, retiring in grand perspective.

It is unnecessary to remind the reader that there is a great deal more than landscape to Mrs. Radcliffe. She is a past mistress of horrors, which she always uses, however, with an eye to their picturesque effect. She makes us see, even if we do not feel, the nightmare scenes through which her puppets pass. The male writers of the bizarre are far less descriptive. Lewis's *Monk* (1795), Moore's *Zeluco* (1786), and Maturin's tales represent not so much pictures as " those struggles of passion when the soul trembles on the verge of the unlawful and the unhallowed." This is particularly true of the latter's masterpiece, *Melmoth the Wanderer* (1820). As he had confessed earlier, the Radcliffian " style of writing was out when I was a boy, and I had not the power to revive it." More accurately he did not need, could not restrict himself to, picturesque vision. Like Byron, Shelley, Scott, and Turner in his later phase, he gives an impression, not a pictorial description, of scenes. The state of mind of the protagonists is what interests him, not their appearance in a succession of landscapes. Just as it was only the second-rate poets who described picturesquely after the Wartons, it was only the second-rate novelists who visualized through a picture frame after Mrs. Radcliffe. Typical of these was T. S. Surr, whose *Winter in London* (1806) is picturesque in a Gilpin-de Loutherbourg style, interesting for its presentation of contemporary English life. The young hero

found himself unawares at the brink of a precipice which overhung a natural cascade, whose waters, tumbling down the craggy sides of a steep cliff, formed at its base a little river which divided the grounds of Roseville Park from those of Beauchamp Abbey. On each side of the eminence he saw a park and mansion : but in nothing were they similar. On his right the ivy mantled towers of Beauchamp Abbey bounded the view of a thickly wooded domain, where huge oaks, the growth of centuries, waved over long dark terraces of grass which the mower's scythe had not visited for years. Grottoes of shell-work surmounted with ill formed images of stone ; hermitages with straw-thatched roofs, formed together a display of taste which, while it impressed the thought " that grandeur once dwelt here " at the same time told the beholder the date of its desertion.

The modern park, to the right, " planted with trees of all species to produce an effect " was obviously by Repton, though " the growing palace of Mr. Sawyer Dickins " that " rose daily higher and higher till the grand portico showed itself above the green waving branches of the newly planted park " should more properly have been baronial. The most picturesque passage is that describing a " masquerade " in Lord Roseville's London house, at which the Prince Regent was present. The house and gardens had been transformed into a number of " scenes "—a Moorish alhambra, a gallery disguised as an Egyptian temple, and the garden of a Turkish seraglio where a pavilion was prepared for the Regent's supper. In contrast to this brilliantly lighted scene the next,

under the skilful management of Carbonel, Loutherbourg and that promising young artist, Kerr Porter,[1] with the assistance of some amateurs of fashion, represented a tract of the dreary desert of Arabia at the hour of midnight.

---

[1] Louis Carrogis Carbonel (1717-1806), perfected the " transparency " ; worked in France. Robert Kerr Porter lived in Reynolds's old studio, 16 Great Newport Street, Leicester Square, and there convened, 20th May 1799, " a select society of Young Painters," including Thomas Girtin and F. L. Francia.

LANDSCAPE, WITH FIGURES

No words can convey to the imagination a just conception of the gloomy grandeur of this panoramic deception. So elegantly was it executed that ladies actually shrieked at the well counterfeited howlings of beasts of prey, and of the hollow whistling blasts of wind, which seemed alternately to scatter and collect heaps of sand. At the extremity of the scene was a well executed design of the ruins of a species of ancient temple. . . . Behind the remains of an uncouth arch, appeared a light issuing through the mouth of a cavern, from the fires of a troop of wandering Arabs, whose camels were seen crouching among the ruins.

De Loutherbourg, pupil of Vernet, scene-painter, royal academician, occultist, and maker of the Eidophusikon, is the archetype of the picturesque painter. As Thomson and Mrs. Radcliffe had transformed pictures into poetry and novels respectively, and the gardeners had formed pictures with real trees and buildings, "Leatherbag" contrived his panorama, which he called the Eidophusikon, so as to realize pictures in all four dimensions. As a landscape painter he will be noticed later. During his first ten years in England (1771-81) his most important work was theatrical scenery design, into which he introduced many novel effects both of painting and lighting. But in 1781 he put his skill to producing an entertainment exclusively scenic, describing it as "Various Imitations of Natural Phenomena, represented by Moving Pictures." It made a great sensation. Reynolds praised it warmly, and "Gainsborough was so delighted with the Eidophusikon that for a time he thought of nothing else, talked of nothing else, and passed his evenings at the exhibition in long succession."[1]

[1] W. H. Pine, *Wine and Walnuts*, 2nd ed., 1824, vol. i, chap. xxi. Gainsborough even made a toy Eidophusikon of his own, shown at the Grosvenor Gallery in 1885. It was formerly in the possession of Dr. Monro, and is stated to have consisted of painted glass slides. These, or a set very like them, known to have been at Monro's house, are still in existence.

The first exhibition consisted of five scenes:

1. Aurora ; or the Effects of the Dawn, with a View of London from Greenwich Park.
2. Noon ; the Port of Tangier in Africa, with the distant View of the Rock of Gibraltar.
3. Sunset ; a View near Naples.
4. Moonlight ; a View of the Mediterranean, the Rising of the Moon contrasted with the Effect of Fire.
5. The Conclusive Scene, a Storm at Sea, and Shipwreck.

Pyne has described some of the scenes which he saw when a boy. The first scene showed the Observatory on the left " conspicuous in its picturesque eminence " and the Hospital at its foot. Beyond lay Deptford and Greenwich, the river winding westwards, the northern hills in the distance, and, in the middle distance, on the flat stage, the pool and port of London, " each mass being cut out in pasteboard. . . . The heathy appearance of the foreground was constructed of cork, broken into the rugged and picturesque form of a sandpit covered with minute mosses and lichens, producing a captivating effect, amounting indeed to reality."[1] When the curtain rose the scene was bathed in the mysterious light of dawn. Gradually the day broke—a streak of saffron, pink light on clouds, then the first rays gilding the tree-tops and vanes—till at length the prospect was flooded with golden light. Subsequently the " conclusive scene " was given topical interest by being adapted to represent the wreck of the " Halsewell " East Indiaman, described at the time as an " exact, awful and tremendous Representation of that lamentable Event." Loutherbourg also devised an alternative *finale* representing an equally sublime scene—" the region of the fallen angels, with Satan arraying his troops on the banks of the Fiery Lake " and the uprising of that Palace of

[1] For Gainsborough's adoption of this practice, see p. 64 *supra*, and note.

Pandemonium described in *Paradise Lost.* Pyne saw

in the foreground of a vista, stretching an immeasurable length between mountains ignited from their bases to their lofty summits with many coloured flame, a chaotic mass rising in dark majesty, which gradually assumed form until it stood, the interior of a vast temple of gorgeous architecture, bright 'as molten brass, seemingly composed of unconsuming and unquenchable fire. In this tremendous scene the effect of coloured glasses before the lamps was fully displayed,—

changing the hues from sulphurous blue and lurid red to livid brightness, whilst resounding peals of thunder added a preternatural horror, heightened " by a variety of groans that struck the imagination as issuing from infernal spirits." [1]

Between the scenes Michael Arne, son of Dr. Arne, played a sonata of Schubert, and at other times Dr. Burney obliged. At the same time " Transparencies " were exhibited. These were another evolution from the habit of regarding things as pictures, and had considerable vogue during the last quarter of the eighteenth century. In effect the transparency was a precursor of the magic lantern, consisting of continuous designs on thin paper, the passage of which from one roller to another, in front of a lamp, revealed to the spectators a procession of figures set in suitable landscapes. Carmontelle introduced the diversion to France in about 1765, and Angelo, the well-known Eton character, claimed that his father initiated the process in England from a *tableau mouvant* that he had seen at Venice, receiving the approbation of Gainsborough, Wilson, and other painters.

Walter Scott accepted the picturesque and fused it into his romances together with all their other ingredients. His minutely described landscapes are directly

[1] The fullest account of the Eidophusikon is to be found in Austin Dobson's *At Prior Park*, 1912.

felt, not seen, as Mrs. Radcliffe saw hers, through a picture frame. Only second-rate writers continued, after *Waverley*, to be conscious of the picturesque.

An important exception was the most sophisticated of novelists, Peacock, who was conscious of everything yet subscribed to none. Throughout his novels the picturesque crops up repeatedly as one of the crotchets that he alternately ridicules and caresses. His footnotes show him to have been familiar with the writings of Price, Knight, Gilpin, Repton, and their reviewers. In *Headlong Hall* (1816) Sir Patrick O'Prism represents the theories of Price and Knight, Marmaduke Milestone those of Repton:

" Sir," said Mr. Milestone, " you will have the goodness to make a distinction between the picturesque and the beautiful."

" Will I ? " said Sir Patrick, " och ! but I won't, for what is beautiful ? That which pleases the eye. And what pleases the eye ? Tints variously broken and blended. Now, tints variously broken and blended constitute the picturesque."

" Allow me," said Mr. Gale (who, with Mr. Treacle, was a very profound critic from Edinburgh), " I distinguish the picturesque and the beautiful and add to them, in the laying out of grounds, a third and distinct character, which I call *unexpectedness*."

" Pray, sir," said Mr. Milestone, " by what name do you distinguish this character when a person walks round the grounds for a second time ? "

In *The Misfortunes of Elphin* (1829)—that gorgeous blend of Welsh legend and nineteenth-century satire— he shows himself as a sincere lover of picturesque scenery—yet not an unconscious one. When the great sea-wall had burst during the storm, and the chief characters were making their escape along its remnants,

The bard, who had something of a picturesque eye, could not help sparing a little leisure from the care of his body to observe the effects before him: the volumed blackness of the storm; the white bursting of the breakers in the faint and scarcely perceptible moonlight; the long floating hair and waving drapery of the young women. . . .

Taliesin's first view of Caer Lleon is made the occasion for a dig at " the sentimental tourist (who, perching himself on an old wall, works himself up into a soliloquy of philosophical pathos on the vicissitudes of empires, interrupted only by an occasional peep at his watch, to ensure his not over-staying the minute at which his fowl, comfortably roasting at the nearest inn, has been promised to be ready)." In *Melincourt* (1817) he had already had at tourists when Mr. Forester remarked, of a road in the Lakes, " I have no wish to exclude the visits of laudable curiosity, but there is nothing I so much dread as the intrusion of those heartless fops, who take their fashionable autumn tour, to gape at rocks and waterfalls, for which they have neither eyes nor ears." Yet in *Crotchet Castle* (1831) one of his most crotchety crotcheteers—Mr. Chainmail— has three glimpses of a lovely nymph in three sensitively painted scenes—a tarn, a ruined castle, and across a chasm:

She was asleep. Below the pool two beetle-browed rocks nearly overarched, leaving just such a space at the summit as was within the possibility of a leap; the torrent roared below in a fearful gulf.

The idealism that Mr. Priestley[1] has observed to have been at the bottom of Peacock's satire, accepted and loved the picturesque. His ideal world, perpetually contrasted with the one produced by " the march of mind," is the world of Gilpin, to whom his clerics bear a remote family resemblance. Yet he could not forget that the very taste that enabled him to behold this ideal world was nothing but a fashion. He expressed this

[1] *Thomas Love Peacock*, by J. B. Priestley (English Men of Letters Series), 1927.

realization through the mouth of the Hon. Mrs. Pin-
money in *Melincourt* :

> Tastes—they depend on fashion. There is always a fashion-
> able taste: a taste for driving the mail—a taste for acting
> Hamlet—a taste for the marvellous—a taste for the simple—a
> taste for the sombre—a taste for the tender—a taste for
> banditti—a taste for ghosts—a taste for the devil—a taste for
> picturesque tours—a taste for taste itself, or for essays on taste ;—
> but no gentleman would be so rash as to have a taste of his own,
> or his last winter's taste, or any taste, my love, but the fashion-
> able taste. Poor dear Mr. Pinmoney was reckoned a man of
> exquisite taste among all his acquaintance; for the new taste,
> let it be what it would, always fitted him as well as his new
> coat. So much for tastes, my dear.

And so much for the taste for the Picturesque.

§ 2

PICTURESQUE PAINTING

> *The picturesque is merely that kind of beauty which
> belongs exclusively to the sense of vision. . . . The eye,
> unassisted, perceives nothing but light, variously graduated
> and modified.*—The Dialogue (Uvedale Price and Payne
> Knight), 1801.

In relation to painting itself, " picturesque " means,
loosely, " reminiscent." With " architectural " architecture and " poetic " poetry, picturesque painting can
be said to be a pastiche—an assembly of conventional
objects conventionally seen adding nothing to our
experience.

I want to give it a more precise significance.

Ruskin[1] used the term as " the degradation (some-

---

[1] *Modern Painters*, vol. v.

times the undeveloped state) of Contemplative Landscape; "—the painting, of which he held Turner to be
the supreme exponent, that is concerned with observing
the powers of nature. He made the term apply to
pictures meant to display the skill of the artist and his
powers of composition, or to provide agreeable forms
and colours, but which lacked intensity of feeling. This
more compact sense of picturesque painting might be
described as the synthesis of the inferior qualities of
both classic and romantic art: Claude's composition
and Rembrandt's technique.

The picturesque phase through which perception
passed between 1730 and 1830 has been shown to have
been the transitional stage between intellectual, classic
art that, generally speaking, stimulates the mind, and the
imaginative art of the nineteenth century that interested
itself rather with emotion or sentiment. Classic art
makes you think, imaginative art makes you feel. But
picturesque art merely makes you see. It records without contemplating. To that extent Ruskin's definition
of picturesque painting holds good.

But what does it see? When the theory of ideal forms
was relinquished as a rationale for painters, they had to
cease thinking what would be the most beautiful shape
for an object, and to look at it as it was, and to paint
that aspect of it that most moved them. The painter,
pure and simple, if he has nothing in him of the draughtsman or sculptor, naturally sees (*a*) qualities in objects
that make him itch, not to model or draw curves, but
to paint, and (*b*) the effects of light. The feeling for
solid form is, essentially, the sculptor's; for design the
draughtsman's. For the painter to address himself to
either, primarily, is unnatural. All three are essential
to a work of art, to a " picture." But for a " painting,"
which is all that the picturesque point of view can aspire
to produce alone, form and rhythm are *ultra vires*.

When painters, then, ceased to look at nature, in

Reynolds's phrase "with the eyes of a poet," they looked at her, as he said of Gainsborough, with the eyes of a painter. They looked for qualities in objects that were asking to be painted; that were, in fact, picturesque. The chief qualities they selected were roughness, lusciousness of texture, glinting, sparkling surfaces, the crumbling and decayed. These they found in the objects now known as picturesque; sandy lanes, dock leaves, gnarled trees, hovels, donkeys, and ruins. Their brushes were attracted to the rendering of these qualities, because they were well suited to paint. No moral feeling entered into the business, though sentiment was attached to many of these objects, particularly to rural scenes and ruins. But there was a great deal of sensuous feeling for texture. With a collection of these objects and qualities, then, the painter made a picture. The objects were, preferably, symbols of affecting ideas, and they were to be rendered "paintily." The picture was to appeal to the imagination educated on old masters.

The most complete examples of pictures that are picturesque in this sense are those by Morland. Apart from the sentiment attached to horses and rural scenes, they have not an atom of feeling beyond the feeling for paintiness—picturesqueness. Every object that they contain has been inserted because it is picturesque—eminently suited for painting.

Apart from picturesque qualities, the painter saw light. Whilst Gainsborough was the founder of the "rough" picturesque, Wilson was the master of light, surpassing Claude. It was he, more than any other, who directed the eyes of eighteenth-century painters to the painting of sunlit atmosphere and, as a consequence, of sunlit surfaces. When the theories of the picturesque came to be worked out, it was with light that they were primarily interested. While Uvedale Price restricted the picturesque to objects themselves, Payne Knight used the word as a term for abstract vision. The picturesque was merely that kind of beauty which belonged exclusively to the sense of vision. And since, in his opinion, the eye unassisted perceived nothing but light variously gradated and modified, picturesque beauty was the beauty of light falling on surfaces in such a way as to irritate the optic nerve agreeably.

Here, then, we have a meaning for picturesque painting with a large application to actual works. To the merely sensuous properties of Morland's objects and technique is added the abstract appreciation of the action of light. Great art, permanent art, is only produced when truth is perceived abstractly, apart from its empirical associations. There is a cow. Morland paints her, delighting in the luscious roughness of her tawny coat. Constable paints her, and we feel the light playing on her angular form, till it has a life of its own, that we instantly recognize as true. Cézanne might paint that cow, and her form would be more intensely significant. Or Van Gogh, and she would be the most vitally red cow we had ever seen, tremendously cowish. These last three interpretations might be crude, but they would be art, because the painters had felt intensely. Constable's cow would, in addition, be picturesque, because the qualities that he felt consciously were those that, at the time, were recognized as picturesque. Similarly Morland's cow would be picturesque, but not art. Only craftsmanship. For Morland only felt " Here is a rough red cow," whereas Constable had felt the flicker of the sunlight on her body.

The development of living, imaginative painting in England can therefore be traced by observing the subjects that interested painters, and the technique they adopted in presenting them. Picturesque painting is the technique that accentuated broken surfaces, or suggested " intricacy " by the skilful application of broad masses of paint; and yet did not pierce through the substance to the life. It is preoccupied with surface, and does not feel intensely. It makes pictures, but not art. But, as in the case of the traveller, the novelist, and the poet, the discoveries of the picturesque painter prepared the way for the more sensitive artists who followed him. In the following appendix I have assembled the principal artists whose work enables us to trace the growing preoccupation with the rough and irregular, and with light. They can only be fully appreciated in relation to the great art they rendered possible, and to the ideas associated with the subjects they painted which have been dealt with in earlier chapters.

A test as to whether a picture is picturesque might be found in the extent to which the colour brown is employed. The eye that appreciated landscape through old masters and poetry definitely loved brown. The eye that saw for itself discovered that brown did not exist, but was a combination of the primary colours. The stories of Sir George Beaumont and the brown tree are almost too hackneyed to quote. "Where do you put your brown tree?" he is said to have asked Constable. " A good picture, like a good fiddle, should be brown " is another pronouncement, ascribed to his love of the mellowing tinge of time on old canvasses. The point to remember is that brown was closely associated with ideas, in their immature state, of romance and sublimity, as " gloom " was in architecture. Isaac d'Israeli[1] wrote a little history of the association, showing how Milton had borrowed the expressions "imbrown" and "brown," which he applied to evening and shade, from the Italian *fa l'imbruno,* found in Boiardo, Ariosto, and Tasso, " who make very picturesque use of it ":

> and where the unpierced shade
> Imbrowned the noon-tide bowers.

---

[1] *Curiosities of Literature,* vol. ii, p. 119, art. "Imbrown and Brown."

Thomson was delighted by the brownness he saw in his picturesque landscapes:

> with quicken'd step
> Brown night retires.—*Summer*, v. 51.

These literary and poetical associations led to the use of brown by painters so long as painting was literary and poetic; so long, in fact, as it was picturesque. When painters ceased to aim at making their pictures like old masters', and instead painted what they felt through their eyes, brownness and picturesqueness disappeared. They had served their purpose.

Note. My use of the term " form " may lead to misunderstanding. I have used it here, and in what follows, in the sense of solidity; that plasticity which Cézanne gave consciously to our hypothetical cow. Constable seems not to have consciously apprehended plasticity. In common with other picturesque painters, he chose subjects of which the texture was " painty," *i.e.*, picturesque. His expression, in addition, of their form was unconscious and raises him above the category of picturesque painters. Picturesque painting, as I use the term, was brought to an end by Cézanne's restoring to art a consciousness of solidity.

THE MOST EMINENTLY PICTUR-ESQUE ENGLISH PAINTERS, 1730-1830

THE list that follows is largely based, as must be any survey of the painting of this epoch, on Colonel M. H. Grant's monumental work, *The Old English Landscape Painters*. Before 1730, when the poems of Thomson and Dyer mark the birth of the picturesque point of view, a native landscape school did not exist. Such landscape painting as there was, was either topographical, recording facts baldly, as in Robert Streater's (1624-1680) *Boscobel House* at Hampton Court; or it had no relation to native scenery or climate, as is shown by the *Landscape* at Painters' Hall by Robert Aggas (1619-1679). The majority of painters, indeed, were foreigners, and all painting with scanty exceptions was derived, whether indirectly or via Holland, from the ideal Italian source. An early exception was Francis Place (1647-1728), who showed considerable interest in cliffs and ruins, while a certain C. F. Vaughan, whose history I have not traced, painted the prospect from Greenwich Hill, *c.* 1670, with a breadth and flow of pigment that is most remarkable.

I have kept the list as short as possible, omitting artists who were primary idealizers, sentimentalists, formists, or otherwise preoccupied, or who are scarcely known. Those included are either picturesque painters at their best or at their worst, interesting themselves in broken surfaces, or broken light, or producing pictures that are picturesque solely by association with Italian or Dutch painting.

NORIE, JAMES (1684-1757). Member of well-known Edinburgh family of artists. His work limited to

Scotland. The "father of Scottish landscape." Had a precocious skill in drawing Gothic architecture, and an appreciation of mellow light.

WOOTTON, JOHN (1686-1765). The horse painter. But an occasional and skilful painter of ideal landscape. A pair of these known to me represent a seaport and a glade in the manner of Claude. Two illustrated by Grant suggest rather Gaspar Poussin.

HOGARTH, WILLIAM (1697-1764). Included here as an early definer, in his *Analysis*, of " Beauty." His rare landscapes partake of that quality. But his handling of paint in his normal subjects is rich and vigorous. An admirer of Titian. In these respects a forerunner of the picturesque.

LAMBERT, GEORGE (1710-1765). May here be taken out of order as the landscape painter extolled by Hogarth, and employed by him for the backgrounds on the great staircase at St. Bartholomew's Hospital. The father of English landscape. A Gasparish manner, but had a love of woodland scenes which he painted with a richness akin to Ruysdael. Pupil of Wootton. Scene painter at Covent Garden.

TAVERNER, WILLIAM (1703-1772). A lawyer, but a considerable painter. A water-colour in the Victoria and Albert Museum shows an interest in bosky trees. Generalized landscapes in oil in style of Gaspar.

TULL, NICHOLAS (?-1762). Called at the time an imitator of Hobbema. Grant illustrates a picture by him of an exceedingly picturesque cottage and water-mill.

SMITH, THOMAS, " of Derby " (?-1767). An early painter of the Lake and Peak Districts. Gray noted, in his *Tour to the Lakes*, that he had recently stayed in the inn at Malham with Vivares the engraver, who, with J. Mason, reproduced many of his landscapes. Father of John Raphael Smith.

SMITH OF CHICHESTER, WILLIAM (1707-1764). Saw even better than J. Lambert, than whom he was older, the soft atmosphere of England and the picturesque qualities of oak foliage.

SMITH OF CHICHESTER, GEORGE (1714-1776). An eye for picturesque scenes, whether cottages or Claudian glades. The same gentleness as his brother, but a rich painter and, in his feeling for the spirit of nature, a finer artist.

SMITH OF CHICHESTER, JOHN (1717-1764). Rarer and weaker.

WILSON, RICHARD (1714-1764). The painting of atmosphere has been the prime contribution of the English Landscape school to European art, and Wilson was the first English painter to reveal its possibilities. Before his visit to Italy (1749-1755) his landscape was either of the clean, topographical order or, as shown in his *Dover* (*c.* 1746), a development from Lambert. At Venice the influence of Zuccarelli, and at Rome of Claude Joseph Vernet, directed Wilson to a more picturesque vision, traceable in the type of scene selected and in a richer quality of paint. From this he evolved his characteristic style, in which the whole landscape is fused in mellow light. There is little attempt at realism; his composition and treatment of trees and foliage is picturesque in its derivation from Claude and such " atmospherists " as Berghem and Both. He was compelled, in order to earn his living, to turn out conventional picturesque compositions. But atmospheric fusion is to be seen in all; indeed, in his later " pot-boilers " it is carried to excess. " Beauty," as defined in the eighteenth century, was the chief quality of Wilson's painting, verging on the sublime in *Niobe's Children*.

In such work as *The Convent*, however (at the Glasgow Corporation Art Gallery), there is a decided feeling for crumbling masonry and irregularity of outline in the architecture. The *Snowdon* at Nottingham is a superb example of Wilson's contribution to the appreciation of English landscape. It represents what Gray and Gilpin went to see in the Lakes. Wilson is the first English landscape painter to pass through the picturesque phase to temperamental observation—to art.

ZUCCARELLI, FRANCESCO, R.A. (1702-1788). In England 1745, 1752-73. One of the greatest decorators of his century. He accepted those scenes and aspects of nature that the Italo-Dutch school had shown to be picturesque, and surpassed his prototypes in the mellowness of his colour and the richness of his paint. But his work shows no aesthetic emotion, and awakes none. His popularity did much to develop the appreciation of picturesque qualities.

COZENS, ALEXANDER. Arrived in England 1745. Died 1786. As drawing master at Eton during most of his life in England, he may be credited with a formative influence on perception among the aristocracy. He gave lessons to George III when Prince of Wales, to Sir George Beaumont, and, no doubt, to Uvedale Price. His work shows a sure recognition of picturesque objects, and of the effective ways for treating and composing them. His practice (as described by Henry Angelo, and, without acknowledgment, by Price) of converting blobs and blots of colour, splashed on to paper, into scenes of rocks and ruins, was essentially picturesque.

SERRES, DOMINIC, R.A. (1722-1793). A Gascon, who took to seafaring, settled in England in 1758, and ended Marine Painter to George III. Occasional landscapes show an affection for picturesque objects, such as cottages, which were to provide his sons with their material.

REYNOLDS, Sir Joshua (1723-1792). Advocated generalization in painting nature. His sketch of Mrs. Thrale's park (Victoria and Albert Museum) verges on impressionism, whilst a great view from Richmond Hill, mezzotinted by J. Jones, recalls forcibly the landscapes of Rubens. His claim to consideration as a picturesque painter lies rather in the influence exerted on contemporaries by the rich quality of paint in his portraits, and his eulogy of Gainsborough in his 14th Discourse.

SANDBY, Paul, R.A. (1725-1809), and Thomas, R.A. (1721-1798). Paul is the *doyen* of English water-colour. A genial personality, the fast friend of Wilson, and, in his age, of Turner and Girtin, whose enormous *œuvre*, spanning two generations, is essentially picturesque. A tendency to idealization he derived, probably *via* Taverner, Zuccarelli, Wilson, or G. Barret senior, from Gaspar and Claude. With him, " all the world's a stage," and its scenery—scenery. An appreciation of Dutch painting is equally evident in his gnarled trees and crumbling edifices (Plate XVI). He converted topography into picturization. Thomas Sandby, his brother, was Deputy Ranger of Windsor Great Park 1746-98, and in that capacity carried the picturesque into practice by planning Virginia Water. His drawings are topographical. Between them the brothers represent consistently and over a long period the type of the picturesque artist.

GAINSBOROUGH, Thomas (1727-1788). From discipleship of the only landscape painting he knew—that of Lambert and Wootton—Gainsborough passed on to an admiration for the Dutch, particularly Jan Wynants. In this early style, of which the finest accessible example is the *Cornard Wood* in the National Gallery, he stresses the roughness, knobbliness, and ruttiness of country scenery, the catching lights on dock and countless oak leaves. Though his manner of painting them changed, his fondness for these picturesque qualities never deserted him. He would bring home bits of bark, moss, rock, etc., and make of them miniature "scenes." In 1760 he moved to Bath, and his Dutch manner before long was abandoned. His landscape painting underwent a revolution. Instead of accurately recording picturesque qualities in picturesque objects, he began to paint what he felt, when looking at them, in a rapid, sensitive calligraphy. The change was from what became Uvedale Price's conception of the picturesque, as having objective existence in certain qualities, to that of Payne Knight, with whom the picturesque was a mode of vision. With Gainsborough, however, the mode of vision was inseparable from the artist's emotion. He felt, poignantly if not deeply, the harmony of colour, the rhythm of forms that his fancy rendered diaphanous. Reynolds said of him that if he did not see with the eye of a poet, he saw with the eye of a painter. The compliment must not be misunderstood. There is poetry and fairyland in Gainsborough's later landscapes, but it is the poetry of paint. Reynolds was only saying that Gainsborough ceased idealizing, on a literary theoretic system derived from Claude, and looked for himself. It cannot be held, however, that he revealed a new aspect of nature, though he perfected a new way of painting it. What he saw, to the end of his days, was the picturesque flicker of light and atmosphere on moist foliage and earth. He painted the picturesque with genius, and to him is directly attributable the cult of the picturesque peasant, hovel, gipsy. But whereas Wheatley and Hamilton sentimentalized them and Morland brutalized them, Gainsborough left his rustics and children as simply " picturesque "—agreeable objects suitable to lanes and woods.

ADAM, ROBERT (1728-1792). Several water-colours in the Victoria and Albert Museum are fantastically picturesque; a castle perched on a crag, a classical landscape with cascade. In the Soane Museum are a series of water-colour compositions of the interiors of Roman ruins *à la* Piranesi. An over-mantel picture at the Royal Society of Arts, representing a " sublime " gorge, if not by him, represents the style of subject he enjoyed. A design for " ruins " is in the Victoria and Albert Museum. For his picturesque attitude to architecture see *supra*, chapter vi, section 1 (Plate XIII, fig. 1).

CLERISSEAU, CHARLES LOUIS (1722-1820). Came to England on the invitation of R. Adam 1771. Remained till 1790. " Famous for the beauty and neatness of his drawings from the antique " (H. Walpole). These were usually classical landscapes or ruins, such as Thermae.

GOUPY, JOSEPH (1729-1763). In England from *c.* 1740 till his death. Gouache was his best medium. In it he copied or adapted after Salvator and the Poussins. Taught Mrs. Delany.

PILLEMENT, JEAN (1728?-1808?). In England 1760-80. An exquisite *pasticheur* of all picturesque painters from Claude to Zuccarelli. His work is usually executed in gouache, water-colour, or pastel, and brilliantly dainty in colouring.

RICHARDS, JOHN INIGO, R.A. (died 1810). Secretary of Royal Academy from 1788. Mainly a scene painter. Executed many topographical pictures. His landscape compositions assemble all the picturesque ingredients—broadly treated trees, blue mountains, castles, earthy foregrounds. His colouring is rich and mellow.

TOMKINS, William, A.R.A. (1730?-1792). Topographer and a notorious copier of Claude and Hobbema, into whom he introduced a dash of Salvator.

TOMKINS, Charles (*c.* 1750-*c.* 1806). A topographical engraver who occasionally painted picturesque scenes in Gainsborough's earlier manner, and Morland's.

JONES, Thomas (1730?-1803). Pupil of Wilson, from whom and from G. Smith of Chichester he habitually stole.

BARRET, George, senior, R.A. (1728-1784). Remained in Dublin till 1763, when Burke, his ardent patron, induced him to come to London. There his landscapes soon obscured Wilson's whence they manifestly are derived. They represent Burke's " beauty," just as Barry, another of his *protégés*, represents his " sublime." Patronized also by Lord Dalkeith, Sir Peter Leicester, and Lock of Norbury, for whom he decorated a circular room with a panorama of the Lake District. An excellent painter who never rose above the picturesque—and consequently commanded consistently high prices.

BEAUCLERK, Lady Diana (1734-1808). Born Spencer, being the eldest daughter of the third Duke of Marlborough. Illustrated Walpole's *Mysterious Mother* " sublimely," and Burger's *Leonore*. A brilliant amateur *pastichiste* of Gainsborough, revelling in picturesque details, such as gnarled boughs and gipsies (Plate III).

WRIGHT, Joseph (of Derby), A.R.A. (1734-1797). Excelled in night scenes. His landscapes are subordinate to his portraits and groups, and are mainly simple topography. But *The Earth Stopper* (exhibited 1773), in the possession of the Hon. Gerald Agar-Robartes is an example of his picturesque treatment of a woodland night scene: the moon silhouettes the conventional trees and the earth stopper works by the glow of a lantern.

MORE, JACOB (of Rome) (*c.* 1735-1795). Native of Glasgow. Had a great reputation in Rome where, in 1785, he was commissioned by the Prince Borghese to decorate rooms in his palace, and in 1787 was visited by the admiring Goethe. A thin and feeble copyist of Claude and Vernet.

LOUTHERBOURG, PHILIP JAMES DE, R.A. (1740-1812). Came to England 1771. Perhaps the greatest painter who can be set down as picturesque. In Paris he worked for the battle painter François Casanova (younger brother of the notorious Jacques), whom he speedily outshone by the richness of his colour and paint. Like most innovators, he was accused of using unwarrantably brilliant colour. To-day we are consequently struck by its splendour. As scene painter to Garrick (1771-76), and subsequently to Sheridan (1776-85), he revolutionized the art, not only in point of colour, but in mechanism and lighting. He was also instrumental in introducing more accurate costume in place of the crinolines and periwigs of the day. Partly to this end he amassed a remarkable collection of armour. His *Eidophusikon*, or scenic entertainment, has been already described. His oil-paintings are dramatically composed, striking in subject, and supremely well painted. He was a magnificent technician, making use of every picturesque quality. The richness of textures is brilliantly reproduced in his vigorously applied pigment. He carried the " picturesque pastoral " scenes of Gainsborough to their furthest possibilities and undoubtedly prepared the way for Morland and Ibbetson. Yet facile, slick, and brilliant as was his painting, it lacks either the spiritual or aesthetic feeling that is needed for art.

MORTIMER, JOHN HAMILTON, A.R.A. (1741-1779). " Our sublime Mortimer," had Wright of Derby as fellow pupil of Thomas Hudson, and imparted to him something of his own passion for violent chiaroscuro. He aimed at being the Salvator Rosa of England, specializing in banditti, caverns, and sublime incidents. In pursuance of Burke's definition of the sublime, he eschewed colour, replacing it by black shadows and interplays of brown. His drawing is vigorous and his technique picturesque.

BAMFYLDE, COPLESTONE WARRE (died 1791). An amateur, squire of Hestercombe, Somerset, a place which he " improved " in the manner of Brown. Exhibited landscapes, some of which were engraved, as that of Stourhead, by Vivares, 1777. He designed the frontispieces to Richard Graves's *Columella* (1779), which consist of imaginary prospects of the Leasowes, Shenstone's garden.

ROOKER, MICHAEL " ANGELO," A.R.A. (1743-1801). Best known for his numerous water-colours. A pupil of Paul Sandby, whose style and subjects he largely reproduced. A picturesque painter of architecture, ruins, and impressive scenery, in which he manages his shadows and stresses the inequalities of surface with picturesque effect (Plate XIII, fig. 2).

HODGES, WILLIAM, R.A. (1744-1797). Best known for his landscapes of Australasia, made when official draughtsman to Captain Cook on his second voyage (1772-75), and landscapes of India, made on the invitation of Warren Hastings (1778-84). The latter were referred to by Reynolds in the

Discourses as having a possible influence on architecture. He selected tropical landscape into Claudian compositions, of which the colouring is brilliant, though rather hard and lacking in chiaroscuro. Made good use of dry scrumbling to suggest rough foregrounds. He is represented at the Victoria and Albert Museum by a picturesquely conceived and broadly treated view of Ludlow Castle.

HEARNE, THOMAS (1744-1817). The picturesque topographer *par excellence*. Much of his output engraved for *The Antiquities of Great Britain*, completed 1807. Executed a set of water-colours of the grounds at Downton Castle for Payne Knight. These, like all his works, are full of picturesque detail but show no attempt at colour. Turner was indebted to him in his early days. He abhorred Turner's painting as entirely lacking in " sentiment."

HACKERT, JOHANN GOTTLIEB (1744-1773), brother of J. P. Hackert, the companion of Payne Knight to Sicily. In England 1772 and died at Bath 1773. His brother exhibited, but is not otherwise recorded, in England till 1791. Both painted ideal landscape, with pearly distance and painty foreground.

TAYLOR, JOHN (of Bath) (*c*. 1745-1806). " If I am not mistaken this young gentleman of Bath is the best landscape painter now living."—Humphrey Clinker, 1766. Smollett particularly admired the rich colour of his foliage and dramatic introduction of gleams of sunlight. His supremacy persisted in the minds of many well informed judges in spite of Gainsborough's activities in the same city. His work is rare and little known, but treats extremely decoratively, with deep tones and rich paint, of architecture in picturesque settings.

ELFORD, Sir William, Bt. (1747-1837). A west country banker who exhibited forty landscapes at the Royal Academy, of correctly picturesque subjects well executed after the manner of Gainsborough.

WHEATLEY, Francis, R.A. (1747-1801). Received some tuition from Wilson, and worked with Mortimer. With the latter executed the decoration of the saloon at Brocket Hall. *The Whistling Oyster Tavern*, in the possession of Lord Woolavington, is a product of this phase; a group of debauchees depicted with black chiaroscuro, but with stronger colouring than Mortimer permitted himself. His typical work might be defined as Gainsborough subjects seen with a sentiment milder than Mortimer's and painted with Wilson's pure colour. His scenes of peasants and cottages, treated with a juicy brush-work, did much to render such objects "picturesque" to contemporary observers.

FARINGTON, Joseph, R.A. (1747-1821). Wilson, Claude, and architecture.

DANIELL, Thomas, R.A. (1749-1840). Ransacked the Far East for the picturesque, including India, Egypt, and China (1784-94). His work had considerable influence in popularizing the Indian style of architecture, by giving it picturesque association. His painting, particularly when reproduced in aquatint, distinguished by the broad treatment of the masses.

RATHBONE, John (1750-1807). "The Manchester Wilson." Achieved a large output of "picturesque beauty." A member of the Morland-Ibbetson group.

BEAUMONT, Sir George Howland, Bt. (1753-1827). The greatest of the connoisseur patrons. His hospitality and his influence felt by all the outstanding landscape painters of his time. His own painting, though he loved and emulated the old masters, is always individual. He never imitated, but went for the picturesque qualities, which their painting revealed, and seized them vigorously. He had indeed a conception of the ideally picturesque to which he strove to approximate all his pictures. Prominent among its components was, of course, the brown tree of the anecdote. He admired brownness for its own sake, finding the subdued tints of an old picture more picturesque than those in nature or in Constable. He saw and thought in terms of the old masters—had, in fact, the picturesque mind. The great result of this possession is the National Gallery, the foundation of which is almost entirely owing to his perseverance, and contains the whole of his private collection. Without the picturesque phase, and without Sir George Beaumont, it is not too much to say that we should not have the National Gallery as it is to-day. Only to the picturesque mind does the existence of a national collection of paintings appear so vital that no labour is too great for its establishment. At other epochs paintings are regarded as aesthetically or spiritually necessary. Only in the picturesque phase was life itself to be approached through a picture gallery.

HAMILTON, WILLIAM, R.A. (1751-1801). " Beautiful " *genre*. His father worked in Adam's office and he himself derived his instruction from Adam's chief decorator Antonio Zucchi. Hamilton sought the picturesque in literature, illustrating in Thomson's *Seasons*, Boydell's *Shakespeare*, and Macklin's *Bible*. An early, and perhaps the most influential, painter of the anecdotal.

WEBBER, JOHN, R.A. (1752-1793). Accompanied Cook's third voyage. Attempted to reproduce the brilliant colour of the tropics without knowing how to manipulate paint.

COZENS, JOHN ROBERT (1752-1799). In 1776 taken by Payne Knight to sketch the Alps. In 1780-83 in Italy in the company of William Beckford. Through the picturesque he attained to the intense feeling for visual phenomena, apart from their labels, that produces art. The possible reactions on one another of Cozens and Knight suggest a large field of speculation for which, unfortunately, we have no data whatever. His first year in Switzerland (1776) produced a vanished *Landscape, with Hannibal in his march over the Alps showing his Army the fertile plains of Italy*—a subject dealt with by Turner in 1812. The influence of Knight may be detected in the choice of the subject, and through him of Gray, who noted a similar subject, *Hannibal passing the Alps; elephants tumbling down the precipices,* as a sublime subject that he had never seen painted. Cozens, however, freed himself effectually from literary and picturesque aspects of nature and felt directly through his eyes.

NICHOLSON, FRANCIS (1753-1844). His life covers the great period of water-colour art, in which medium he painted, always picturesquely, sometimes better, the dales and fells of the Pennines, and of other mountainous districts.

○ BIGG, WILLIAM REDMORE, R.A. (1755-1828). Inherited from his teacher, Edward Penny, his penchant, as Col. Grant expresses it, for the minor sentimentalities. His scenes contain a wealth of picturesque features, and generally a cottage.

STOTHARD, THOMAS, R.A. (1755-1834). An illustrator of exquisite sensibility. In oils, his glowing, broken colour, derived from the Venetians, renders him an essentially picturesque painter.

CATTON, CHARLES, JUNIOR (1756-1819). An admirable, but almost forgotten painter of picturesque scenes, usually of rural life, with a technique as vigorous as James Ward's or Morland's.

ROWLANDSON, THOMAS (1756-1827). His brilliance as a draughtsman of the grotesque and, on occasion, of the beautiful, supplements his claim to be considered one of the masters of the picturesque. Indeed, no other artist so obviously delighted in the country life of England for picturesqueness itself. He loved the gnarled tree for its gnarledness, the hovel for its delapidation, the hollow way for its rich crumbling banks. His every figure has the " irregularity of outline " that delighted the picturesque eye in a ruin or a cow.

BOURGEOIS, SIR PETER FRANCIS, R.A. (1756-1811). As a social product Bourgeois represents completely the picturesque phase. Son of a Swiss watchmaker, he was intended for a commission in the English army, but, under the influence of Desenfans, the picture dealer and dilettante, he directed himself to art, studying for two years under de Loutherbourg. In 1779 he was appointed Court Painter to the King of Poland—a sinecure, since that king had no court and shortly ceased to be a king, but not before he had conferred a knighthood on Bourgeois. Desenfans left him the great collection of pictures that he had assembled for the same monarch, prior to the latter's deposition, and Bourgeois bequeathed it to Dulwich College, where it hangs in Soane's characteristic gallery: a monument, in its mixture of masterpieces and obscurities, to the point of view that valued a picture, not as a work of art, but as a collection of picturesque objects and qualities. The Dulwich gallery is a " period room." The student of the picturesque appreciates not the masterpieces, but the jumble. It is of value to him for what it omits even more than for what it contains. It embalms the range of art on which the picturesque point of view was formed. Bourgeois's own painting is amply represented, and, as we should expect, is de Loutherbourg minus that master's one virtue: intensity. Bourgeois was facile, vigorous, learned in the manners of the Dutch, and wholly deficient in aesthetic impulse. He made picturesque pictures.

HOPPNER, JOHN, R.A. (1758-1810). His only large, known landscape, *Gale of Wind* (1794), in the Tate Gallery is not very exciting. In his portraits, however, the handling of the paint and the landscape backgrounds have all the qualities that picturesque writers required of a painter. An uncommon drawing in the possession of Mr. P. M. Turner shows an exceedingly picturesque landscape: a castle on a hill overshadows a torrent and stormy trees (Plate XXVIII).

NASMYTH, ALEXANDER (1758-1840). An Admirable Crichton of the picturesque: engineer, *architetto-pittore*, even architect, town planner, landscape gardener, scene, portrait, and landscape painter. Made models for the lay-out and grouping of the New Town, Edinburgh, and, as we have seen (p. 223), for Dunglass. His painting consists in clear and atmospheric presentments of picturesque scenes.

IBBETSON, JULIUS CAESAR (1759-1817). To Morland's subjects and de Loutherbourg's vigour Ibbetson brought a sensitiveness to atmosphere, and of handling, that makes him one of the greatest of the "little masters." His pictures, invariably picturesque, sometimes approximate to art.

MONRO, DR. THOMAS (1759-1833). His evening classes made of 8 Adelphi Terrace a temple of the picturesque. Drawings by Gainsborough and

Cozens, and prints, were copied by young artists. His own wash drawings portray picturesque ideas.

MORLAND, George (1763-1837). The Correggio of the picturesque. He saw nothing but picturesque qualities, and painted them as he saw them with mastery. Of feeling, whether imaginative or aesthetic, he had not an ounce. His enormous *œuvre* is supplemented by the output of numerous imitators, such as Thomas Hand, David Brown, William Cowden.

ARNALD, George, A.R.A. (1763-1841). An industrious and picturesque topographer, especially of scenes in gentlemen's parks.

WESTALL, Richard, R.A. (1765-1836). Elder brother of William (who accompanied voyages of exploration). In water-colours he raised sentimental illustration to beauty, with exquisite line and considerable feeling for form. Payne Knight found in his oil-painting the embodiment of his personal conception of " beauty," in that its rustic types illustrated " those tender feelings which we call pathetic," while at the same time it contained rich, clear colour. He possessed at least seven pictures by him, still at Downton Castle; among them *Storm in Harvest* (Plate XII), which he considered one of the three "most interesting and affecting pictures that the art has ever produced."

BARRET, George, junior (1767-1842). A lover of golden light. His rich, crumbling, rather heavy technique, both in oils and water-colour, proceeds directly from picturesque theory. His subjects are nothing if not picturesque, and his compositions contain a plethora of approved objects, grouped on the best principles.

CROME, John (1768-1821). Picturesque as were

Crome's subjects, and the qualities that he painted so richly, it is only on second thoughts that we notice the fact. To an eye for the picturesque, formed, like his technique, on the Dutchmen, he added the instinct of a great artist. Without, possibly, realizing it, he was fundamentally moved by form and relations of form. With rustic subjects and East Anglian sunlight he achieves the monumental.

LAWRENCE, Sir Thomas, P.R.A. (1769-1821). As good a painter as Sargent, with as great a love of landscape, though not, unfortunately, as great an output of it. He longed to be free of the commissions that, since his prodigious youth, had rained upon him, and to paint " sublime History." And " the best historical painters," he said, " have always been good painters of landscape." In this he shared the sentiments of his friend and patron Payne Knight, for whom he painted one of his few landscapes—or history pieces—" Homer reciting the Iliad " (Plate VIII), now at Downton. Knight's Hellenism may have suggested the subject and insisted on the beauty of the attendant figures, but the liquid paint, the luscious colour, and the glitter of sky and foliage, are characteristically Lawrence and picturesque. Psychologically he was passionately, and literally, romantic—in the *Mysteries of Udolpho* strain, as Col. Grant aptly points out, and, left to himself, would have surpassed Fuseli and John Martin in quest of the sublime. Like Mrs. Radcliffe he could not separate emotion from landscape painting. He had no interest in picturesque objects as such. He had passed through that stage, to be able to feel fiercely through his eyes and to splash on the paint as a relief. Yet only in his backgrounds and rare landscapes was he free to indulge in such relief.

On his portraiture, as on himself, he imposed a courtly, urbane restraint.

BARKER, Thomas (of Bath) (1769-1847). Put, in youth, to copying Dutch landscape pictures, he extended his scope to include Gainsborough's subjects and method. As for the latter and for Taylor, the presence of picturesque scenery round a watering place simplified the way to popularity. Capable at times of aesthetic feeling, as shown in the noble landscapes at the National and Tate Galleries, Barker was habitually and constitutionally a picturesque painter, with imagination and force. In his hey-day Barker built Doric House on Salem Hill, Bath, which stands to this day. The façade is of two orders and the effect architecturally picturesque. On the staircase he painted, 30 feet by 12 feet, the *Massacre at Scio*, a subject that thrilled Haydon when he saw it, and was subsequently to inspire Delacroix.

WARD, James, R.A. (1789-1859). Might be called the Michelangelo of the picturesque. He was early inspired to ape Morland with skill. Teniers, de Loutherbourg, and Paul Potter followed as exemplars, from whom he learnt his cool tonality, his exuberant brush-work, and his treatment of cattle-hide. As an animal painter no one excelled him in picturesque handling. Then in 1803 he saw Rubens' *Château de Stein*, newly imported by Sir George Beaumont. Its glory called up all his powers, latent and developed. He would rival it. His effort resulted in that masterpiece of the picturesque, *St. Donats Castle, Fighting Bulls*, in the Victoria and Albert Museum (Plate VI). Is any picturesque object, or pathetic circumstance, or romantic association lacking? Sir George Beaumont held Rubens' own work " gross and vulgar " beside it. And it was rejected by the Royal

Academy. A masterpiece it undoubtedly is, but of the picturesque, not of art. It is an assembly of features and qualities. Its strength is that of sinew, not of conception. It is a gorgeous exhibition of painting, but of design, feeling, or aesthetic movement it is as innocent as a de Loutherbourg. The *Harlech Castle* in the National Gallery is a pendant with a change of scene. One other supreme effort he made: the *Gordale Scar* in the Tate Gallery. Colossal in subject and abnormally large for a landscape (in dimension 131 inches by 140 inches), the picture is the ruin of a high endeavour. It is practically indecipherable in its present position. Sir George Beaumont had deemed the scene " beyond the range of art." Ward's great effort does not persuade us that he was wrong.

REINAGLE, Ramsay Richard, R.A. (1775-1862). Excellent journeyman painter of well chosen picturesque scenes.

GIRTIN, Thomas (1775-1802).
TURNER, J. M. W. (1775-1851).
CONSTABLE, John (1776-1837).

Not only the accident that they were born almost within a year of one another makes it convenient to treat these three great artists together. Each developed a different aspect of picturesque vision to the full extent to which the scope of this book permits us to trace it.

The painting of Constable exactly embodies Payne Knight's conception of picturesque vision: an abstract appreciation of colour, light, and shadow not for the objects they enable the mind to perceive, but for the " moderate and varied irritation of the optic nerve " which they produce. With Constable, as with Knight, no particular forms were significant in themselves, but only such objects as

displayed " intricacy of parts, colour, and surface."
Indeed, Constable did not consciously interest
himself in form. What did interest him passionately was, as Knight described the business of a
painter to be, " to imitate the visible qualities of
bodies, separating them " from habitual associations. He made, what Thomas Reid observed had
rarely been done, " the visible appearance of
objects of sight a subject for reflection," independent of their identity. This led him to the discovery
of the means to reproduce brilliant colour by the
juxtaposition of tints—a method that enormously
impressed the French at the " Salon des Anglais "
held in 1824, and eventually led to impressionism.
We have seen how, in other pursuits, the picturesque led men from insensitiveness in face of
nature to appreciation—through pictures, poetry,
romance; and finally through the abstract appreciation of colour and light. Constable alone, of
artists yet encountered, was able largely to divest
his eyes of tradition and his hand of trickery. He
painted, with entire truth, what he fervently felt
through his eyes. As Mr. Clive Bell has recently
phrased it, whilst his predecessors fitted nature to
a picture, Constable fitted pictures to nature. So
late as 1849 his work was unintelligible to many
connoisseurs. Thus Stanley, in his edition of
Bryan: " He neither imitated the ancient masters,
nor the modern; whether he really copied nature
time will discover. . . . When showers fall, instead
of verdant freshness, his trees are covered with
fleeces of snow. . . . His admirers consider that
the scattered lights are sparkling touches of genius.
All this may be so ; it is useless to dispute on a
matter of taste."

Girtin, in his short life, never got free of topography, from which he derived his livelihood.

But in the recording of romantic views he went far beyond his contemporaries in design. Even if he was painting Bridgenorth or Kirkstall, he saw, primarily, forms, and in his picture combined them by sensitive arrangements of tone. The " breadth " of his vision—his capacity for untroubled masses of tones—is his picturesque quality. How admirably he applied this to the rendering of a scene objectively picturesque is seen in his *Hollow Lane* (Plate X), in the Victoria and Albert Museum.

Turner's painting comprehends and glorifies all the ideals of the picturesque. His three phases illustrate the three meanings of the word. His first, topographical, phase shows us ruins and picturesque, that is irregular, buildings. His great middle period was occupied by competing, on their own ground, with his landscape painting predecessors, in order to prove that a Claude, a Wilson, a Salvator, a Cuyp could not make a prospect nearly so picturesque as could he, Turner. To this process of idealizing the picturesque he brought a gorgeously romantic imagination, and a passion for colour for its own sake. That tag of Campbell's—" 'Tis distance lends enchantment to the view "—which epitomizes the romantic preference for uncertainty and illusion over knowledge, describes perfectly the enchantment that Turner throws over his presentments of picturesque scenes, and over men and women who gaze at them. In his last phase he achieved the abstract colour-vision envisaged by the three friends in Uvedale Price's *Dialogue* (1801), when Mr. Seymour observed: " I can imagine a man of the future, who may be born without the sense of feeling (that is, of touch) being able to see nothing but light variously modified, and that such a way of considering nature

[272]

would be just, for then the eye would see nothing but what in point of harmony was beautiful." Mr. Seymour went on to confess that such " pure abstract enjoyment of vision, our inveterate habits will not let us partake of." In such a picture as the *Drawing Room, Petworth*, in the National Gallery, Turner contrived to forget the habits of a lifetime that informed him that such and such lines were a chair, those and those a mantelpiece. He tore off the labels, eliminated even the forms, and left only " light variously modified." Picturesque aestheticism, with light as its fundamental cause of emotion, has Turner's last phase as its culmination. A century ago Turner and the picturesque had the refreshing newness of Cézanne and significant form.

From this point it is unnecessary to pursue the methods of a cataloguer. With scarcely an exception every painter was more or less picturesque till the Pre-Raphaelites began painting tracts, and, in our own times, the movements of the later nineteenth century in France made themselves felt. A Cotman, a de Wint could approach Constable and Turner in the power of their presentments of picturesque objects, but could not surpass them. The Rev. John Thompson of Duddingston (1778-1840) became the Turner of Scotland and the pictorial counterpart of Walter Scott. His full, heavy colour at times is almost dissociated from representation, and his sparkling light is admirably picturesque. He lacked, however, Constable's instinct for form and Turner's feeling for the structure of natural growths; defects that keep him within the category " picturesque." But his colour-technique carried picturesque painting into the neighbourhood of Monticelli (Plate XXVII). A painter whose reputation rests entirely on the picturesque is David Cox. His *Treatise on*

Landscape Painting indicates a mind educated on Burke and Price, and proceeds in the form of recipes:

> A cottage or village scene requires soft and simple admixture of tones, calculated to produce pleasure. . . . On the contrary, the structures of greatness and antiquity should be marked by a character of awful sublimity. . . .

His painting has the virtue of suggesting the fresh air, but apart from that is a monotonous shorthand adapted to " catching lights " on rank grass and gnarled trees. He was better with architecture.

More completely a disciple of Burke, via Turner, was John Martin (1789-1854). One day he will come into the reputation he deserves, if only as a curiosity. His biography has already been written (*John Martin, Painter*, by Mary L. Pendered, 1923). He was of the race of supermen with feet of clay, along with James Ward, Francis Danby, Haydon, and the architects of the colossal. Nineveh, Babylon, Sodom and Gomorrah, Paradise, and Hell were his subjects. For an illustrator of Milton some will say Blake was the born artist, but others Martin. It is the difference between linear and picturesque majesty.

A final development of picturesque painting reached its climax in the group of travelling painters who popularized France, revolutionary Italy, and the Near East: Samuel Prout (1783-1850), David Roberts (1798-1864), James Holland (1800-1870), J. F. Lewis, R. A. (1805-1876), and W. J. Muller (1812-1845). At their best in water-colours, these artists painted with extraordinary skill a riot of picturesque features and incidents. Muller and Lewis in particular were gorgeous colourists, and chose subjects—whether from Europe or Asia Minor—that no healthy man failed to enjoy. Prout is the master of dilapidation. Mouldering cusping, rugged statuary, and gaily coloured market-women perpetuate in his pictures the picturesque " quaintness " of Normandy and Breton towns.

By the middle of the century, however, the picturesque in England was being swamped by quaint architectural views and quainter anecdotage. The tradition of Gilpin and Knight, Constable and Turner, was more fruitful among the French. The spirit of the picturesque passed into the Elysian fields of Barbizon, among Diaz's scintillating tree-trunks, Dupré's and Troyon's sheep, and the dawns of Corot.

There it should have rested, after a century's hard work in the bosoms of poets and gardeners, travellers, architects, and painters. But no. It is still in request to write for the newspapers, and to sit on the Council for the Preservation of Rural England.

NOTES ON THE ILLUSTRATIONS

PLATE IV (facing p. 36)

Niccolo Poussin. *Oils.*
This type of picture created the eighteenth century's conception of ideal landscape. The trees are less generalized than those of Claude, and there is a clearer apprehension of form, particularly in the disposition and design of the architecture.   *Louvre.*

PLATE V (facing p. 37)

Salvator Rosa. *Oils.*
Ruins, banditti—or persons suggestive of them— and ships in various picturesque positions. *Modena.*

PLATE VI (facing p. 52)

James Ward, R.A. *Oils* ($51\frac{3}{4}$ in. $\times$ $89\frac{1}{2}$ in.).
A masterpiece of picturesque painting, based on Rubens. The picture represents graphically the "high colouring" that James Thomson introduced into poetry and that Gilpin advocated in descriptive writing. See Appendix.   *Victoria and Albert Museum.*

PLATE VII (facing p. 53)

Claude Lorraine. *Oils.*
James Thomson's description of the approach to the Castle of Indolence (p. 45) might have been taken from this picture. The castle in the distance is the kind of building that stimulated the picturesque movement in architecture.   *Louvre.*

PLATE VIII (facing p. 68)

Sir Thomas Lawrence, P.R.A. *Oils* (40 in. $\times$ 50 in.).
Painted for Richard Payne Knight, in whose house— Downton Castle—it still hangs. The colours are rich

and scintillating. The light breaks picturesquely over a suggested landscape and catches the dark green foliage in glints of brilliance.

PLATE IX (facing p. 69)

Richard Payne Knight, by Lawrence. He is here portrayed perusing a volume on gems, with a specimen of his collection of antique bronzes at his elbow.

Downton Castle.

PLATE X (facing p. 84)

Thomas Girtin. *Water-colour* (16⅜ in. × 12 1/16 in.). This is a subject that invariably excited the picturesque eye. The description of a similar lane on p. 71 might have been taken from this picture. The version reproduced is now considered to be a copy, but is superior, for present purposes, to an authenticated sketch of the same subject in the British Museum.

Victoria and Albert Museum.

PLATE XI (facing p. 85)

This is one of a series of four " Seasons." Poussin has chosen the Deluge to represent winter. Great as a work of art from whatever attitude it is criticized, we can see how disciples of Burke would find it sublime, and those of Price picturesque. The latter includes it in his imaginary picture gallery. See p. 76. *Louvre.*

PLATE XII (facing p. 100)

Payne Knight owned this picture and much admired its pathos in addition to its picturesque qualities, such as the contrast of light and shade. *Oils* (24 in. × 31 in.).

Downton Castle.

THE PICTURESQUE

Plate XIII (facing p. 101)

Fig. 1

R. Adam. *Water-colour* ($9\frac{5}{8}$ in. × $12\frac{3}{16}$ in.).
One of the architect's numerous compositions that attest his appreciation of the picturesque.

Victoria and Albert Museum.

Fig. 2

M. A. Rooker, A.R.A. *Water-colour* ($14\frac{3}{8}$ in. × $10\frac{13}{32}$ in.).
Wokey Hole was early recognized as particularly picturesque. Here it is presented in a style typical of the early water-colour painters.

Plate XIV (facing p. 116)

Aquatint from the Rev. W. Gilpin's *Observations on Cumberland and Westmorland.* He thus describes it: " An illustration of that kind of wild country of which we saw several instances, as we entered Cumberland. In general, the mountains make the most considerable part of these scenes. But when any of them is furnished with a distant view of a lake, the landscape is greatly inriched."

Plate XV (facing p. 117)

Aquatint from the Rev. W. Gilpin's *Observations on the Highlands of Scotland.* " A scene . . . particularly picturesque." Both these illustrations are generalizations composed of picturesque qualities.

Plate XVI (facing p. 132)

Paul Sandby, R.A. *Body colour* ($27\frac{5}{8}$ in. × $41\frac{5}{8}$ in.).
A landscape clearly derived from Claude, and rendered picturesque by the great gnarled beech tree.

[280]

Similar scenes were created in many parks by the landscape gardeners of the time.

Victoria and Albert Museum.

PLATE XVII (facing p. 133)

Fig. 1

Repton designed this adjunct to a Gothic mansion with an eye on the chapter houses of mediaeval cathedrals. In winter it could be converted into a conservatory by filling in the arches with glazed partitions. Aquatint from *The Theory and Practice of Landscape Gardening*, 1803.

Fig. 2

A " scenic design " for a dairy disguised as a ruin. J. B. Papworth is best known for his admirable classic architecture. Coloured print from *Hints on Ornamental Gardening*, 1823.

PLATE XVIII (facing p. 148)

Fig. 1

T. Gainsborough, R.A. *Distemper washed with gum* ($11\frac{11}{12}$ in. $\times$ $15\frac{11}{12}$ in.).

Some of the wilder picturesque gardens aimed at creating such traditionally romantic scenes as this.

Fig. 2

One of the water-colours executed in 1798 by T. Hearne for R. Payne Knight, of the grounds at Downton Castle.

PLATE XIX (facing p. 149)

From H. Repton's *Theory and Practice of Landscape Gardening*, 1803. In Fig. 1 the " slide " is in position showing the ground as it was. In Fig. 2 the slide is removed, showing his projected treatment of it. It will be seen that he has very cleverly made use of existing trees and woods. The scheme was not carried out.

PLATE XX (facing p. 164)

Fig. 1

Payne Knight's park at Downton Castle. By T. Hearne. The gorge of the River Teme lent itself to picturesque treatment.

Fig. 2

This "bath house" at Downton consists of two circular vaulted chambers, one of which contains a bath fed by a spring. Such structures are not uncommon in the parks of this period. Considerable efforts were made that this one should be picturesque.

PLATE XXI

Scotney Castle, Kent. A scene composed on lines suggested by Uvedale Price's books, c. 1837.

PLATE XXII

A village green by John Nash, the architect of Regent's Street.

PLATE XXIII (facing p. 181)

Fig. 1

From James Malton's *Essay on Cottage Architecture*, 1798 (second edition). "The fashion of the windows and the square bow are, in my opinion, extremely beautiful. The pillars (of the porch) are merely oak stumps; or, what is better, they may be made of heart of oak roughly carved in imitation of the bark of a tree, and painted so as to resemble it."

[282]

Fig. 2

" Crotchet Castle . . . the castellated villa of a retired citizen." T. L. Peacock. From *Designs for Rural Retreats*, J. Malton, 1802.

PLATE XXIV (facing p. 196)

Dunglass was built 1807-13, partly in the style of Vanbrugh.

PLATE XXV (facing p. 197)
Fig. 1

Lithograph from *Village Architecture*, by P. F. Robinson, 1830.

Fig. 2

Lithograph from *The Landscape Architecture of the Great Painters of Italy*, by T. L. Meason, 1827.

PLATE XXVI (facing p. 212)
Fig. 1

Aquatint from Francis Goodwin's *Rural Architecture*, 1835.

Fig. 2

Aquatint from J. Thomson's *Rural Retreats*, 1827. See p. 224.

PLATE XXVII (facing p. 213)

The Rev. J. Thomson of Duddingston, H.R.S.A. *Oil* (14 in. × 19 in.).

Impressionism has here been reached through the picturesque. " Beyond a low rocky foreground on the left, where two women sit, a high isolated mass of rock crowned by a square towered castle rises from a quiet sea on the right, against an ominous sky of cumulous cloud." The latter are of a golden hue, the rock of purples and black, and the seaweed in the foreground a rich orange. *National Gallery, Edinburgh.*

PLATE XXVIII (facing p. 228)

An exceedingly rare example of Hoppner's landscape work. His eye is shown to have been as picturesque as we should deduce from the quality of his paint. Black and white chalk on grey paper ($12\frac{1}{2}$ in. × $9\frac{3}{4}$ in.).
In the collection of Percy Moore Turner, Esq.

PLATE XXIX (facing p. 229)

The affinity between Constable's treatment of broken colour and light, and Payne Knight's definition of picturesque vision is clearly illustrated.

All the pictures from Downton Castle are reproduced by the courteous permission of Mr. C. A. Boughton Knight, the descendant of Richard Payne Knight.

INDEX

A Bibliography is to be found under "Books"

[285]

INDEX

INDEX

INDEX

INDEX

on skylines, 203; on the relation of painting and gardening, 173; on the use of pictures, 134; on town planning, 205; on Vanbrugh (Sir John), 198, 202.

Prideaux, S. T., 115.

Priestley, J. B., 243.

Prospects, famous, 41, 42, 72, 86, 103, 125, 174, 201, 251, 255.

Prout, Samuel (1783-1850), 274.

Pugin, Augustus Welby (1811-1852), 165, 194, 230.

Puritan abhorrence of art, 24.

Pynacker, Adam (1622-1673), 11.

Pyne, William Henry (1770-1843), 118, 239, 240.

Quincey, Quartremere de (1755-1849), 200, 201.

Radcliffe, Mrs. Ann (1764-1823), 1, 32, 231, 233.

Raphael Sanzio (1483-1520), 9, 29, 227.

Rathbone, John (1750-1807), 262.

Rectories, 73, 77, 183.

Reform Club, The, London, 217.

Regent's Park, London, 166, 220.

Regent Street, London, 208.

Reid, Dr. Thomas (1710-1796), 78, 271.

Reinagle, Ramsay Richard (1775-1862), 270.

Religion, effect on appreciation of scenery, 6, 8, 51.

Rembrandt (1607-1669), 11, 28, 67, 70, 76.

Reni, Guido (1575-1642), 66, 75.

Repton, Humphry (1752-1818), 32, 69, 105, 180, 209, 238; his acquaintance with Sir Uvedale Price, 164; his career, 162; his conception of gardening, 170; his informal partnership with John Nash, 165; Knight's (R. Payne) ridicule of, 171; on the relation of painting and gardening, 161; poetry of, 163.

Reynolds, Sir Joshua (1723-1792), 52, 60, 62, 63, 66, 115, 128, 186, 187, 218, 255, 260; on Sir John Vanbrugh, 192; Sir Uvedale Price on, 205.

Rhone, river, France, 27.

Richards, John Inigo (d. 1810), 257.

Richardson, Jonathan (1665-1745), 28, 29, 35.

Samuel (1689-1761), 31.

"Richness," 178, 180, 181, 182, 185.

Rievaulx Abbey, Yorks, 103.

Rivers, 47, 116, 117, 130, 132, 138.

Roads, effects of, 7, 86, 115, 140; state of, 101; Young's (Arthur) reports on, 101.

Roberts, David (1798-1864), 274.

Robinson, Peter Frederick (1776-1858), 210, 224, 225.

William, 174, 184.

Rock gardens, 174.

Rocks and crags, 7, 9, 10, 21, 25, 26, 36, 37, 39, 41, 42, 47, 48, 54, 76, 85-89, 91, 94, 99, 100, 102, 104, 109, 112, 113, 116, 117, 120, 129, 138, 152, 157, 176.

Romano, Giulio (1492-1546), 227.